McGraw-Hill's

500
World History
Questions

Volume 1: Prehistory to 1500

Also in McGraw-Hill's 500 Questions Series

McGraw-Hill's

500

World History

Questions

Volume 1: Prehistory to 1500

Ace Your College Exams

Jon Sterngass, PhD

New York   Chicago   San Francisco   Lisbon   London   Madrid   Mexico City
Milan   New Delhi   San Juan   Seoul   Singapore   Sydney   Toronto

1 2 3 4 5 6 7 8 9 10   QFR/QFR   1 9 8 7 6 5 4 3 2

ISBN   978-0-07-178058-2
MHID   0-07-178058-0

e-ISBN   978-0-07-178059-9
e-MHID   0-07-178059-9

Library of Congress Control Number 2011944588

McGraw-Hill products are available at special quantity discounts to use as premiums
and sales promotions or for use in corporate training programs. To contact a
representative, please e-mail us at bulksales@mcgraw-hill.com.

This book is printed on acid-free paper.

CONTENTS

INTRODUCTION

Congratulations! You've taken a big step toward achieving your best grade by purchasing *McGraw-Hill's 500 World History Questions, Volume 1.* We are here to help you improve your grades on classroom, midterm, and final exams. These 500 questions will help you study more effectively, use your preparation time wisely, and get the final grade you want.

This book gives you 500 multiple-choice questions that cover the most essential course material. Each question has a detailed answer explanation. These questions give you valuable independent practice to supplement your regular textbook and the groundwork you are already doing in the classroom.

You might be the kind of student who needs to study extra questions a few weeks before a big exam for a final review. Or you might be the kind of student who puts off preparing until right before a midterm or final. No matter what your preparation style, you will surely benefit from reviewing these 500 questions that closely parallel the content, format, and degree of difficulty of the questions found in typical college-level exams. These questions and their answer explanations are the ideal last-minute study tool for those final days before the test.

Remember the old saying "Practice makes perfect." If you practice with all the questions and answers in this book, we are certain that you will build the skills and confidence that are needed to ace your exams. Good luck!

—Editors of McGraw-Hill Education

CHAPTER 1

Prehistory and the Neolithic Revolution

1. Paleolithic humans
   (A) domesticated animals
   (B) discovered agriculture
   (C) organized themselves based on a well-defined social hierarchy
   (D) formed exclusively matriarchal societies
   (E) relied on foraging

2. In which of the following regions did native peoples NOT develop agriculture?
   (A) southern Asia
   (B) southwestern Asia
   (C) Australia
   (D) northern Africa
   (E) Andean highlands

3. All of the following are means of determining the approximate dates of human cultures in the Mesolithic and Neolithic eras EXCEPT
   (A) stratigraphy
   (B) cosmic microwave background (CMB) radiation
   (C) paleontology
   (D) paleobotany
   (E) typology

4. It is believed that women in early Neolithic society
   (A) usually accompanied men on hunting expeditions
   (B) usually led the clan
   (C) were expected to devote themselves solely to child care
   (D) experienced a rigid sexual division of labor
   (E) were probably the first farmers

5. Which of the following is the correct chronological sequence of eras?
   (A) Paleolithic, Neolithic, Iron Age, Chalcolithic
   (B) Paleolithic, Bronze Age, Iron Age, Chalcolithic
   (C) Neolithic, Bronze Age, Paleolithic, Chalcolithic
   (D) Chalcolithic, Iron Age, Bronze Age, Paleolithic
   (E) Neolithic, Chalcolithic, Bronze Age, Iron Age

6. The knowledge of agriculture
   (A) was confined to river valley cultures
   (B) arose in different areas of the world around the same time
   (C) was usually passed from one culture to another
   (D) diffused throughout the Eastern Hemisphere only
   (E) developed first in Mesoamerica

7. All of the following are true of the Bering land bridge EXCEPT that it
   (A) allowed wooly mammoths to travel from Asia to North America
   (B) disappeared about 12,000 BCE
   (C) was close to 1,000 miles north to south at its widest point
   (D) existed during the Pleistocene ice ages
   (E) enabled Paleo-Indians to colonize Asia from North America

8. The Lascaux cave paintings could be used as a primary source
   in a study of
   (A) Paleolithic humans
   (B) Neolithic humans
   (C) the Nok culture
   (D) ancient Austronesian peoples
   (E) *Australopithecus robustus*

9. The Neolithic Revolution refers to
   (A) the invention of metallurgy
   (B) the ability to create fire at will
   (C) the extinction of the Neanderthals that allowed *Homo sapiens sapiens*
       to populate the planet
   (D) the transition from hunting and gathering to agriculture
   (E) the development of tool-making capabilities by humans

10. Most Neolithic cultures included all of the following EXCEPT
    (A) religious beliefs
    (B) tools
    (C) sundials
    (D) artwork
    (E) fire

11. Piltdown Man shows that
    (A) the large modern brain preceded the modern omnivorous diet
    (B) scientists can sometimes be dishonest or naive
    (C) the "missing link" came from England
    (D) species can sometimes make gigantic evolutionary leaps
    (E) there is no such thing as a "missing link"

12. The first humans probably evolved in
    (A) Africa in the Pleistocene era
    (B) Asia in the Jurassic era
    (C) Africa in the Cretaceous era
    (D) Asia in the Permian era
    (E) Africa in the Carboniferous era

13. The earliest species to be classified in the same *Homo* species as modern humans is
    (A) *Homo erectus*
    (B) *Homo habilis*
    (C) *Australopithecus robustus*
    (D) Java Man
    (E) Peking Man

14. Which of the following artifacts is likely to be from the Neolithic period?
    (A) An aqueduct
    (B) A codex
    (C) A representation of a goddess of vegetation
    (D) An iron plow
    (E) Glyphs

15. All of the following are true about Lucy, a fossilized skeleton found by Donald Johanson in 1974, EXCEPT that
    (A) she was found in Ethiopia
    (B) she is classified as an *Australopithecus afarensis*
    (C) her skeleton implied that an increase in brain size preceded bipedalism in human evolution
    (D) she probably lived about 3.2 million years ago
    (E) she was a hominid

16. Determining the age of an ancient culture by counting the layers created by melts of water from a receding ice sheet is known as
    (A) aquachronology
    (B) geochronology
    (C) dendrochronology
    (D) paleobotany
    (E) carbon 14 dating

17. Neanderthals
    (A) were first discovered in Africa in the 1960s
    (B) walked like a chimp or an orangutan
    (C) became extinct because they failed to develop tools
    (D) lived on earth between about 1 million and 600,000 years ago
    (E) coexisted with modern humans for at least 10,000 years

18. The Iron Age
    (A) preceded the Stone Age
    (B) preceded the Bronze Age
    (C) left few artifacts, because iron is so malleable
    (D) led to new forms of implements, weapons, and pottery
    (E) began about 12,000 BCE

19. Scientists believe that the first people whose brains and bodies were close to those of modern-day humans—*Homo sapiens*—appeared about how many years ago?
    (A) 4 million
    (B) 1 million
    (C) 400,000
    (D) 40,000
    (E) 10,000

20. Hunter-gatherer societies were first supplanted by societies based on the domestication of plants and animals about
    (A) 1 million BCE
    (B) 400,000 BCE
    (C) 100,000 BCE
    (D) 40,000 BCE
    (E) 10,000 BCE

21. Which event occurred after the domestication of sheep, pigs, and goats?
    (A) The invention of the wheel
    (B) The development of language
    (C) The use of stone tools
    (D) The creation of so-called Venus figurines
    (E) None of the above

22. All of the following are true of the Neolithic Revolution EXCEPT that it led to
    (A) new irrigation and food-storage technologies
    (B) trading economies
    (C) the development of nonportable art and architecture
    (D) centralized administrations and political structures
    (E) the discovery of fire making

23. As of 2012, the best-preserved Neolithic archaeological site is
    (A) Selçuk
    (B) Nineveh
    (C) Tel Maresha
    (D) Çatal Hüyük
    (E) Cahokia

24. All of the following are true of Jericho EXCEPT that
    (A) it is located in present-day Palestinian territories
    (B) contrary to popular belief, it lacked thick city walls
    (C) it became a trade center connecting Anatolia with places around the Red Sea
    (D) it relied on the cultivation of wheat and barley
    (E) it is the oldest continuously inhabited city in the world

25. Bronze is
    (A) a metal primarily used for making warriors' helmets
    (B) a medal awarded to the third-place winner in the mammoth-killing contest
    (C) an alloy usually composed of copper and tin
    (D) an alloy composed of tin and arsenic
    (E) soft and malleable

CHAPTER 2

Egypt and Mesopotamia

26. Cities developed in Mesopotamia between 4000 and 1000 BCE because its inhabitants learned how to
- (A) irrigate dry land through intricate canal systems
- (B) conceptualize law codes to govern their inhabitants
- (C) develop long-range trade routes with distant cultures
- (D) construct large ceremonial centers for religious purposes
- (E) create the agricultural system known as the Mediterranean polyculture

27. The neo-Assyrians
- (A) destroyed the culture of the Sumerians
- (B) were masters of carved stone relief sculpture
- (C) were highly skilled administrators
- (D) were uninterested in the transmission of knowledge
- (E) were noted for their leniency toward people they conquered

28. "For six days and six nights the winds blew, torrent and tempest and flood overwhelmed the world, tempest and flood raged together like warring hosts. When the seventh day dawned, the storm subsided, the sea grew calm, and the flood was stilled. I looked at the face of the world, and there was silence, all mankind turned to clay . . ."

This passage is from the
- (A) *Rubaiyat*
- (B) Hebrew book of Exodus
- (C) Egyptian *Book of the Dead*
- (D) Rigveda
- (E) *Epic of Gilgamesh*

29. What was the result of the battle of Megiddo in about 1479 BCE?
    (A) Thutmose III reestablished Egyptian dominance in Palestine.
    (B) The Assyrian Ashurbanipal effectively ended the Babylonian Empire.
    (C) Nabopolassar evicted the Hyksos from Egypt.
    (D) Kyan's victory gave Babylon control of the vast wealth of Lydia.
    (E) Sargon the Great was defeated by the Sumerians.

30. The alphabet was invented in
    (A) Babylonia
    (B) Israel
    (C) Sumer
    (D) Phoenicia
    (E) Assyria

31. Which of the following ancient cultures was situated near the Persian Gulf?
    (A) Indus Valley
    (B) Nubia
    (C) Yellow River valley
    (D) Egypt
    (E) Sumer

32. Religious leaders in Mesopotamian society enjoyed high social status because of their ability to discover the will of the gods through
    (A) monotheism
    (B) *ma'at*
    (C) divination
    (D) wisdom literature
    (E) apotheosis

33. At the battle of Carchemish in about 605 BCE,
    (A) the Persians defeated the Egyptians
    (B) the Egyptians defeated the Hebrews
    (C) the neo-Assyrians defeated the Babylonians
    (D) the neo-Assyrians defeated the Persians
    (E) the Babylonians defeated the Egyptians and neo-Assyrians

34. All of the following are true of the Phoenicians EXCEPT that they
    (A) were masters of long-distance trade
    (B) adopted Hebrew monotheism
    (C) traded with the Hebrews
    (D) influenced the development of the Roman alphabet
    (E) manufactured glass for trade

35. Religious traditions in the New Kingdom of Egypt
    (A) could determine the success or failure of the king
    (B) did not play a major role in the lives of ordinary people
    (C) initiated the transition to monotheism
    (D) greatly reduced the importance of a belief in the afterlife
    (E) resemble religious traditions still practiced in Egypt today

36. Sumerians probably invented writing in order to
    (A) praise the gods
    (B) record business transactions
    (C) keep detailed genealogical records
    (D) codify centuries of miscellaneous laws
    (E) write poetry

37. All of the following were true of the Hittites EXCEPT that they
    (A) were skillful charioteers
    (B) established a kingdom in north-central Anatolia
    (C) used iron metallurgy
    (D) reached the height of their power around the 14th century BCE
    (E) briefly expanded into Egypt

38. The Hebrews achieved their first truly national organization
    with a creation of a monarchy under Saul in the
    (A) 1900s BCE
    (B) 1600s BCE
    (C) 1300s BCE
    (D) 1000s BCE
    (E) 700s BCE

39. King Hammurabi's law code was written in about
    (A) 3200 BCE
    (B) 2700 BCE
    (C) 2200 BCE
    (D) 1700 BCE
    (E) 1200 BCE

40. The Hebrew Bible established a religion based on all of the following
    EXCEPT
    (A) monotheism
    (B) a covenant relationship
    (C) a refusal to practice idolatry
    (D) God's active role in history
    (E) a deterministic view of ethics

41. The Egyptian pharaoh who is sometimes considered monotheistic was
    (A) Akhenaton
    (B) Nefertiti
    (C) Ramses
    (D) Hashepsut
    (E) Amose

42. All of the following are true of the neo-Assyrian Empire EXCEPT that
    (A) it was overthrown by the Medes and the Chaldeans
    (B) its later capital was at Nineveh
    (C) its religious cult of Ishtar emphasized love, war, fertility, and sex
    (D) it conquered Jerusalem and destroyed the kingdom of Judah
    (E) it built huge temples to the people's gods

43. All of the following are true about the ancient kingdom of Kush
    EXCEPT that
    (A) its kings ruled Egypt for a century
    (B) it was an ancient Nubian state centered in present-day Sudan
    (C) around 600 BCE, the capital was moved from Napata to Meroë
    (D) it was intimately connected with the 25th Dynasty of Egypt
    (E) it differed from Egypt in its disdain for pyramids

44. King Sargon of Akkad tried to establish an empire because he wanted
    greater control of
    (A) his subjects
    (B) foreign irrigation systems
    (C) natural resources for metallurgy
    (D) seaports to export surplus agriculture
    (E) a supply of slaves

45. Women in the Old Kingdom in Egypt
    (A) were allowed to own land
    (B) were forbidden to serve in the government
    (C) were excluded from religious rituals
    (D) could not make wills
    (E) were not permitted to divorce

46. The Egyptian concept of *ma'at* can be roughly translated as
    (A) pharaoh
    (B) afterlife
    (C) justice
    (D) bounty of the Nile
    (E) goodness

47. The treaty signed about 1274 BCE following the battle of Kadesh
   (A) signified the end of the Hittite Empire
   (B) established Assyrian rule over Nineveh
   (C) led to the enslavement of the Hebrew people
   (D) established peace between the Egyptian and Hittite Empires
   (E) represented a truce between the Assyrians and the Hebrews

48. The female pharaoh of the 18th Dynasty who was famous for her prolific building spree was
   (A) Sobekneferu
   (B) Neferneferuaten
   (C) Hatshepsut
   (D) Khentkaus I
   (E) Nitocris

49. All of the following are true regarding the neo-Babylonian Empire EXCEPT that
   (A) it was established by the Chaldeans
   (B) King Nebuchadnezzar II drove the Egyptians out of Syria
   (C) it preserved a great deal of the ancient literature of the Near East
   (D) it was culturally conservative and intellectually stagnant
   (E) one of its greatest achievements was the Ishtar Gate

50. The Akkadian Empire is often considered the world's first empire. It collapsed around 2200 BCE, when it was attacked by the
   (A) Sumerians
   (B) Egyptians
   (C) Assyrians
   (D) Hebrews
   (E) Gutians

51. King Hammurabi's law code
   (A) categorized society according to a social hierarchy
   (B) expressed the majority of the population's view of justice
   (C) gave women the same legal rights as men
   (D) aimed to ensure that more powerful citizens were protected by the law
   (E) was always practiced exactly as written

52. All of the following are true regarding Egypt's New Kingdom EXCEPT that
   (A) the leaders were known as pharaohs
   (B) most of the temples remaining in Egypt today were built during this time
   (C) the rulers engaged in foreign wars to promote Egypt's interests
   (D) it was followed by the Second Intermediate Period
   (E) Egyptian control extended into Asia at this time

53. The end of the neo-Assyrian empire was caused by
   (A) economic crises
   (B) depopulation
   (C) climate change
   (D) internal rebellions
   (E) the spread of the bubonic plague

54. Most modern European languages are derived from
   (A) Hebrew
   (B) Semitic
   (C) Minoan
   (D) Indo-European
   (E) Linear B

55. The powerful monarch who strengthened Egypt by uniting Upper and Lower Egypt into a single centralized kingdom around 3000 BCE was
   (A) Akhenaton
   (B) Menes
   (C) Ramses
   (D) Amenhotep
   (E) Thutmose

56. The New Kingdom began around 1567 BCE after Egypt was liberated from the
   (A) Sumerians
   (B) Assyrians
   (C) Hittites
   (D) Hyksos
   (E) pharaohs

57. Which statement best applies to Pentateuchal law in the Hebrew Bible?
    (A) It applied equally to all Hebrew people.
    (B) It called for vicarious punishments.
    (C) It assigned the death penalty for property crimes.
    (D) It was concerned solely with ritual matters.
    (E) It was adopted by the Babylonians.

58. The word *Mesopotamia* is Greek for "land between two rivers."
    These two rivers are the
    (A) Euphrates and Nile
    (B) Murat and Tigris
    (C) Kara Su and Tigris
    (D) Euphrates and Tigris
    (E) Nile and Tigris

59. What is the correct chronological order (from oldest to most recent)
    for the following empires?
    (A) Persia; neo-Babylonia; neo-Assyria
    (B) Neo-Assyria; Persia; neo-Babylonia
    (C) Neo-Assyria; neo-Babylonia; Persia
    (D) Neo-Babylonia; neo-Assyria; Persia
    (E) Neo-Babylonia; Persia; neo-Assyria

60. All of the following are associated with the Sumerians in the third
    millennium BCE EXCEPT
    (A) ziggurats
    (B) organized irrigation systems
    (C) cuneiform
    (D) a number system based on the number 60
    (E) a religious system based around the god Ashur

CHAPTER **3**

Persia and Greece

61. Minoan culture is associated with
    (A) Crete
    (B) Malta
    (C) the hilltops on the Peloponnese peninsula in southern Greece
    (D) Sicily
    (E) Rhodes

62. Mycenaean and Minoan cultures were similar in all of the following ways EXCEPT in
    (A) constructing similar types of burial chambers
    (B) engaging in maritime trade
    (C) developing a written language
    (D) engaging in wars of conquest
    (E) transmitting some of their culture to classical Greece

63. "The unexamined life is not worth living" is a famous sentiment expressed by
    (A) Socrates
    (B) Solon
    (C) Aristotle
    (D) Cicero
    (E) Cleisthenes

64. All of the following are true of Zoroastrianism EXCEPT that
    (A) it is a religion and philosophy based on the teachings of the prophet Zoroaster
    (B) it was once one of the world's largest religions
    (C) it was founded some time before the sixth century BCE in ancient Sparta
    (D) good and evil are believed to have distinct sources
    (E) its most important religious texts are known as the Avesta

65. What happened at the battle of Opis in 539 BCE?
    (A) The Persians defeated the Hebrews.
    (B) The Babylonians defeated the Egyptians.
    (C) The kingdom of Judah defeated the Sumerians.
    (D) The Hittites defeated the neo-Babylonians.
    (E) The Persians defeated the neo-Babylonians.

66. The Persian Empire that displaced the neo-Babylonian Empire is known as
    (A) the Achaemenid Empire
    (B) the Macedonian Empire
    (C) the Ptolemaic Empire
    (D) the Median Empire
    (E) none of the above

67. Female citizens of the Greek polis did NOT have
    (A) access to the justice system
    (B) protection from being sold into slavery
    (C) respected roles in public religious ceremonies
    (D) the freedom to live without a male guardian
    (E) any control over property rights

68. Which of the following is true of Athenian democracy?
    (A) Court trials were held without the use of juries.
    (B) It was a direct democracy.
    (C) It had a single chief executive.
    (D) Anyone who reached the age of 18 could vote.
    (E) Unfavorable decisions could not be appealed to a higher court.

69. All of the following are true regarding Herodotus EXCEPT that
    (A) he is frequently called the "father of history"
    (B) he wrote a history of the Peloponnesian Wars
    (C) he studied cultures other than that of the Greeks
    (D) he lived in the fifth century BCE
    (E) his writing was known for large digressions

70. King Darius I extended the power of the Persian Empire by
    (A) cutting back on building projects
    (B) lowering taxes
    (C) organizing a large royal army
    (D) establishing one official state religion
    (E) building a large navy

71. Solon balanced reforms that granted political power to ordinary citizens by expanding the role of the
    (A) archons
    (B) Areopagus Council
    (C) laborers
    (D) Council of 400
    (E) Delian League

72. In 371 BCE, Thebes broke the power of Sparta at the battle of
    (A) Plataea
    (B) Syracuse
    (C) Leuctra
    (D) Chaeronea
    (E) Thymbra

73. Evidence from documents found at the palace of Knossos reveal that Mycenaean culture supplanted Minoan culture in Crete about
    (A) 8000 BCE
    (B) 2200 BCE
    (C) 1800 BCE
    (D) 1400 BCE
    (E) 1000 BCE

74. All of the following are true of the Greeks in the so-called Dark Ages (c. 1000–750 BCE) EXCEPT that
    (A) large settlements decreased in population or disappeared
    (B) the population became more mobile
    (C) the people lost their knowledge of writing
    (D) trade virtually disappeared
    (E) herding animals became more common

75. All of the following were great Greek writers of tragedy EXCEPT
    (A) Aristophanes
    (B) Euripides
    (C) Sophocles
    (D) Aeschylus
    (E) none of the above

76. The poems *Theogony* and *Works and Days* were written by
(A) Homer
(B) Pindar
(C) Hesiod
(D) Bacchylides
(E) Archilochus

77. The philosophers who most influenced Greek thinking during the Archaic Age were from
(A) the Peloponnese peninsula
(B) Ionia
(C) Crete
(D) Athens
(E) Lesbos

78. In Plato's *Symposium* (385 BCE), the participants all assume that serious love will be between
(A) a man and his wife
(B) a mother and her children
(C) an older man and an adolescent boy
(D) an adolescent boy and girl
(E) a man and his mistress

79. Greek colonization accomplished all of the following EXCEPT
(A) increased communication among Mediterranean peoples
(B) the spread of Greek language and culture
(C) the foundation of cities such as Syracuse and Naples in the western Mediterranean
(D) the building of a centralized state
(E) facilitation of trade among the polis

80. The Greeks defeated the Persians at Marathon in 490 BCE because the Greeks had
(A) strong warships known as triremes
(B) heavier hoplite weaponry
(C) numerical superiority in infantry
(D) many skilled archers
(E) the best fighters in the world (the Spartans)

81. The geography of ancient Greece
    (A) unified the city-states
    (B) made farmland scarce
    (C) prevented overseas trade
    (D) made city-states vulnerable to overseas invasion
    (E) led to large-scale cattle ranches

82. Bearing male children brought special honors to a woman in ancient Athens because
    (A) male children were necessary to protect and support their parents
    (B) male children were automatically assumed to be legitimate
    (C) female children were regularly sold into slavery
    (D) only men could pass Athenian citizenship on to their offspring
    (E) female children were not citizens

83. All actions of the Peloponnesian League were approved by
    (A) Athens
    (B) Sparta
    (C) Thebes
    (D) Corinth
    (E) Macedonia

84. All of the following are basic beliefs of Zoroastrianism EXCEPT that
    (A) humans are born as sinners and have a compulsion to be sinful
    (B) water and fire are agents of ritual purity
    (C) the world is a battlefield between good and evil forces
    (D) there is an afterlife
    (E) there will be an ultimate judgment day

85. Hippocratic medical doctrine included all of the following EXCEPT that it
    (A) made little or no mention of a divine role in sickness and cures
    (B) influenced the oath that modern medical graduates initially swear to uphold
    (C) was the first to propose the germ theory of disease
    (D) emphasized clinical experience over abstruse theory
    (E) stressed the idea of a crisis in the progression of a disease

86. The term *Greek colonization* can be misleading because
(A) there was minimal official state involvement in new settlements
(B) women did not participate in establishing new settlements
(C) the Greeks had little cultural impact on the areas they settled
(D) most Greek settlements were economic failures
(E) the Greeks settled in Magna Graecia with much greater frequency than in western Asia

87. One of Pericles's major reforms was
(A) paying people for serving in public office
(B) expanding the right of citizenship to foreigners
(C) reducing the number of military campaigns against Sparta
(D) increasing the political rights of women
(E) reducing the court role of the Areopagus Council

88. In fifth-century BCE Athenian democracy, who had the right to vote?
(A) Men residing within the polis
(B) Male and female citizens
(C) Male citizens
(D) Landowning men
(E) Only those men who possessed more than 1,000 drachmas in real property

89. One of the greatest Greek lyric poets, whose work deals with passion and love for various people and both genders, was
(A) Homer
(B) Lesbos
(C) Sappho
(D) Terence
(E) Praxilla

90. Athens defended its dominance over its allies in the Delian League by arguing that
(A) its allies were useless
(B) it needed to keep the league strong enough to protect Greece from the Persians
(C) its contributions to the naval fleet gave it the right to dominate its allies
(D) the money collected from member tributes was needed for public building projects
(E) if the league were weak, Sparta would take over Greece

91. All of the following are true of the ancient Greek Olympic games EXCEPT that
    (A) they took place every four years
    (B) they were celebrated for more than 1,000 years
    (C) women were allowed to participate under certain conditions
    (D) they also featured religious celebrations
    (E) they were Panhellenic

92. *The History of the Peloponnesian War* was written by
    (A) Herodotus
    (B) Thucydides
    (C) Xenophon
    (D) Polybius
    (E) Arrian

93. Socrates's opponents charged him with
    (A) impiety
    (B) supporting Sparta
    (C) being a member of the Thirty Tyrants
    (D) violent attacks against citizens
    (E) mentoring oligarchs and tyrants

94. In the golden age of Athens (c. 450 BCE), slaves probably made up what percentage of the city's population of 300,000?
    (A) 2 percent
    (B) 15 percent
    (C) 33 percent
    (D) 50 percent
    (E) 75 percent

95. The Greek military formation that dominated battlefields during the classical Greek and Hellenistic periods was known as a(n)
    (A) hoplite
    (B) cohort
    (C) aspis
    (D) sarisa
    (E) phalanx

96. All of the following were true of the Parthenon EXCEPT that
   (A) it was built as a house for the goddess Athena
   (B) only priests and priestesses could enter the temple
   (C) the sculptural frieze portrayed Athenian citizens in the presence of the gods
   (D) subtle curves and inclines were used to produce the illusion of completely straight lines
   (E) it broke with precedent by being constructed near, but not on, the Athenian acropolis

97. The Persian War is best described in the works of
   (A) Aeschylus
   (B) Aristophanes
   (C) Euripides
   (D) Sophocles
   (E) Homer

98. In ancient Greece, some itinerant professional teachers of philosophy and oratory were associated with moral relativism and manipulation of rhetoric. They were called
   (A) Sophists
   (B) Stoas
   (C) Archons
   (D) Triremes
   (E) Stoics

99. The Greeks defeated Persia in which crucial naval battle that helped save Greece's independence?
   (A) Plataea
   (B) Salamis
   (C) Marathon
   (D) Syracuse
   (E) Actium

100. The Minoans developed their agriculture through the use of
   (A) iron plows
   (B) irrigation with water pumps drawn by oxen
   (C) Mediterranean polyculture
   (D) Aegean dairy farming
   (E) Grecian monocropping

101. All of the following were true of the Persians EXCEPT that
    (A)   their language was related to those of the Aryans and Hittites
    (B)   they treated conquered peoples in a manner similar to that adopted by the Assyrians
    (C)   they spread a new religion across their empire
    (D)   they were efficient administrators
    (E)   they established an effective system of communication

102. In its golden age, Athens achieved its great wealth through all of the following EXCEPT
    (A)   Delian League tributes
    (B)   spoils taken from conquered Persian outposts
    (C)   taxes on trade goods
    (D)   the sale of triremes to its allies
    (E)   booming seaborne commerce

103. Which of the following statements is true of ancient Greek pottery?
    (A)   Because of its fragile nature, very little Greek pottery has survived.
    (B)   Greek vases were mostly made using the coil method, because the Greeks did not possess potter's wheels.
    (C)   There was an international market for Greek pottery from the eighth to the fourth century BCE.
    (D)   Greek pottery is unique in that human figures are never depicted.
    (E)   Black- and red-figure techniques were both used in Athens during the golden age.

104. The Thirty Tyrants was a popular name for
    (A)   the Persian council of war under Xerxes
    (B)   the leaders who successfully overthrew the Hellenic League
    (C)   the dictators who ruled Athens directly after the Persian wars
    (D)   a pro-Spartan oligarchy in Athens
    (E)   the consecutive series of Spartan rulers between 476 and 431 BCE

105. The decisive event of the Peloponnesian War was
    (A)   the Athenian invasion of Sicily
    (B)   Pericles's funeral oration
    (C)   the battle of Naupactus
    (D)   the rule of the Thirty Tyrants
    (E)   the battle of Marathon

106. The end of the golden age in Athens can be attributed to
(A) a widespread rejection of democracy
(B) the Persian conquest
(C) the plague
(D) the Macedonian conquest of Athens
(E) the Peloponnesian War

107. At the time of an Athenian mother's death,
(A) her children inherited her dowry
(B) her husband inherited her dowry
(C) her parents regained her dowry
(D) her husband and sons split her dowry
(E) her dowry was confiscated by the state

108. The Royal Road
(A) was built by the Persians to invade Greece
(B) was built by the Persians to cross the Hellespont
(C) was maintained for more than 3,000 miles
(D) connected Athens to Greek colonies in Anatolia
(E) was used by Persian couriers to travel from Susa to Sardis

109. In classical Greece, religious sacrifices were held for all of the following reasons EXCEPT
(A) providing an occasion for the community to assemble
(B) eliminating sick or injured animals through animal sacrifice
(C) reaffirming the community's ties to the divine world
(D) benefiting the worshippers' personal relationship with the gods
(E) trying to provide divine protection from disaster

110. All of the following are true of freestanding Greek sculptures in the fifth century BCE EXCEPT that
(A) they were meant to be seen by the public
(B) women were usually portrayed in the nude
(C) physiques and postures became more naturalistic than those of the Archaic Age
(D) musculature was anatomically correct
(E) faces were portrayed as calm rather than smiling as in the Archaic Age

CHAPTER 4

The Hellenistic World

111. The occupation of Jerusalem by Antiochus IV led to a Jewish revolt that is celebrated today in the Jewish holiday of
(A) Rosh Hashanah
(B) Hanukkah
(C) Yom Kippur
(D) the Sabbath
(E) Passover

112. All of the following are true of Alexander the Great EXCEPT that
(A) he led a combined Macedonian and Greek army against Persia
(B) he wanted to receive the same honors as a god
(C) he modeled himself on Achilles, the hero of Homer's *Iliad*
(D) his soldiers were intensely loyal and would follow him anywhere
(E) he spread Greek colonists and culture through ancient southwestern Asia

113. Alexander the Great smashed Darius III and ended the Persian (Achaemenid) Empire at the battle of
(A) Gaugamela (Arbela)
(B) Ipsus
(C) Chaeronea
(D) Issus
(E) Thymbra (Sardis)

114. In *The Republic*, Plato wrote about
(A) a system for international peace
(B) the importance of monotheism for a successful city-state
(C) ideal forms of government
(D) why poets should play an important role in a city-state's government
(E) why people should avoid caves

115. The Diadochi were
- (A) an informal group of realistic Hellenistic sculptors
- (B) peripatetic philosophers
- (C) rival successors to Alexander the Great
- (D) the dynasty of Macedonian kings that succeeded Alexander
- (E) the advisers to Mithradites who helped created the kingdom of Pontus

116. After the Peloponnesian War, Athens's economy slowly revived because of trade and
- (A) a production boom in the silver mines
- (B) plunder taken from military expeditions
- (C) the production of goods in homes and small shops
- (D) the return of soldiers from the war
- (E) the destruction of the Long Walls in 393 BCE

117. The influence of Greek culture during the Hellenistic period was strongest among
- (A) urban populations in Egypt and southwestern Asia
- (B) farmers in the Persian countryside
- (C) the Romans
- (D) the people of western India
- (E) merchants in North Africa and southern Europe

118. Aristotle's followers were known as
- (A) Sophists
- (B) Republicans
- (C) Peripatetics
- (D) Academicians
- (E) Stoics

119. All of the following are true of Stoicism EXCEPT that
- (A) its followers believed human actions had meaning if taken in the pursuit of virtue
- (B) its followers believed politics were incompatible with virtue
- (C) its followers believed fate controlled everything
- (D) it was founded by Zeno of Citium
- (E) its philosophy advocated equal citizenship for women

120. Menander is famous as
- (A) one of the greatest writers of Greek tragedies
- (B) the man who moved Hellenistic sculpture to a more emotional perspective
- (C) the best-known representative of Athenian New Comedy
- (D) the originator of the idea of philosophical materialism
- (E) the ingenious architect who laid out the street plan for Alexandria, Egypt

121. All of the following are true of Arsinoë II EXCEPT that she
- (A) began the tradition of Ptolemaic sibling marriages
- (B) played a major role in politics in Thrace
- (C) was a coruler of Egypt
- (D) maneuvered to have Seleucus conquer the kingdom of Lysimachus
- (E) was the oldest surviving child of Ptolemy I

122. The percentage of the population of the Hellenistic kingdoms that worked as peasant farmers was about
- (A) 20 percent
- (B) 40 percent
- (C) 60 percent
- (D) 80 percent
- (E) 99 percent

123. The person who is often called the "father of geometry" is
- (A) Archimedes
- (B) Euclid
- (C) Pythagoras
- (D) Hipparchus
- (E) Thales

124. Plato's philosophy held that the absolute virtues were the only true reality, and he called them
- (A) dialogues
- (B) forms
- (C) guardians
- (D) auxiliaries
- (E) helots

125. Artistic expression in the Hellenistic kingdoms focused largely on
   (A) the lives of monarchs
   (B) political issues
   (C) individual emotions
   (D) foreign policy
   (E) city life

126. The research institute in Alexandria was called the
   (A) Museum
   (B) Lyceum
   (C) Academy
   (D) Stoa
   (E) *Pinakes*

127. In 301 BCE, at the battle of Ipsus,
   (A) Alexander the Great captured northern India
   (B) Ptolemy II became sole ruler of Egypt and declared himself pharaoh
   (C) Antigonus's defeat led to the final breakup of Alexander's empire
   (D) Seleucus lost control of Persia to Egyptian forces under Cassander
   (E) the Diadochi took over the old Persian Empire

128. All of the following are true of Archimedes EXCEPT that he
   (A) invented Greek fire
   (B) explained the principle of the lever
   (C) invented the screw pump known as Archimedes's screw
   (D) discovered the principle of buoyancy that bears his name
   (E) made several noted mathematical discoveries

129. Women in Hellenistic culture excelled as
   (A) monumental sculptors
   (B) neo-Platonist philosophers
   (C) masters of epigrammatic poetry
   (D) New Comedy playwrights
   (E) writers with royal patronage

130. One of the main ways Macedonian kings maintained effective rule was through
   (A) support from powerful nobles
   (B) alliances with Greek city-states
   (C) sustaining a large slave population
   (D) infrequent military invasions
   (E) downplaying their ethnic heritage

131. All of the following are true of Alexandria in Egypt EXCEPT that
(A) the city no longer exists because Julius Caesar burned it down in 48 BCE
(B) it had the largest Jewish population in the world during the Hellenistic period
(C) it had an extraordinary library
(D) its lighthouse was one of the so-called Seven Wonders of the Ancient World
(E) it was located on the Mediterranean Sea

132. Local men could advance within the administration of the Hellenistic kingdoms by learning
(A) rhetoric
(B) geometry
(C) philosophy
(D) Greek
(E) mathematics

133. *Laocoön and His Sons* is a famous Hellenistic
(A) historical painting
(B) sculpture
(C) opera
(D) comedy of manners
(E) tragedy

134. During the Hellenistic period, all of the following were forms of religious expression EXCEPT
(A) the worship of healing divinities
(B) ruler cults
(C) the cult of Isis
(D) the cult of Caracalla
(E) Jewish worship at the Second Temple

135. Aristarchus of Samos is known as the
(A) first scientist in Europe to dissect cadavers
(B) developer of the *paideia* school of child-rearing
(C) originator of the theory that the world is made of atoms
(D) genius behind the first geometric axioms
(E) creator of a heliocentric model of the solar system

136. Epicureans taught all of the following EXCEPT that
   (A) the universe is infinite and eternal
   (B) women and slaves could be regular members of their school
   (C) all human knowledge is based on experience and perception
   (D) active citizenship is an overrated way to achieve happiness
   (E) the gods reward and punish humans in this life, not the next one

137. For their service in the royal armies of the Hellenistic kingdoms, professional soldiers from Greece and Macedonia received
   (A) weapons
   (B) slaves
   (C) land grants
   (D) precious stones
   (E) pensions

138. The so-called successor kings to Alexander divided his empire into which three new kingdoms?
   (A) Macedonian, Persian, and Egyptian
   (B) Antigonid, Seleucid, and Ptolemaic
   (C) Attalid, Macedonian, and Ptolemaic
   (D) Seleucid, Bactrian, and Parthian
   (E) Ptolemaic, Cassandran, and Antipaterian

139. In Book II of *Politics*, Aristotle wrote, "Even when laws have been written down, they should not always remain unaltered." This is the basic principle behind
   (A) checks and balances
   (B) federalism
   (C) amendments to a constitution
   (D) the three-fifths compromise
   (E) division of powers

140. All of the following are true about the battle of Chaeronea in 338 BCE EXCEPT that
   (A) it ended Greek independence for decades
   (B) it led to the creation of a federation of Greek states
   (C) the winning general was Alexander the Great
   (D) the forces of Athens and Thebes were destroyed
   (E) it unified Greece under Macedonian control

141. All of the following were true of Philip II EXCEPT that
- (A) he was the father of Alexander the Great
- (B) he was assassinated in 336 BCE
- (C) he was a skilled military innovator and leader
- (D) his ultimate goal was to conquer Greece
- (E) he formed the League of Corinth

142. Diogenes was a
- (A) Stoic
- (B) Epicurean
- (C) Peripatetic
- (D) Cynic
- (E) Neoplatonist

143. The wealthy capital of the kingdom of the Attalids in western Anatolia was
- (A) Pergamum
- (B) Bactra
- (C) Antioch
- (D) Cyrene
- (E) Tyre

144. Basic characteristics of Hellenistic culture included all of the following EXCEPT
- (A) the overwhelming impact of royal wealth
- (B) a concentration on private rather than public matters
- (C) an increased interaction among diverse peoples
- (D) a shared culture based on the use of the Macedonian language
- (E) a fusion of the ancient Greek world with the cultures of the Middle East and southwestern Asia

145. All of the following advanced the fields of science or anatomy in the Hellenistic age EXCEPT
- (A) Ctesibius
- (B) Erasistratus
- (C) Praxagoras of Cos
- (D) Herophilos of Chalcedon
- (E) Praxiteles of Athens

CHAPTER 5

The Roman Republic and Empire

146. All of the following helped to spread Christianity EXCEPT
   (A) its acceptance as the official religion of Rome in the third century CE
   (B) the Pax Romana
   (C) the Silk Road
   (D) the missionary efforts of Paul of Tarsus
   (E) Roman roads

147. The last Hellenistic kingdom to fall to the Romans was the
   (A) Antigonid kingdom
   (B) Seleucid kingdom
   (C) Ptolemaic kingdom
   (D) Anatolian kingdom
   (E) Etruscan kingdom

148. Defeat at which battle marked the end of the Roman Empire's expansion into northern Europe?
   (A) Teutoburg Forest
   (B) Pharsalus
   (C) Beth-horon
   (D) Milvian Bridge
   (E) Pydna

149. The First Triumvirate consisted of
   (A) Jupiter, Diana, and Neptune
   (B) Julius Caesar, Pompey, and Crassus
   (C) Livy, Ovid, and Virgil
   (D) Octavian, Marc Anthony, and Lepidus
   (E) Julius Caesar, Pompey, and Catiline

150. Which group invaded Rome in 410 CE and sacked the city?
(A) Huns
(B) Visigoths
(C) Gauls
(D) Ostrogoths
(E) Vandals

151. Hypatia was
(A) a mathematician who was murdered by a Christian mob
(B) the head of a guardian cult that was sacred to Roman women
(C) the daughter and only biological child of Augustus
(D) the first notable female architect to publish a book that survived
(E) the most noted Christian martyr from Diocletian's Great Persecution

152. The Romans dated their city's founding to the year
(A) 753 BCE
(B) 509 BCE
(C) 600 BCE
(D) 44 BCE
(E) 31 BCE

153. All of the following are true of Augustus's reign EXCEPT that he
(A) was a patron of the arts and literature
(B) initiated a period of relative peace known as Pax Romana
(C) dramatically enlarged the empire
(D) reformed the Roman system of taxation
(E) dismantled the principate and replaced it with a new system
of government

154. *The Metamorphoses* was written by
(A) Virgil
(B) Horace
(C) Ovid
(D) Hypatia
(E) Martial

155. All of the following are true of homosexuality in ancient Rome EXCEPT that
    (A) it was regarded as an ordinary part of the range of human experience
    (B) men's acceptance of a passive role was considered worthy of contempt
    (C) Roman emperors remained heterosexual to bolster the family structure of the Roman state
    (D) male writers of books and legal codes were not as interested in lesbianism as in male love
    (E) legislation against homosexuality did not become common until the reign of the Christian emperors

156. All of the following are true of the Etruscans EXCEPT that
    (A) their culture peaked about 500 BCE
    (B) they were famous for their gold work and pottery
    (C) they had a tremendous influence on Roman religious beliefs and architecture
    (D) their alphabet was based on Greek models
    (E) they were especially influential southeast of the Tiber River

157. Roman policy toward granting citizenship differed from Greek policy in that Roman citizenship
    (A) included slaves
    (B) included children of freedmen
    (C) excluded women
    (D) excluded freed slaves
    (E) included all foreigners

158. A man climbing the ladder of Roman political office, from least powerful to most powerful, would progress according to the following order:
    (A) quaestor, aedile, praetor, consul
    (B) quaestor, praetor, aedile, consul
    (C) aedile, quaestor, consul, praetor
    (D) consul, praetor, aedile, quaestor
    (E) aedile, quaestor, praetor, consul

159. The Gracchi were
    (A) Roman deities who supposedly protected the emperor when he traveled outside the Roman city limits
    (B) reformers who wanted to expand the *insulae*
    (C) decurions under the principate
    (D) *curiales* who became Christian ascetics in the late 400s CE
    (E) brothers who tried to limit the size of the latifundia

160. In 404 CE, Emperor Honorius established the new capital of the western empire in
- (A) Milan
- (B) Byzantium
- (C) Ravenna
- (D) Naples
- (E) Avignon

161. The Edict of Milan in 313 CE
- (A) outlawed polytheism
- (B) included Jesus in the imperial cult
- (C) made Christianity the official state religion
- (D) tried to avoid angering traditional believers
- (E) made the Lord's day a holy occasion each week

162. Eventually, Christianity became the religion of the overwhelming majority of people in the empire for all of the following reasons EXCEPT that
- (A) it offered the social advantages and security of belonging to the emperor's religion
- (B) it drew believers from women as well as men of all classes
- (C) it assured people of personal salvation
- (D) it nourished a strong sense of community
- (E) it was popular among Roman soldiers and spread with the legions across the empire

163. A free marriage was one in which
- (A) a wife could freely divorce her husband
- (B) a husband and wife owned all their property in common
- (C) a wife could conduct business without a male guardian
- (D) a wife lived under her father's power rather than her husband's
- (E) a woman had to wait for her father to die before marrying

164. The doctrine of Cicero that combined strands of Greek philosophy and Roman values is called
- (A) *pax deorum*
- (B) *humanitas*
- (C) Stoicism
- (D) *mos maiorum*
- (E) *paideia*

165. The Council of Nicaea met in 325 CE to settle the controversy over
    (A) the position of women in the church
    (B) marriage
    (C) Donatism
    (D) the celibacy of priests
    (E) Arianism

166. Emperor Nero
    (A) modeled familial harmony as a way of connecting with *mos maiorum*
    (B) encouraged religious tolerance in the empire
    (C) supported deflation of the currency, which angered the masses
    (D) was the first emperor of the Julio-Claudian Dynasty
    (E) embarked on an ambitious building program after the Great Fire

167. All of the following are true regarding Augustine's position on sexual desire EXCEPT that
    (A) it influenced western Christianity for more than a thousand years
    (B) it ennobled virginity and sexual renunciation as the highest virtues
    (C) it praised sexual intercourse between loving spouses
    (D) it led to calls for celibate priests and bishops
    (E) it blamed events in the Garden of Eden for the disconnect between human will and passions

168. All of the following reasons have been given for the decline of the Roman Empire EXCEPT that
    (A) military dictatorship failed to provide protection from invaders
    (B) the population increased beyond the empire's ability to support it
    (C) large estates at the fringe became self-sufficient and broke away
    (D) debasement of the currency helped ruin the economy
    (E) citizens stopped participating in government

169. Under Diocletian's tax reforms, the coloni (tenant farmers)
    (A) were forced to serve in the military
    (B) had to pay for shortfalls in tax collection out of their own pockets
    (C) had to leave the farm to seek menial work in the city
    (D) lost the freedom to move from one plot of land to another
    (E) moved farther from urban areas to avoid higher taxes

170. The Anglo-Saxons invaded Britain in the fifth century CE after
the Romans
    (A) withdrew their army from Britain in order to defend Italy from
        the Visigoths
    (B) taxed the Angles and Saxons on the continent to the point
        of starvation
    (C) refused to grant the Anglo-Saxons asylum from the marauding Huns
    (D) drove the Anglo-Saxons from their homelands north of the Danube
        River
    (E) made an agreement with the Jutes and Celts to divide England
        into three parts

171. The concept of *patria potestas* meant
    (A) the Roman Republic had priority in the Roman value system
    (B) constant vigilance was required to keep the Roman legions strong
    (C) a Roman father had complete ownership and control of his
        household's property
    (D) it was the duty of Roman citizens to protest if they thought
        the republic was wrong in its policies
    (E) it was an honor to die for one's country

172. All of the following are true of the reign of Marcus Aurelius EXCEPT that
    (A) he wrote *The Meditations*
    (B) he had to defend the empire from invaders from the north and east
    (C) he was the last of the so-called Five Good Emperors
    (D) Pax Romana essentially came to an end with his death
    (E) he imposed new tax burdens on the *curiales*

173. All of the following were battles of the Punic Wars EXCEPT
    (A) Cannae
    (B) Lake Trasimeno
    (C) Metaurus River
    (D) Zama
    (E) Actium

174. All of the following were popular belief systems of the Roman Empire
except
    (A) Mithraism
    (B) the Eleusinian mysteries
    (C) the cult of Isis
    (D) Waldensianism
    (E) Stoicism

175. Which of the following is true of the coinage of the Roman Empire?
  (A) Roman coinage steadily gained in value as the empire matured.
  (B) Roman coins were almost worthless by 300 CE.
  (C) Roman emperors often deflated the currency to keep prices under control.
  (D) Counterfeit coins helped reduce governmental expenses in the later Roman Empire.
  (E) Gold coins gradually replaced silver coins after 229 CE.

176. Spartacus was
  (A) the leader of an unsuccessful slave revolt against the Roman Republic
  (B) the Roman general who reformed the republic's armies
  (C) the richest man in Rome, who influenced politics between the triumvirates
  (D) one of a pair of brothers who advocated giving land to poor Romans
  (E) the *pontifex maximus* who ordered Julius Caesar to surrender his command in 53 BCE

177. All of the following are true of Constantine EXCEPT that
  (A) he evolved the idea of an ecumenical council
  (B) he subdivided the Roman Empire into a tetrarchy
  (C) he was the first Roman emperor to convert to Christianity
  (D) he was a superb general
  (E) he issued the Edict of Milan

178. At the time of Jesus, the Jewish religious sect that believed in a communal life dedicated to asceticism and abstinence was the
  (A) Essenes
  (B) Bar Kohbites
  (C) Pharisees
  (D) Sadducees
  (E) Zealots

179. Voting procedures in the assemblies of the early Roman Republic permitted
  (A) each individual to receive one vote
  (B) large groups to receive more votes than smaller ones
  (C) each group, defined by status and wealth, to receive one vote
  (D) the crowd to vote by applauding or hissing after the public speeches
  (E) the Plebeian Council to have much more power than the Tribal Assembly

180. An unintended effect of Diocletian's Great Persecution was
- (A) the elimination of Christianity in the eastern empire
- (B) that Christians began to outnumber polytheists
- (C) the conversion of Constantine to Christianity
- (D) that many polytheists became sympathetic toward the persecuted Christians
- (E) that the empire suffered severe economic dislocations from the removal of Christians from influential mercantile positions

181. The Vestals
- (A) were one of many female priesthood groups
- (B) were responsible for checking the virginity of the emperor's wife
- (C) had no power in the republic because they were women
- (D) tended the eternal flame of Rome
- (E) could not own property or make a will

182. Which of the following statements is true of *curiales* in the fourth century CE?
- (A) Roman citizens competed to join the curial class.
- (B) The burdens of the position discouraged socially minded volunteers.
- (C) Reforms by Domitian and Constantine lightened the tax-collecting problems of the *curiales*.
- (D) The situation of *curiales* was transformed as Christians and soldiers filled the previously inaccessible positions.
- (E) Constantine and Valens abolished the positions because of the difficulties in filling them.

183. To get rid of their enemies, the Second Triumvirate used
- (A) proscription
- (B) indictments
- (C) popular mobs
- (D) trial before assembly
- (E) star chambers

184. The immediate cause of the end of the Roman Empire was
- (A) poor harvests
- (B) the vastness of the empire, which made efficient rule impossible
- (C) non-Roman members of the army
- (D) inefficient leadership
- (E) the movement of Germanic tribes through the empire to Rome

185. Which of the following ancient cultures used a postal service?
  (A) Ancient Egypt
  (B) Ancient China
  (C) The Persian Empire
  (D) The Roman Empire
  (E) All of the above

186. All of the following are true of Julius Caesar EXCEPT that
  (A) he was the only member of both the First and Second Triumvirates
  (B) he was adored by his army
  (C) his power as dictator offended the *optimates*
  (D) his victory at Pharsalus in 48 BCE ended his rivalry with Pompey
  (E) his victories over Vercingetorix established Roman dominance in Gaul for the next 500 years

187. All of the following were noted scientists of the Roman Republic or Empire EXCEPT
  (A) Gerard of Cremona
  (B) Hero of Alexandria
  (C) Galen
  (D) Ptolemy
  (E) Pliny the Elder

188. Plautus and Terence are associated with Roman
  (A) philosophy
  (B) epic poetry
  (C) comedy
  (D) tragedy
  (E) science

189. Roman baths were
  (A) open only to members of the elite
  (B) an effective way to fight the spread of communicable disease
  (C) often used as centers for exercising and socializing
  (D) open only to men
  (E) common in Rome but rare in the provinces

190. "Arms and the man I sing, the first who came,
Compelled by fate, an exile out of Troy,
To Italy and the Lavinian coast . . .
Till he should build his town
And bring his gods to Latium, whence, in time,
The Latin race, the Alban fathers rose
And the great walls of everlasting Rome."

These words were written by
(A) Homer
(B) Aeneas
(C) Virgil
(D) Lucan
(E) Lucretius

191. All of the following were important philosophical thinkers during
the time of the Roman Empire EXCEPT
(A) Origen
(B) Philo
(C) Plotinus
(D) John Scotus Eriugena
(E) Porphyry

192. The excavation of Pompeii reveals what life was like in a Roman city
in about
(A) 170 BCE
(B) 70 BCE
(C) 70 CE
(D) 170 CE
(E) 270 CE

193. The plebeians ultimately won their demands during the so-called Struggle
of the Orders by
(A) staging a revolt
(B) threatening the safety of patrician citizens
(C) speaking in the public assemblies
(D) refusing military service
(E) amending the Twelve Tables to allow them to make laws

194. The temporary office to which the Roman Senate appointed Sulla and which he then used to reorganize the government in favor of his own social class was
(A) senator
(B) consul
(C) dictator
(D) emperor
(E) aedile

195. The hierarchical system that imposed mutual obligations on members of Roman society was called the
(A) *mos maiorum*
(B) patron-client
(C) *patria potestas*
(D) decurion
(E) *insulae*

CHAPTER 6

China: Hsia to Han

196. The Silk Road
- (A) comprised land routes only
- (B) was actually misnamed, since the network had nothing to do with the transport of silk
- (C) connected land routes to Indian Ocean trade
- (D) stopped to the east of Mediterranean trade routes
- (E) was protected from one end to the other by pastoral nomads

197. Which best describes the form of government established in the early years of the Han Dynasty?
- (A) A form of feudalism was combined with a centralized autocracy.
- (B) Local lords forced the emperor to divide China into decentralized fiefdoms.
- (C) The emperor maintained control over the empire without consulting the Chinese bureaucracy.
- (D) The Han Dynasty was one of three competing kingdoms in China, each with a warlord or emperor.
- (E) Feudalism was abolished, creating a manpower surplus that allowed the creation of great building projects.

198. "Under heaven nothing is more soft and yielding than water
Yet for attacking the solid and the strong, nothing is better
It has no equal
The weak can overcome the strong
The supple can overcome the stiff
Under heaven everyone knows this
Yet no one puts it into practice."

This quotation is from
(A) the Rigveda
(B) the Tao Te Ching
(C) *The Analects*
(D) the Bhagavad Gita
(E) *The Mengzi*

199. Iron-tipped plows were first used in
(A) the Han Dynasty
(B) the Warring States period
(C) the Three Kingdoms period
(D) the Hsia Dynasty
(E) the Shang Dynasty

200. All of the following are basic beliefs of Confucianism EXCEPT that
(A) compromise and patience are necessary in all matters
(B) there should be respect for age and authority
(C) the family is the foundation of society
(D) society should be ordered, and everyone should do what is expected
(E) human nature is essentially evil and must be constrained by laws and rituals

201. All of the following are inventions and advances attributed to the Han Dynasty EXCEPT
(A) a calendar of 365 days
(B) porcelain
(C) paper
(D) the Grand Canal
(E) the seismograph

202. All of the following are true regarding the Warring States period
EXCEPT that
(A) there was mass migration to cities
(B) iron replaced bronze as the dominant metal used in warfare
(C) fear of anarchy led to the development of new philosophical systems
(D) it ended with the unification of China under the Qin (Ch'in)
Dynasty
(E) its artists excelled in the development of wood-block printing

203. It is commonly accepted that the greatest disciple of Confucius was
(A) Mencius
(B) Mozi
(C) Sun Tzu
(D) Yang Zhu
(E) Xunzi

204. Which of the following was a major accomplishment of the Shang
Dynasty?
(A) The invention of gunpowder
(B) The invention of paper
(C) The invention of the compass
(D) The invention of a pictographic and ideographic writing system
(E) The invention of iron-tipped plows

205. What is the proper order of these early Chinese dynastic periods?
(A) Hsia, Shang, Zhou, Qin, Han
(B) Hsia, Qin, Han, Shang, Zhou
(C) Shang, Hsia, Han, Zhou, Qin
(D) Hsia, Qin, Shang, Zhou, Han
(E) Shang, Zhou, Qin, Hsia, Han

206. All of the following are true of the Qin Dynasty EXCEPT that it
(A) created a strong central government
(B) began constructing the Great Wall
(C) followed legalistic principles
(D) encouraged freedom of thought
(E) standardized writing, weights, and measures throughout the empire

207. In Shang China, the economy depended primarily on
  (A) animal husbandry
  (B) trade
  (C) farming
  (D) hunting and gathering
  (E) tribute and plunder from conquest

208. All of the following are true of Chinese Legalist philosophy EXCEPT that
  (A) its followers believed humans were inherently evil
  (B) it was the basic governing philosophy of the Qin Dynasty
  (C) its proponents believed the government that governs best, governs least
  (D) it was founded by Shang Yang about 350 BCE
  (E) its followers believed in strict censorship

209. All of the following were true of the Shang EXCEPT that
  (A) they spoke a Sino-Tibetan language
  (B) they fought on horseback and in chariots
  (C) they expanded irrigation systems on the Yellow (Huang He) River
  (D) they tried to break down the social stratification of Chinese society
  (E) they began silkworm cultivation in China

210. The concept of the mandate of heaven was
  (A) the Zhou Dynasty's justification to rule
  (B) opposed by Mencius as contradictory to Confucian philosophy
  (C) identical to the European concept of the divine right of kings
  (D) rejected by the Han because their dynasty was not founded by a noble
  (E) of little effect on Chinese history after the Tang Dynasty

211. All of the following were reasons for the collapse of the Han Empire EXCEPT
  (A) the power of local warlords led to the deterioration of the central state
  (B) attacks by the Xiongnu overwhelmed Han defenses
  (C) peasant rebellions reduced support for the emperor
  (D) epidemic diseases led to population decline
  (E) tribute payments weakened the treasury

212. An important military development of the Warring States period was
  (A) the invention of gunpowder
  (B) the casting of individual weapons
  (C) the widespread use of chariots
  (D) the cultural diffusion of the phalanx
  (E) the use of elephants to intimidate opposing forces

213. Sun Tzu is famous as the author of
  (A) *The Analects*
  (B) the Four Books
  (C) *The Mengzi*
  (D) *The Six Secret Teachings*
  (E) *The Art of War*

214. All of the following are true about the Zhou Dynasty EXCEPT that it was
  (A) relatively brief
  (B) followed by the Qin Dynasty
  (C) the dynasty during which the use of iron was introduced to China
  (D) the apex of Chinese bronzeware creation
  (E) the dynasty during which the Chinese written script evolved into its modern form

215. The powerful and feared first empress of the Han Dynasty was
  (A) Empress Lu Zhi
  (B) Lady Qi
  (C) Princess Lu Yan
  (D) Empress Dowager Cixi
  (E) Empress Wu Zetian

216. The oldest form of Chinese writing was
  (A) merchant records on rice paper
  (B) dynastic genealogies carved on stone
  (C) questions to priests on animal bones
  (D) tax rolls on paper
  (E) lists of sacrifices to the gods on silk

217. All of the following are true of the Chinese bureaucracy under the Han EXCEPT that
   (A) it administered the Chinese government
   (B) its members were highly paid and highly respected
   (C) qualification took years to complete
   (D) it was restricted to members of the upper classes
   (E) its members had mastered the Chinese alphabet

218. The Terracotta Army is associated with which dynastic period?
   (A) Shang Dynasty
   (B) Qin Dynasty
   (C) Hsia Dynasty
   (D) Three Kingdoms period
   (E) Han Dynasty

219. According to traditional sources, the first Chinese dynasty was the
   (A) Shang
   (B) Hsia
   (C) Zhou
   (D) Qin
   (E) Han

220. All of the following are true about Mohism EXCEPT that
   (A) it was a rival of Confucianism
   (B) its followers rejected offensive warfare
   (C) Mozi wanted to eliminate music and extraneous ritual from Chinese worship
   (D) it particularly emphasized devotion to one's family
   (E) its followers believed in ghosts and spirits

221. According to Confucian thought, all of the following are hierarchical relationships that guarantee stability EXCEPT
   (A) friend to friend
   (B) sibling to sibling
   (C) wife to husband
   (D) subject to emperor
   (E) eldest son to father

222. The Han Dynasty was established by Liu Pang at
(A) the battle of Red Cliffs
(B) the battle of P'eng-ch'eng
(C) the battle of Lan-t'ien
(D) the siege of Chu-liu
(E) the battle of Kai-Hsia (Giaxia)

223. All of the following are true of the Three Kingdoms period EXCEPT that
(A) it was extremely bloody
(B) technological innovation thrived
(C) it is an obscure period that has basically been forgotten
(D) it followed the Han Dynasty
(E) the population decreased significantly

224. The Taoist concept of complementary opposites is known as
(A) yin and yang
(B) de and li
(C) e and fa
(D) shu and lian
(E) yi and ren

225. All of the following are true of Emperor Wu of Han EXCEPT that
(A) his reign was one of the longest in Chinese history
(B) he expanded Chinese borders as far as present-day Kyrgyzstan in the west
(C) he established a centralized state
(D) he developed the Silk Road
(E) he followed Mohist principles regarding offensive warfare

CHAPTER 7

India Through the Gupta Empire

226. Which religion spread primarily through the efforts of traders and merchants?
    (A) Shinto
    (B) Zoroastrianism
    (C) Jainism
    (D) Buddhism
    (E) Judaism

227. People in Neolithic Asia probably cultivated all of the following EXCEPT
    (A) millet
    (B) rice
    (C) spices
    (D) poi
    (E) bananas

228. All of the following are true of the empire of Chandragupta Maurya EXCEPT that it
    (A) adopted Buddhism as a unifying force throughout the empire
    (B) became the first unified, centralized government in India
    (C) used standardized coinage to make trade more efficient
    (D) established governmental control of mining and shipbuilding
    (E) formed a powerful military

229. The summer monsoons in India blow
    (A) northeast off the Indian Ocean
    (B) south across the dry Asian interior
    (C) southwest from the Pacific Ocean
    (D) west from southeast Asia
    (E) east from the Indian Ocean, the Persian Gulf, and the Red Sea

230. All of the following were true of women in the Gupta Empire EXCEPT that
    (A) they could own and inherit property
    (B) child marriage became more common
    (C) widows with sons were not permitted to remarry
    (D) female infanticide was occasionally practiced
    (E) they could not participate in sacred rituals or study religion

231. In its current form, the *Manusmriti* (laws of Manu)
    (A) was probably written during the Mauryan Empire
    (B) attempted to validate the high caste position of the Brahmans
    (C) preached gender equality in religious practice but not in economic matters
    (D) attempted to mitigate the social inequality of the caste system
    (E) was probably written during the Gupta Empire

232. Mathematical and scientific achievements of the Gupta Empire include all of the following EXCEPT
    (A) new developments in surgery
    (B) Indian numerals and the decimal number system
    (C) accurate calculation of the value of pi and the circumference of the earth
    (D) the concept of zero
    (E) the spinning wheel for spinning thread or yarn from wool

233. "As man discards worn out clothes
    To put on new and different ones,
    So the embodied self discards its worn-out bodies
    to take on new ones. . . .
    Death is certain for anyone born,
    and birth is certain for the dead;
    since the cycle is inevitable
    you have no cause to grieve!"

    In this passage, Lord Krishna is explaining to the warrior Arjuna
    (A) the existence of heaven and hell
    (B) the importance of nirvana
    (C) the doctrine of reincarnation
    (D) the meaning of karma
    (E) the way to achieve buddhahood

234. All of the following are true of the *Mahabharata* and the *Ramayana*
EXCEPT that
   (A) they both probably took their final form during the Mauryan period
   (B) they are both epic poems
   (C) they are both longer than *The Iliad* and *The Odyssey* put together
   (D) they are both written in Sanskrit
   (E) they both contain digressions into Hindu mythology and philosophy

235. "The Brahmin was his mouth, his two arms made the Kshatriya;
his two thighs made the Vaishya; and from his feet was made the Sudra."

This passage from the Rigveda deals with the origin of
   (A) Indian monarchial rule
   (B) slavery after the collapse of the Indus Valley culture
   (C) the caste system
   (D) humanity
   (E) the earth according to Hindu legend

236. All of the following are true of Jains EXCEPT that
   (A) they are vegetarians
   (B) they believe Mahavira established the central historical beliefs
        of Jainism
   (C) they practice nonviolence
   (D) their religion has basically been absorbed into Hinduism
        in modern times
   (E) adherents who conquer their inner enemies are called *jinas*

237. One of the main reasons for the collapse of the Gupta Empire was
   (A) peasant revolts
   (B) invasions by the Huns
   (C) the Muslim conquest of northern India
   (D) the disloyalty of the southern vassals
   (E) all of the above

238. The Tamil people
   (A) invaded India in the second millennium BCE
   (B) are native to southern India and Sri Lanka
   (C) speak an Indo-European language
   (D) converted to Islam to avoid the caste system
   (E) live around the Indo-Gangetic plain because of its alluvial soil

239. Buddhism declined in India for all of the following reasons EXCEPT that
   (A) Buddhist monks became preoccupied with philosophy
   (B) changes in Hinduism favored a new personal relationship with major deities
   (C) the fall of the Han Dynasty decreased merchant support for Buddhist monasteries
   (D) the Upanishads were reinterpreted to rival Buddhist teachings
   (E) the more popular Theravada Buddhism was gradually supplanted by Mahayana Buddhism in India

240. Kalidasa was
   (A) the Sanskrit poet who wrote *Abhijnanasakuntalam*
   (B) the Hindu sage who wrote the *Ramayana*
   (C) the monk who first spread Buddhism to Tibet and Nepal
   (D) the Hindu deity with the body of a boy and the head of an elephant
   (E) the Guptan ruler who extended the empire to the Himalayas

241. All of the following are true of Ashoka the Great EXCEPT that
   (A) he helped spread Buddhism to Sri Lanka
   (B) he promoted vegetarianism
   (C) he was the grandson of Chandragupta Maurya
   (D) he issued Rock and Pillar Edicts
   (E) his empire helped spread the use of Indian numerals

242. Within a century after Ashoka's death,
   (A) Alexander the Great conquered northern India
   (B) Chandragupta established his capital at Patna
   (C) Buddhism virtually disappeared in India
   (D) India fragmented into small warring states
   (E) music festivals and dances were outlawed

243. All of the following are true regarding Theravada Buddhism EXCEPT that
   (A) it is the oldest surviving Buddhist school of thought
   (B) it is the main religion of continental southeast Asia and Sri Lanka
   (C) it deemphasizes the role of ritual
   (D) it tends to be more liberal and accessible than Mahayana Buddhism
   (E) its main scriptures are in Pali, not Sanskrit

244. The custom of sati describes
   (A) exorbitant gifts of gold at Hindu weddings
   (B) the naming ceremony following the birth of a Brahmin child
   (C) the traditional lighting of a lamp to a Hindu deity in the morning
   (D) the self-immolation of a widow after her husband's death
   (E) a particular kind of ritual murder and robbery of travelers in India

245. The Four Noble Truths are most closely associated with
   (A) Hinduism
   (B) the laws of Manu
   (C) Sikhism
   (D) Jainism
   (E) Buddhism

246. All of the following are major river systems of the Indian subcontinent EXCEPT
   (A) the Indus
   (B) the Brahmaputra
   (C) the Ganges
   (D) the Syr Dar'ya
   (E) all of the above are major river systems of the Indian subcontinent

247. The classical empires of the Han, Romans, and Gupta experienced all of the following prior to their downfall EXCEPT
   (A) the dissolution of their empires into numerous local governments
   (B) economic decline
   (C) major conflicts between political and religious authorities
   (D) the need to hold off foreign tribes along their borders
   (E) internal political weakness before their downfall

248. The Indus Valley culture (fl. c. 2600–1700 BCE) is often associated with the city of
   (A) Margao
   (B) Madras
   (C) Pataliputra (present-day Patna)
   (D) Bamiyan
   (E) Harappa

249. All of the following are true of the so-called Aryan invasion theory EXCEPT that
   (A) it has been controversial for more than a century
   (B) it now attempts to explain the collapse of the Indus Valley culture
   (C) most scholars believe it to be false
   (D) DNA evidence seems to support it
   (E) it has often had a racial component

250. Puranas are
   (A) women who had a special dispensation to own property in the Gupta Empire
   (B) a form of stupa that has official status as law
   (C) the lowest caste in Hinduism
   (D) a type of religious text
   (E) specialized infantrymen from the Mauryan Empire

CHAPTER 8

Byzantium

251. The key to the prosperity of Constantinople was its crucial location on the
    (A) Caspian Sea
    (B) Red Sea
    (C) Tiber River
    (D) Baltic Sea
    (E) Bosporus Strait

252. The movement that shook the Byzantine Empire between 726 and 843 was known as
    (A) Monophysitism
    (B) Arianism
    (C) Pelagianism
    (D) Nestorianism
    (E) iconoclasm

253. The first major military challenge to the Byzantine Empire came in the late sixth and early seventh centuries from the
    (A) Slavs
    (B) Avars
    (C) Sassanids
    (D) Arabs
    (E) Bulgars

254. Tensions between Eastern and Western Christianity
    (A) were resolved after the fall of Constantinople in 1453
    (B) were settled by the Fourth Crusade
    (C) resulted in a split between the popes and patriarchs in 1054
    (D) involved only practical and not doctrinal differences
    (E) were ignored by the patriarch Photios the Great so he could pursue his classical studies

255. All of the following are true of the so-called Macedonian renaissance of the ninth and tenth centuries EXCEPT that
(A) it is sometimes called the first Byzantine renaissance
(B) Basil II subjected all of Bulgaria to Byzantine rule
(C) Emperor Constantine VII Porphyrogenitos wrote books on geography and history
(D) relations with the Roman Catholic Church improved
(E) Photios the Great helped convert the Slavs to Christianity

256. The earliest Christian coenobitic monasticism emerged in
(A) Russia
(B) Greece
(C) Anatolia
(D) Persia
(E) Egypt

257. Byzantines flocked to hippodromes, mixing sports rivalry with
(A) theatrical presentations
(B) religious festivals
(C) political partisanship
(D) inaugurations of government officials
(E) declarations of anathema against Muslims

258. The Byzantine Empire did all of the following EXCEPT
(A) bar women from witnessing wills
(B) outlaw prostitution
(C) make divorce and remarriage more difficult than under older Roman law
(D) require women to veil their heads as a sign of modesty
(E) institute stiffer legal penalties for sexual offenses

259. *Pronoia* refers to
(A) the mid-tenth-century reform of the monasteries
(B) the policy of the Byzantine Empire toward the Crusader states
(C) the deflation of the currency under the Comnenian Dynasty
(D) a system of land grants in the Byzantine Empire
(E) a Christological heresy regarding the nature of Jesus's humanity

260. All of the following are true of Hagia Sophia EXCEPT that
    (A) it was commissioned by Justinian I
    (B) it was the largest cathedral in the world for almost 1,000 years
    (C) it was noted for its stunning figurative mosaics
    (D) it was sacked and destroyed during the Fourth Crusade
    (E) its enormous dome was supported by construction devices known as pendentives

261. All of the following are true of the Palaeologan Dynasty EXCEPT that
    (A) it ended with the fall of Constantinople in 1453
    (B) political chaos and military defeats prevented a renewal of art and literature
    (C) Michael VIII Palaeologus tried to rebuild Constantinople
    (D) the migration of Byzantine scholars to western Europe helped spark the Renaissance in Italy
    (E) civil wars helped undermine Byzantine recovery

262. Some scholars believe the reorganization of Byzantium into military districts in the seventh century led to
    (A) poor farmers being pushed off their lands
    (B) the creation of a class of farmer-soldiers
    (C) a shift in education from a secular to a religious focus
    (D) Eastern Orthodox bishops receiving more authority in civil matters
    (E) all of the above

263. All of the following are true of Justinian I EXCEPT that he
    (A) encouraged increasing tolerance for polytheists
    (B) prohibited male homosexual relations
    (C) nearly bankrupted the East with his wars to reunify the empire
    (D) relied heavily on his wife, Theodora
    (E) embellished Constantinople with magnificent and costly architecture

264. The spread of Christianity and the increased restrictions placed on polytheists led to
    (A) the expansion of pagan Neoplatonism
    (B) the publication of the Codex
    (C) the immigration of many Latin-speaking scholars to Constantinople
    (D) the popularization of Ambrose's writings on Christian ethics
    (E) the closing of the Athenian Academy around 530

265. Ravenna (in northern Italy) is famous for
   (A) Hagia Sophia
   (B) its church architecture in the Greek Orthodox style
   (C) its fabulous mosaics
   (D) its proto-Gothic architecture
   (E) its realistic Byzantine/Roman wall painting

266. Western European soldiers sacked Constantinople in the
   (A) First Crusade
   (B) Second Crusade
   (C) Fourth Crusade
   (D) Fifth Crusade
   (E) Seventh Crusade

267. All of the following are true of the so-called Plague of Justinian
EXCEPT that it
   (A) was probably some variant of bubonic plague
   (B) killed about half of Constantinople's population
   (C) reduced Byzantine tax revenues by leaving many farms vacant
   (D) led to a shortage of Byzantine army recruits and the hiring of
       mercenaries
   (E) killed more than 65 percent of the people of the Byzantine Empire

268. Which ruler was responsible for the *Corpus Iuris Civilis* (*Body of Civil Law*)
codifying Roman law?
   (A) Constantine
   (B) Leo III
   (C) Manuel I
   (D) Justinian I
   (E) Alexius I

269. Monophysites believed that
   (A) Jesus was more divine than human
   (B) Jesus was more human than divine
   (C) original sin did not taint human nature
   (D) good and evil were distinct principles with separate origins
   (E) the material world was created by an intermediary (Demiurge)
       rather than directly by God

270. Emperor Leo III (the Isaurian)
(A) defended Constantinople against the Muslim siege from 717 to 718
(B) sided with the iconodules
(C) usurped power from the Macedonian dynasty
(D) made peace with Kievan Rus and supported its conversion to Christianity
(E) blinded 99 out of every 100 Bulgarian prisoners

271. Byzantine contact with western Europe continued through
(A) Venetian traders
(B) Russian traders
(C) Jewish traders
(D) Muslim traders
(E) Syrian traders

272. All of the following are true of John Chrysostom EXCEPT that he
(A) was known for his eloquence
(B) attacked Jews in his sermons
(C) was the archbishop of Constantinople
(D) supported the theater and horse races against attacks by ascetic Christian moralists
(E) preached against the abuse of authority

273. Kievan Rus
(A) developed close economic and cultural ties with Byzantium
(B) could not compete with western Europe in wealth and power
(C) was able to repel the Mongol invasions
(D) encouraged the Vikings to invade western Europe
(E) refused to trade slaves after the population adopted Christianity in the 10th century

274. Stylites were
(A) Byzantine infantrymen who had formerly been slaves
(B) eunuchs who had high court positions and served the emperor
(C) farmer-soldiers from the *themes*
(D) Muslim adventurers who fought for the Byzantines in the 11th and 12th centuries
(E) Christian ascetics who lived on pillars

275. Anna Comnena is famous for writing
- (A) *The Spaneas*
- (B) *The Secret History*
- (C) *The Alexiad*
- (D) *The Universal Chronicle*
- (E) *Digenis Acritas*

276. All of the following were true of eunuchs in the Byzantine Empire EXCEPT that
- (A) they could become generals
- (B) they could become patriarch of Constantinople
- (C) they could become *parakoimomenos*
- (D) they could become emperor
- (E) they could become civil servants

277. The Byzantines lost control of most of Anatolia in the battle of
- (A) Adrianople
- (B) Edessa
- (C) Solachon
- (D) Kleidion
- (E) Manzikert

278. Byzantine literature is almost entirely concerned with
- (A) Acritic songs
- (B) religious expression
- (C) the compilation of encyclopedias of classical knowledge
- (D) popular poetry
- (E) heroic and epic tales

279. Which of the following is sometimes considered the last major historian of the ancient world as well as the first Byzantine historian?
- (A) Procopius of Caesarea
- (B) Niketas Choniates
- (C) George Acropolites
- (D) Michael Attaleiates
- (E) Joannes Cinnamus

280. All of the following are true of the reign of Emperor Manuel I Comnenus EXCEPT that
  (A) he invaded Italy
  (B) the Seljuk Turks crushed his army at Myriocephalon
  (C) he invaded Fatimid Egypt
  (D) he hated western Europeans
  (E) he maneuvered against Frederick Barbarossa

CHAPTER 9

Islam

281. Both Muslims and Jews deny the
  (A) importance of prayer
  (B) prophetic teachings of the Hebrew Bible
  (C) importance of circumcision
  (D) worship of one God
  (E) divinity of Jesus

282. *Islam* is the Arabic word for
  (A) submission
  (B) prophet
  (C) truth
  (D) recitation
  (E) faith

283. The Abbasids moved the capital of the Muslim world to
  (A) Baghdad
  (B) Jerusalem
  (C) Cordoba
  (D) Damascus
  (E) Cairo

284. All of the following were true of the Bedouin tribal society that existed before the rise of Islam EXCEPT that
  (A) the Kaaba was an important religious shrine
  (B) the clan was the main social institution
  (C) men often had more than one wife
  (D) commercial trade was not practiced because it was considered unmanly
  (E) traditions were transmitted primarily through oral poetry and storytelling

285. The Fatimid Caliphate
   (A) was one of a number of Shiite caliphates
   (B) reached its apex in the 14th century
   (C) crushed the Ottoman Turks at Qatwan
   (D) ruled Egypt for more than two centuries
   (E) consistently persecuted Jews and Christians

286. All of the following are true of the Seljuk Turks EXCEPT that
   (A) their expansion led directly to the First Crusade
   (B) their alliance with the Ottomans helped doom the Byzantine Empire
   (C) they were the first Turks to settle in Anatolia
   (D) they came from the central Asian steppes
   (E) they conquered Baghdad in 1055

287. The Mughal Empire was founded by
   (A) Badr al-Jamali
   (B) Baibars
   (C) Babur
   (D) Bayezid I
   (E) Barkyaruq

288. All of the following are true of Sufism EXCEPT that
   (A) *dhikr* (the perpetual remembrance of God) is a central concept
   (B) Sufis have often served as missionaries for Islam
   (C) to combat orthodox opposition, Sufi devotional practices have been codified
   (D) the Persian poet Rumi was a Sufi mystic
   (E) it has frequently emphasized asceticism and mysticism

289. Women in the period of the Abbasid Caliphate
   (A) increasingly appeared in public records and events
   (B) were all confined to harems
   (C) were considered chattels
   (D) were thought by men to be sexually passive and restrained
   (E) adopted the use of the veil after encounters with Byzantine and Persian culture

290. A madrasa is
   (A) a Muslim legal document
   (B) a Muslim slave of Christian origin
   (C) the military marching band of the Janissaries
   (D) a Muslim school
   (E) a Christian vassal of an Ottoman overlord

291. After the battle of Badr, Muslims attacked this group because they failed to convert to Islam.
(A) Nestorian Christians
(B) Jews
(C) Meccan merchants
(D) The Quraysh tribe
(E) Polytheists

292. Which statement regarding women in the early days of Islam (before 750) is true?
(A) Women benefited from the fact that Islam was not a patriarchal religion.
(B) The Koran permitted female infanticide.
(C) Women could not engage in business activities.
(D) A woman's testimony in court was not equal to a man's testimony.
(E) Women were freed from male dominance by the sharia.

293. All of the following were true of Janissaries EXCEPT that they
(A) were noted for their horsemanship and fearless cavalry attacks
(B) went into battle accompanied by *mehter* music played by military bands
(C) were originally composed of Christian boys levied through the *devshirme* system
(D) were the first soldiers of a regular army to wear unique uniforms
(E) were the elite soldiers of the Ottoman Empire

294. Which of the following statements is true regarding the Koran?
(A) The Koran assumes some familiarity with the stories in Jewish and Christian scriptures.
(B) The canon of the Koran was finalized during the Abbasid Caliphate.
(C) Muslims believe the Koran is Muhammad's explanation of God's words to him.
(D) The Koran is organized by the length of suras, with shorter suras coming first.
(E) The word *Koran* means "truth" in Arabic.

295. All of the following are true of the Umayyad Caliphate EXCEPT that
(A) it was overthrown in 750 CE
(B) it established Arabic as the official state language
(C) it was still expanding when it was overthrown by the Abbasids
(D) the Umayyads transformed the caliphate from a religious institution to a dynasty
(E) it was noted for its poetry and architecture

296. All of the following are true of the Ottomans EXCEPT that
- (A) victories at the battles of Kosovo and Nicopolis placed much of the Balkans under their rule
- (B) Ottoman expansion reached its peak in the 16th century
- (C) they were originally a nomadic tribe out of Arabia
- (D) they conquered Constantinople in 1453
- (E) Bursa and Edirne were early capitals of their empire

297. By the 11th century, the characteristics that united the Islamic world did NOT include
- (A) language
- (B) trade networks
- (C) intellectual life
- (D) loyalty to a single ruler
- (E) the Koran

298. Which of the following is NOT a correct statement concerning the beliefs of Islam?
- (A) All Muslims must acknowledge that there is one God called Allah and that Muhammad is his prophet.
- (B) All Muslims must pray five times a day while facing Mecca.
- (C) All Muslims must fast during the daylight hours during the month of Ramadan.
- (D) All Muslims must contribute to the support of the poor and needy.
- (E) All Muslims must make at least one pilgrimage (hajj) to either Mecca or Medina during their lifetime.

299. "A Book of Verses underneath the Bough,
A Jug of Wine, a Loaf of Bread—and Thou
Beside me singing in the Wilderness—
Oh, Wilderness were Paradise enow!"

This quatrain was written by
- (A) Omar Khayyam
- (B) Averroes
- (C) Judah Halevi
- (D) Kahlil Gibran
- (E) Rumi

300. All of the following are true of Muslim economics EXCEPT
that Muslims
- (A) participated in the trans-Sahara trade
- (B) invented the double-entry bookkeeping system
- (C) traded with Russia via the Byzantine Empire
- (D) developed the forerunners of present-day checks
- (E) traded actively in the Indian Ocean

301. The Mamluk soldiers who emerged in the Islamic world
- (A) fought only for a single ruler
- (B) were mercenaries who maintained their own mounts and arms
- (C) were tied to specific estates by oaths of loyalty
- (D) moved about independently rather than in groups
- (E) were crushed by the Mongols at Ayn Jalut

302. All of the following are true of Maimonides EXCEPT that
- (A) his *Mishneh Torah* is still used as a standard compilation
of Jewish law
- (B) he served as court physician to Saladin
- (C) his *Guide for the Perplexed* attacked the relevance of philosophy
to Jewish theology
- (D) he wrote the *Guide for the Perplexed* in Arabic
- (E) he was the most influential Jewish thinker of the Middle Ages

303. All of the following are true of the Cordoba Caliphate EXCEPT that
- (A) it was in al-Andalus
- (B) it competed with the Umayyad Caliphate for dominance over
the Muslim world
- (C) Mozarabs played an important role its culture
- (D) religious toleration was widely practiced
- (E) it was important in the translation of Greek classics

304. Which Muslim city is associated with a famous medieval school
of translators?
- (A) Isfahan
- (B) Toledo
- (C) Marrakech
- (D) Acre
- (E) Lisbon

305. All of the following are classic works of Islamic architecture EXCEPT the
    (A) Taj Mahal (India)
    (B) Alhambra (Spain)
    (C) Selimiye Mosque (Turkey)
    (D) Sankore Madrasa (Mali)
    (E) Cairo Geniza (Egypt)

306. The city that served as a crucial place for the establishment
of Muhammad's new religion was
    (A) Jerusalem, because of its large Jewish population
    (B) Constantinople, because it was the capital of the Byzantine Empire
    (C) Medina, because Muhammad's earliest supporters were located there
    (D) Jidda, because the Red Sea port was crucial to controlling the Arabian peninsula
    (E) Mecca, because it had a prior reputation as a religious and commercial center

307. Which of the following statements is true regarding the so-called Pirenne thesis, named after medieval historian Henri Pirenne?
    (A) The failure of Islam to advance technologically after 1200 was caused by inherent flaws in the religion.
    (B) Medieval Islam actually pioneered representative democracy.
    (C) The Muslim failure to take Constantinople until 1453 doomed Islamic states to second-class political status after 1500.
    (D) The "fall of Rome" was caused not by German invasions but by the movement of Islam into the Mediterranean.
    (E) Islamic philosophy, technology, and scientific culture saved western Europe from barbarism.

308. The dispute between Shiite and Sunni began over the
    (A) choice of caliphs to succeed Muhammad
    (B) definitive form of the Koran
    (C) treatment of subjects in the conquered territories
    (D) acceptability of secular poetry
    (E) role of eschatology in Islam

309. A hadith is a
    (A) Seljuk tax on Christian residents of Anatolia
    (B) form of land ownership common in al-Andalus
    (C) Mamluk cavalry soldier
    (D) story about Muhammad that carries the force of law
    (E) type of erotic Persian poetry that is still written today

310. All of the following are true regarding slavery in Muslim lands EXCEPT
that
(A) Islam discouraged the enslavement of free Muslims
(B) Muslims never enslaved Europeans in large numbers
(C) the Koran did not abolish slavery
(D) Arab slave traders enslaved more than five million Africans between
650 and 1800
(E) Muslim rulers in Africa participated in the slave trade

311. The author of the extremely influential book *The Canon of Medicine* (1025)
was known in Europe as
(A) Averroes
(B) Rhazes
(C) Avicenna
(D) Albertus Magnus
(E) Albucasis

312. Compared to the Macedonian renaissance (c. 870–1025) and Carolingian
renaissance (c. 790–900), the Islamic renaissance (c. 790–1050) more
strongly emphasized
(A) the study of classical literature
(B) art
(C) mathematics
(D) the exegesis of religious texts
(E) architecture

313. El Cid (Rodrigo Diaz)
(A) defeated the Muslim armies in France and saved western Europe
(B) is despised in present-day Spain because he spent many years fighting
for the Muslims
(C) won his reputation fighting against the Fatimid Caliphate
(D) is associated with the Spanish city of Madrid
(E) exemplifies the complexity of politics in medieval Spain

314. All of the following were decisive Muslim victories EXCEPT
(A) the battle of Tours (Poitiers) in 732
(B) the battle of Manzikert in 1071
(C) the battle of Constantinople in 1453
(D) the second battle of Taraori in 1192
(E) the battle of Hattin in 1187

315. The work of Al-Khwarizmi, Ibn al-Haytham, Ibn Sina, and Ibn Rushd demonstrated that
    (A) medieval Islamic and Christian societies developed in isolation
    (B) Islam is naturally hostile to science and philosophy
    (C) Islamic thinkers influenced medieval European thought
    (D) Islamic thinkers made their work more accessible by writing in Latin
    (E) the concept of jihad was alien to Islamic thought

316. All of the following are true of jihad EXCEPT
    (A) it is a religious duty of Muslims
    (B) it is not one of the Five Pillars of Islam
    (C) in medieval Islam, Muslims were allowed to enslave prisoners taken in jihad
    (D) the word never appears in the Koran
    (E) the word means "struggle" in Arabic

317. The Muslim counterpart to Marco Polo would be
    (A) Ibn Battuta
    (B) Hakim
    (C) Nur ad-Din
    (D) Tariq ibn Ziyad
    (E) Hasan ibn Sabah

318. The last major city of the Outremer was captured by Muslims in
    (A) 1104
    (B) 1187
    (C) 1191
    (D) 1291
    (E) 1365

319. In 630, the prestige of Islam was increased and many tribes converted when
    (A) Muhammad removed the idols from the Kaaba
    (B) Muhammad took control of Mecca
    (C) Muhammad completed the *Hijra*
    (D) Muhammad conquered Jerusalem
    (E) the Koran was written

320. Ibn Rushd (Averroes) is best known for his work in
  (A) poetry
  (B) philosophy
  (C) optics
  (D) medicine
  (E) law

CHAPTER 10

Sub-Saharan Africa

321. In the time of the Ghana Empire, trans-Saharan trade was especially active in which two commodities?
(A) Amber and silver
(B) Gold and salt
(C) Ivory and animal skins
(D) Ebony and cowry shells
(E) Jade and exotic woods

322. All of the following were barriers to Africa's economic development EXCEPT
(A) the pervasiveness of disease-carrying insects
(B) the lack of navigable rivers
(C) the difficult geography
(D) the lack of natural resources
(E) all of the above

323. All of the following are major African cultures that originated after 100 CE EXCEPT
(A) Songhai
(B) Zimbabwe
(C) Mali
(D) Kush
(E) Kongo

324. The ancient kingdom of Axum was located in present-day
(A) Ethiopia
(B) Kenya
(C) Tanzania
(D) Sudan
(E) Mali

325. All of the following are true of the Bantu migrations EXCEPT that
- (A) they took place over 2,000 years
- (B) the Bantu took their knowledge of agriculture and iron metallurgy with them
- (C) the evidence for this expansion is primarily archaeological
- (D) the Bantu moved to lands previously occupied by hunter-gatherers such as the Khoisan
- (E) they moved primarily south and east out of western Africa

326. Mansa Musa
- (A) was a king of Ghana
- (B) sacked Timbuktu in 1325
- (C) lived in the 12th century
- (D) made a famous hajj to Mecca
- (E) distrusted learning as an impediment to holiness

327. The Kanem Empire
- (A) was unusual in that most of its people did not convert to Islam
- (B) exported ostrich feathers, slaves, and ivory
- (C) controlled trade in the Cameroon-Congo region
- (D) relied on a powerful infantry to dominate the region
- (E) reached the apogee of its power in the 10th century

328. All of the following are true of Timbuktu EXCEPT that
- (A) it is a town in present-day Mali
- (B) it is located about 10 miles north of the Congo River
- (C) it is noted for the Sankore Madrasa
- (D) it flourished because of its location on trans-Saharan trading routes
- (E) at one time, it had the largest library in Africa

329. All of the following are true regarding the city of Great Zimbabwe EXCEPT
- (A) its massive walls were built without mortar
- (B) it flourished through trade with Axum to the north
- (C) it profited from taxing traders from the gold fields of central Africa
- (D) it traded with Asia through the city of Sofala
- (E) its accomplishments were the subject of modern-day controversy

330. The coffee bean first originated in present-day
- (A) Ethiopia
- (B) South Africa
- (C) Ivory Coast
- (D) Uganda
- (E) Kenya

331. All of the following reasons have been suggested for the decline of the kingdom of Ghana EXCEPT that
- (A) drought was affecting the land and its ability to sustain cattle and cultivation
- (B) Songhai warriors under Sundiata invaded the kingdom from the east
- (C) Almoravid Muslims invaded Ghana from the north
- (D) new gold fields at Bure (present-day Guinea) were out of Ghana's commercial reach
- (E) shifts in trade routes weakened Ghana's economy

332. All of the following reasons have been suggested for the cause of the Bantu migrations EXCEPT
- (A) a population increase in western Africa
- (B) the introduction of new crops such as the banana
- (C) Bantu development of livestock husbandry and expansion to find new grasslands
- (D) the use of iron that permitted new ecological zones to be exploited
- (E) climate changes that forced people out of the Sahara and pressured the proto-Bantu

333. Sonni Ali is associated with which empire?
- (A) Kush
- (B) Benin
- (C) Ghana
- (D) Mali
- (E) Songhai

334. The kingdom of the Kongo
- (A) was a Shona kingdom
- (B) was founded, according to recent estimates, between 500 and 1000 CE
- (C) was a decentralized state typical of central Africa
- (D) depended on raising and trading bananas and yams
- (E) was located in western central Africa

335. All of the following are cities on the Swahili coast EXCEPT
  (A) Sofala
  (B) Abidjan
  (C) Shanga
  (D) Kilwa
  (E) Mombasa

336. The Songhai Empire
  (A) had its capital at Jenne (present-day Djenne)
  (B) controlled the Congo River trade
  (C) collapsed after it was invaded by the Portuguese
  (D) replaced the Malian Empire in western Africa
  (E) refused to trade in slaves, unlike the Malian Empire

337. All of the following are major rivers in Africa EXCEPT
  (A) Zambezi
  (B) Kasai
  (C) Orange
  (D) Limpopo
  (E) all of the above are major African rivers

338. Which of the following statements is true regarding Bantu settlements?
  (A) Cohort groups could sometimes wield considerable power.
  (B) The Bantu were animists but did not believe in ancestor spirits.
  (C) Bantu society did not have gender-differentiated tasks.
  (D) Contrary to popular myth, the Bantu believed that land could
       be bought and sold.
  (E) Most of the African topsoil layer was alluvial and thick.

339. Which of the following statements is true regarding the influence of Islam
  in sub-Saharan Africa?
  (A) African women tended to have fewer privileges than Islamic women.
  (B) The lower classes were more eager to convert to Islam than were
       the elite.
  (C) Contacts with Islam were generated by transatlantic trade.
  (D) African rulers feared that conversion to Islam would undermine their
       authority.
  (E) Converts to Islam often blended Islam and their tribal beliefs.

340. The Akan people were famous for their
   (A) detailed bronze plaques (which were really made of brass)
   (B) beautiful gold weights
   (C) ancient rock art
   (D) life-sized terra-cotta heads
   (E) intricate ivory carvings

341. All of the following are true regarding the kingdom of Axum EXCEPT that
   (A) most of the population converted to Christianity in the 4th century CE
   (B) it became rich connecting the Roman Empire with sub-Saharan Africa
   (C) it traded through the Red Sea trade network
   (D) its culture is noted for its large stone obelisks
   (E) it flourished until about the sixth century CE

342. An object believed to have supernatural powers or a man-made object that has power over others is known as a
   (A) griot
   (B) animistic stele
   (C) fetish
   (D) millet
   (E) Sahel

343. All of the following are true regarding the banana EXCEPT that
   (A) it resulted in a population increase among the Bantu
   (B) it was domesticated in Africa as early as 5000 BCE
   (C) its path was traced through linguistic connections
   (D) it was transported via the Indian Ocean to Madagascar
   (E) it was transported by Malayan sailors

344. All of the following are true regarding Nok culture EXCEPT that
   (A) its terra-cottas are the oldest-known figurative sculpture south of the Sahara
   (B) it flourished between about 500 BCE and 200 CE
   (C) it was one of the earliest sub-Saharan African centers of ironworking
   (D) it was located in present-day Tanzania
   (E) its ultimate fate is unclear

345. Camels were first used extensively for trade across the Sahara in about
  (A) 150 BCE
  (B) 150 CE
  (C) 450 CE
  (D) 750 CE
  (E) 1050 CE

CHAPTER 11

European Middle Ages

346. Which of the following areas did NOT experience a social system based on feudalism?
(A) France
(B) Japan
(C) Spain
(D) Germany
(E) Great Britain

347. The Great Schism from 1378 to 1417 involved
(A) rival popes
(B) Christianity and Islam
(C) Guelphs and Hohenstaufens
(D) Catholics and Protestants
(E) Franciscans and Dominicans

348. Monasticism was
(A) only practiced by Christians
(B) limited to men
(C) common in Buddhism
(D) opposed to education as a deterrent to religious faith
(E) a complete withdrawal of the religious from the secular community

349. All of the following were results of the Black Death that swept through Europe in the 1300s EXCEPT
(A) social unrest
(B) an increase in wages
(C) more rigidity between social classes
(D) labor shortages
(E) population loss

350. Under the code of chivalry, a knight was committed to defending
    (A) his lord on earth and his lord in heaven
    (B) his king and the king's entire family
    (C) his lover and all her relatives
    (D) his fellow knights and their servants
    (E) whoever paid him the most money in advance

351. "It is also not without great rashness that he dares to dispute about those things which do not pertain to philosophy but are matters of pure faith, for example that the soul may suffer hellfire, and that he dares to say the teachings of the [Catholic Church] on this point should be rejected. With equal reasoning, he could argue about the Trinity."

                      —Thomas Aquinas

In this quotation, Aquinas is arguing with
    (A) Siger de Brabant and Latin Averroists
    (B) Duns Scotus and Franciscan theology
    (C) William of Ockham and conciliarism
    (D) John Wycliffe and Bogomilism
    (E) Paul of Samosata and the Paulician movement

352. The Saxons
    (A) lived in present-day Sicily
    (B) held regular meetings of freemen
    (C) eventually defeated Charlemagne to preserve their independence
    (D) were converted to Arian Christianity
    (E) were unknown to the Romans

353. The standard for monastic life in western Europe that influenced many aspects of Catholic worship is called
    (A) the Monastic Code
    (B) the Columban Rule
    (C) the Rule of Saint Benedict
    (D) the Rule of Saint Basil
    (E) the Rule of the Master

354. "Now's the time for pleasure,
Lads and lasses take your joy together
Before it passes.
With the love of a maid aflower
With the love of a maid afire,
New love, new love,
Dying of desire."

This quotation is from
(A) *Carmina Burana*
(B) the *Summa Theologica* of Thomas Aquinas
(C) the Bayeux Tapestry
(D) the *Decretum Gratiani*
(E) *The Song of Roland*

355. All of the following are true of a late medieval guild EXCEPT that it
(A) regulated prices and work hours
(B) set quality standards
(C) generally did not accept women
(D) served social as well as economic needs
(E) usually avoided religious activities as outside its organizational purpose

356. The murder of Thomas Becket was the culmination of a dispute between Henry II and the church over
(A) royal taxes
(B) the Investiture Controversy
(C) the right to appoint bishops
(D) the jurisdiction of the courts
(E) Becket's role in Henry's coronation

357. Which event occurred in the 13th century?
(A) The Fourth Lateran Council was held.
(B) Gutenberg introduced the printing press.
(C) The Hundred Years' War began.
(D) The First Crusade captured Jerusalem.
(E) Archbishop Thomas Becket was murdered in Canterbury Cathedral.

358. Clovis's law code established the wergild to defuse feuds between clans through
(A) imprisonment
(B) loss of property
(C) compensation
(D) executions
(E) vassalage to the king

359. All of the following are true regarding the three-field system EXCEPT that it
(A) began in Europe during the Carolingian Empire
(B) was more efficient than the older two-tier system
(C) depended on heavy plows and always used oxen as draft animals
(D) rotated the crops planted on each field
(E) had a seasonal basis

360. Before 1215, polyphony
(A) was primarily sacred in nature
(B) was mainly written in French
(C) was always committed to memory
(D) did not exist in Europe
(E) was most prevalent in Gregorian chants

361. Which of the following statements is true regarding Gothic sculpture and architecture, as opposed to the Romanesque style?
(A) Gothic sculpture was expressed on a flat surface.
(B) Gothic sculpture was renowned for its naturalistic, three-dimensional depiction of the human figure.
(C) Gothic architecture replaced the massive stained-glass windows common in 11th-century churches with flying buttresses.
(D) Gothic sculpture never appeared in cathedrals, which were meant to be austere places.
(E) Gothic sculpture was pioneered by Gian Lorenzo Bernini.

362. All of the following are true of the Hussites EXCEPT that
(A) Jan Zizka was a military genius
(B) they combined theological radicalism with fervent nationalism
(C) John Huss was burned at the stake despite receiving the promise of safe conduct from the Council of Constance
(D) they organized Mount Tabor according to Hussite beliefs, including strict separation of church and state
(E) they challenged papal authority

363. Papal prestige was greatly increased in early medieval Europe through the work of
(A) Pelagius
(B) Gregory the Great
(C) Leo III
(D) Saint Columba
(E) Pope Zachary

364. The Vikings
(A) established colonies in present-day Newfoundland
(B) took part in the invasions of the Roman Empire in the fifth century
(C) traded with western Europe but not with Russia
(D) failed to establish permanent colonies on Iceland
(E) wore horned helmets

365. The Great Famine of 1315–1317 was caused by overpopulation and
(A) a dramatic drop in wages
(B) an increase in warfare, banditry, and piracy in the early 1300s
(C) the Hundred Years' War
(D) the Black Death
(E) a succession of severe winters and rainy summers

366. The Waldensians were condemned by the church because
(A) the church disagreed with their theology
(B) they advocated giving away all belongings for the benefit of the poor
(C) they allowed their lay members to preach
(D) they refused to acknowledge papal supremacy
(E) they were encouraging dualistic heresies

367. All of the following are true of the great English peasant revolt of 1381 EXCEPT that
(A) peasants complained about the Hundred Years' War
(B) it was triggered by attempts to collect the poll tax of 1377
(C) King Richard II originally agreed to their demand to abolish serfdom
(D) it was the last major peasant revolt in England in the Middle Ages
(E) Wat Tyler emerged as one of the leaders

368. All of the following are true of the coronation ceremony on Christmas Day in 800 EXCEPT that
   (A) it implied a privileged position for the pope
   (B) Pope Leo III gave Charlemagne the title of Byzantine emperor
   (C) the rulers in Constantinople were upset with the pope's actions
   (D) it took place in Rome
   (E) Charlemagne was displeased with the way things transpired

369. A unique system of rule in the sixth and seventh centuries that linked churchmen, the king, and the great landowners was created by
   (A) Byzantium
   (B) the Lombards
   (C) the Visigoths
   (D) the Anglo-Saxons
   (E) the Jutes

370. In the papal bull *Unum sanctam*, Pope Boniface VIII declared that
   (A) the actions of the French Estates General were not binding
   (B) Philip IV was excommunicated
   (C) kings had the right to tax their clergies in times of national emergency
   (D) Christians, whether clergy or secular, represented one sacred world and should try to work together
   (E) it was necessary for the salvation of every person to be subject to the pope

371. All of the following are true of Joan of Arc EXCEPT that
   (A) she was accused of witchcraft and burned at the stake
   (B) she referred to herself as La Pucelle
   (C) she helped lift the siege of Orléans
   (D) she strengthened Charles VII's legitimacy by standing with him at his coronation in Rheims in 1429
   (E) Charles VII tried desperately to save her

372. All of the following were medieval historians EXCEPT
   (A) Gregory of Tours
   (B) Boethius
   (C) Bede
   (D) Einhard
   (E) Geoffrey of Monmouth

373. All of the following are true of Frederick II EXCEPT that
   (A) he revamped the government of Sicily in the Constitutions of Melfi in 1231
   (B) his participation in the Sixth Crusade was a success, even though he never won a battle
   (C) he is associated with the quarrels between the Guelphs and the Ghibellines
   (D) he intervened in northern Italian affairs with the support of the pope
   (E) he was fascinated by science and philosophy

374. All of the following are true regarding Pope Innocent III EXCEPT that he
   (A) worked to unify the German states as a counterbalance to French power and interference in Italy
   (B) presided over the Fourth Lateran Council
   (C) supported the Franciscans and Dominicans, even though some of their beliefs were similar to those of heretical groups
   (D) insisted that Christians confess their sins to a priest at least once a year
   (E) preached a crusade against the Albigensian heretics in Languedoc

375. In 1215, England's Magna Carta
   (A) guaranteed individual liberties to all Englishmen
   (B) established England as a constitutional monarchy under King Richard
   (C) intensified the conflict between church and state
   (D) increased the wealth of the English nobility
   (E) never specifically mentioned habeas corpus or trial by jury

376. All of the following are true of Beguines EXCEPT that
   (A) their male counterparts were known as Beghards
   (B) they were particularly popular in northern Europe
   (C) they lived in religious communities without permanent vows or an established rule
   (D) they devoted their lives to philanthropy such as the care of lepers, the sick, and the poor
   (E) although they were declared heretical at the Fourth Lateran Council of 1215, it did not stop their growth

377. What was the anticlerical movement of John Wycliffe called
by its opponents?
    (A) Lollardy
    (B) The Brethren of the Free Spirits
    (C) Albigensianism
    (D) Proto-Protestantism
    (E) Humanism

378. In northern Germany, towns on the Baltic and North Seas were linked
in a powerful trading alliance called the
    (A) Swabian League
    (B) Swiss Confederation
    (C) Hohenstaufen League
    (D) Hanseatic League
    (E) Teutonic Knights

379. The Magyar advance into western Europe was checked at the battle of
    (A) Poitiers (Tours)
    (B) Bouvines
    (C) Stamford Bridge
    (D) Nicopolis
    (E) Lechfeld

380. All of the following are true of troubadours EXCEPT that
    (A) they were patronized by Eleanor of Aquitaine
    (B) one of the first and most noteworthy was Duke William IX
        of Aquitaine
    (C) they sang their poetry unaccompanied by music
    (D) they celebrated the doctrine of *fin'amors*
    (E) their poetry had an Islamic origin

381. Charlemagne's empire was split into three sections in the Treaty of Verdun
because
    (A) the economic burden of managing such a large empire was too great
    (B) he could not decide which of his sons should inherit the empire
    (C) his grandsons were fighting with each other over who should succeed
        him
    (D) after the feudal system was established, powerful local lords refused
        to allow a distant king
    (E) a single ruler could no longer meet the myriad demands of the
        aristocrats for land and rewards

382. All of the following are true of the Franciscans EXCEPT that
 (A) they refused to allow women into their order
 (B) they ministered to the sick
 (C) they originally advocated a harsh life of poverty
 (D) they often lived and preached in urban areas
 (E) their success can be viewed as paradoxical

383. Slavery in Europe in the early Middle Ages was
 (A) practiced so rarely it was insignificant
 (B) eliminated by Charlemagne's time
 (C) discussed in the New Testament
 (D) vehemently supported by the church
 (E) inherited from both German and Roman traditions

384. Which of the following statements is NOT true regarding the payment of interest in the Middle Ages?
 (A) Interest of any kind is forbidden in Islam.
 (B) Medieval Jews forbid collecting interest from other Jews but not from Christians.
 (C) Thomas Aquinas believed that usury was a violation of natural moral law.
 (D) The Council of Vienne (1311) declared that usury could be permitted if it was a "reasonable" rate.
 (E) Christians pushed Jews into moneylending by forcing them out of other occupations.

385. *The Mabinogion* is
 (A) the earliest extant troubadour song
 (B) a tale of courtly love by Christian of Troyes
 (C) an oral epic from Scandinavia that is still occasionally performed in Norway
 (D) a collection of medieval Welsh stories
 (E) the Scottish stone on which medieval Scottish kings were crowned

386. The papal reform movement of the 11th and early 12th centuries is most closely associated with
 (A) Pope Leo IX
 (B) Pope Alexander II
 (C) Humbert of Silva Candida
 (D) Pope Gregory VII
 (E) Pope Stephen IX

387. During the Inquisition, unrepentant heretics were
- (A) killed and buried
- (B) burned at the stake
- (C) banished from the area
- (D) quarantined in their homes
- (E) imprisoned until they recanted

388. All of the following are true of Hildegard of Bingen EXCEPT that she
- (A) was a student and lover of Peter Abelard and later became a respected abbess
- (B) was respected by Bernard of Clairvaux and Frederick Barbarossa
- (C) produced major works of theology, mysticism, and visionary writings
- (D) wrote one of the earliest examples of liturgical drama
- (E) wrote treatises about the medicinal uses of plants, animals, trees, and stones

389. According to Pope Urban II, the goal of the First Crusade was to
- (A) drive out the Jews living in Christian lands
- (B) provide assistance to the struggling armies of the Byzantine emperor Alexius I
- (C) obtain land and booty by sacking Constantinople
- (D) reclaim the Holy Land from the Muslims
- (E) rid western Europe of the surplus young, landless males who were constantly stirring up trouble

390. All of the following are true of the Domesday Book EXCEPT that
- (A) it was commissioned by William I years after the Battle of Hastings
- (B) it consulted Anglo-Saxon tax lists
- (C) it revealed that slavery was extinct in England
- (D) there was theoretically no appeal against its judgment
- (E) it was unique among medieval European records in its completeness

391. "Whan that Aprill, with his shoures soote
The droghte of March hath perced to the roote. . . .
Thanne longen folk to goon on pilgrimages
And palmeres for to seken straunge strondes
To ferne halwes, kowthe in sondry londes;
And specially from every shires ende
Of Engelond, to Caunterbury they wende,
The hooly blisful martir for to seke
That hem hath holpen, whan that they were seeke."

This passage was written by
(A) William Langland
(B) John Gower
(C) Julian of Norwich
(D) Geoffrey Chaucer
(E) John Wycliffe

392. All of the following are true regarding the Cistercians EXCEPT that they
(A) developed as a response to calls for greater asceticism
(B) experienced their greatest expansion under Saint Bernard of Clairvaux
(C) transformed marginal European lands into productive agricultural estates
(D) worried constantly about whether they were saved, and worshipped a distant and judgmental God
(E) gave ordinary men from nonaristocratic backgrounds an opportunity to lead monastic lives

393. Which statement is true regarding the First Crusade?
(A) It marked the first time that Jews were systematically persecuted in Europe.
(B) The Crusaders' worst attacks on Jews took place in Poland and the Ukraine.
(C) The Crusaders attacked the Jews because of their reputation as moneylenders.
(D) Until this time, Jews had integrated well into European society.
(E) Attacks on Jews were an aberration, as European attitudes toward heterodox people were becoming more liberal by the century.

394. The Concordat of Worms dictated that during the investiture ritual,
   (A) the secular and spiritual symbols of the ceremony would be separated
   (B) a churchman would touch the bishop's head with a scepter
   (C) the emperor or his representative would give the symbols of the ring
       and the staff to the bishop
   (D) emperors were forbidden to be present
   (E) churchmen would receive a legal document in place of a ring and
       a staff

395. Frederick Barbarossa overcame the limits that German princes traditionally
   placed on royal authority by
   (A) handing out duchies to princes
   (B) requiring the princes to publicly acknowledge his primacy
   (C) allowing the pope to name bishops
   (D) seizing the castles and territories of the most powerful princes
   (E) forcing them to go on the Third Crusade and so eliminating them
       temporarily from internal German politics

CHAPTER 12

The Mongols

396. Because of the battles of Hakata Bay, the Mongols failed twice to conquer
   (A) Java and Sumatra
   (B) Persia
   (C) China
   (D) Korea
   (E) Japan

397. Which of the following statements characterizes the Yuan Dynasty?
   (A) It developed rigid social class hierarchies.
   (B) Peasant uprisings were responsible for its establishment.
   (C) Trade collapsed because of its warlike nature.
   (D) It was overthrown by outside invaders.
   (E) It suffered because of its nonexpansionist nature.

398. What was the Mongol capital before Kublai Khan moved it to Khanbaliq (now Beijing) in 1272?
   (A) Bayan Tumen (Choibalsan)
   (B) Hangzhou
   (C) Ulan Bator
   (D) Karakorum
   (E) Samarkand

399. The Mamluks defeated the Mongols and ended the Mongol threat to dominate the Middle East at the battle of
   (A) Ayn Jalut
   (B) Bokhara
   (C) Jan
   (D) Diarbekr
   (E) Baghdad

400. Scholars believe one possible reason for the Mongols' expansion out of their traditional homelands was
- (A) economic necessity brought on by climate changes
- (B) increasing numbers of Christian missionaries settling in the East
- (C) the desire for luxury goods in China
- (D) provocations from Muslim rulers
- (E) the search for Prester John

401. All of the following were long-standing effects of the Mongol invasions of Europe EXCEPT that they
- (A) set back the development of democracy in Hungary
- (B) brought the cultures of Asia into contact with the European world
- (C) increased trade between Europe and Asia
- (D) made it easier for Christianity to spread to Asia
- (E) stimulated the search for exotic goods

402. The Yuan Dynasty included all of these present-day areas EXCEPT
- (A) Xinjiang
- (B) Tibet
- (C) Taiwan
- (D) Yunnan
- (E) Laos

403. All of the following are true regarding the Mongol occupation of Russia EXCEPT that
- (A) it lasted for about 200 years
- (B) the Mongols allowed Russian princes to rule if they paid obeisance to the khan
- (C) the Mongols heavily taxed the Russian church
- (D) the Mongols standardized the collection of taxes
- (E) the Mongols captured Kiev in 1240

404. When the Mongols reached Baghdad, the capital of the Abbasid Caliphate, in 1258, they
- (A) were turned back by the Mamluks
- (B) negotiated a peace treaty with the Abbasids
- (C) moved on to Damascus rather than besiege the city
- (D) compelled the city to surrender and assimilated its cultural treasures into the Mongol Empire
- (E) destroyed the city and massacred most of its inhabitants

405. All of the following were reasons for the outstanding success of Mongol military tactics EXCEPT that
   (A) the Mongol bow was unmatched for accuracy, force, and reach
   (B) the Mongols excelled at siege warfare
   (C) the Mongols devised two- and three-pronged military assaults and complex flanking operations
   (D) the Mongols were extremely disciplined in battle
   (E) the Mongol armies traveled very light and were able to live largely off the land

406. All of the following are true of Ivan III EXCEPT that he
   (A) was nicknamed Ivan the Terrible
   (B) tripled the territory of the state
   (C) was the first Muscovite prince to claim an imperial title
   (D) ended the dominance of the Mongols in Russia
   (E) renovated the Kremlin in Moscow

407. Music dramas written under the Yuan Dynasty
   (A) emphasized Confucian conservatism
   (B) mocked and satirized the Mongols
   (C) looked to Buddhist legends for themes
   (D) supported the elimination of the imperial examination system
   (E) had to be approved by Mongol censors before they could be performed

408. All of the following are true regarding the Mongols in southeastern Asia in the late 1200s EXCEPT that they
   (A) invaded Vietnam (Dai Viet and Champa) several times and forced it to pay tribute
   (B) invaded Korea several times and turned it into a forced ally
   (C) invaded the kingdom of Burma (Myanmar) and destroyed it
   (D) launched two major invasions of Japan but were unsuccessful both times
   (E) invaded and occupied Java

409. The decisive event in the Mongol defeat of the Song Dynasty was
   (A) the siege of Xianyang
   (B) a series of succession crises in the Mongol Empire
   (C) the sudden death of Ogodei Khan
   (D) the defeat of the Russians at Kiev
   (E) the establishment of Pax Mongolica

410. All of the following are true regarding Marco Polo's life and travels EXCEPT that
(A) he worked for Ogodei Khan as an ambassador for 24 years
(B) he came from a family of Venetian merchants
(C) his book was a medieval "bestseller"
(D) he visited India and Sumatra
(E) some scholars question whether he actually went to China

411. All of the following are true regarding Mongol gender relations EXCEPT that
(A) Mongol women were allowed to speak in tribal councils
(B) polygamy was commonly practiced
(C) the influence of foreign cultures tended to restrict women in the later Mongol Empire
(D) immediate remarriage was required after a husband's death
(E) Mongol women refused to adopt the Chinese practice of foot binding

412. The Yuan Dynasty in China was responsible for all of the following measures EXCEPT
(A) dismissing most Confucian scholars
(B) forbidding marriage between the Mongols and the Chinese
(C) preventing the Chinese from learning the Mongol language
(D) eliminating civil service examinations
(E) dividing the population of China into three major groups

413. Which of the following is a true statement about Mongol invasions between 1200 and 1500?
(A) While Mongols were able to convert Russia to Islam, they failed to spread Muslim beliefs throughout India.
(B) Mongols adopted elements of Chinese culture, which were then spread to other parts of Asia.
(C) Mongol invasions were successful in China and Japan but unsuccessful in Korea.
(D) Mongol rule in Russia helped build a peaceful society based on Russian traditions.
(E) The Mongols' occupation of Egypt was much less bloody than their occupation of eastern Europe.

414. The Mongol invasions of Europe began in the
  (A) 1170s
  (B) 1200s
  (C) 1230s
  (D) 1260s
  (E) 1290s

415. The Golden Horde refers to the khanate that made up
  (A) Russia
  (B) Persia and most of the Middle East
  (C) China
  (D) southeastern Asia
  (E) India

416. All of the following are true regarding Genghis Khan EXCEPT that he
  (A) delegated authority based on merit and loyalty rather than family ties
  (B) instituted the great law
  (C) was tolerant of other religions
  (D) allowed his generals considerable autonomy
  (E) caused a succession crisis by failing to name a successor

417. The Yassa was
  (A) the administrative assistant to the khan who was responsible for the day-to-day running of each khanate
  (B) the secular code of Mongol law
  (C) the Mongol bureaucracy that governed China after the Confucian scholars were dismissed
  (D) a Mongol special tax on Muslims in Il-Khanate
  (E) the Mongols' name for their cavalry bow

418. All of the following have been suggested as ways in which Mongol rule affected Russian national development EXCEPT that
  (A) Russian rulers thought of the state as their private domain
  (B) Russian rulers emphasized autocratic power
  (C) Russian rulers favored Kiev over Moscow because of its resistance to Mongol rule
  (D) Russian rulers divided the population into a landholding elite and a vast majority of taxpayers
  (E) Russian rulers stressed personal loyalty and a system of service to rulers

419. All of the following are true regarding Tamerlane (also known as Timur) EXCEPT that he
  (A) refused to attack fellow Muslims
  (B) fancied himself the successor to the Mongol Empire
  (C) sacked Delhi and massacred tens of thousands of citizens
  (D) was a great patron of the arts
  (E) weakened the Christian church in much of Asia

420. The Pax Mongolica had the unintended consequence of
  (A) restricting the flow of ideas because of Mongol intellectual conservatism
  (B) hurting European economies because nascent national states instituted tariffs
  (C) reducing the Eurasian population because of the constant warfare that preceded it
  (D) allowing the Black Death to spread more quickly along trade routes
  (E) making it easier for Ming troops to travel within China and destroy the Yuan Dynasty

Tang/Song China and Southeastern Asia

421. Tu Fu (Du Fu) and Li Po (Li Bai) were noteworthy Tang Dynasty
(A) poets
(B) emperors
(C) calligraphers
(D) astronomers
(E) mathematicians

422. Which of the following is the proper sequence of Chinese dynasties?
(A) Tang, Song, Shang, Ming, Han
(B) Shang, Han, Tang, Song, Ming
(C) Han, Shang, Song, Tang, Ming
(D) Shang, Han, Song, Tang, Ming
(E) Song, Tang, Shang, Ming, Han

423. All of the following were accomplishments during the Song Dynasty EXCEPT the
(A) issuance of paper money
(B) formation of a standing navy
(C) first use of gunpowder
(D) invention of papermaking
(E) invention of moveable-type printing

424. Wu Zetian (also known as Wu Zhao) is famous as the
(A) greatest poet of the Song period
(B) only female Chinese emperor
(C) inventor of the calligraphy style still in use in China today
(D) supposed inventor of wood-block printing
(E) monk who spread Pure Land Buddhism to China

425. The production of beautiful light green celadon pottery in the 11th century is best associated with present-day
(A) China
(B) Cambodia
(C) Korea
(D) Thailand
(E) Laos

426. All of the following are true of the Silk Road during the Tang Dynasty EXCEPT that
(A) the Muslims checked Tang control of central Asia at the battle of Talas in 751
(B) Tang emperors paid special attention to managing the vast western regions
(C) trade was much greater in the first half of the Tang Dynasty than in the second half
(D) Tang China had an excellent transportation network
(E) the eastern terminus of the road was at Hangzhou

427. Chinese rulers of the Tang and Song Dynasties
(A) provided China with a decentralized government
(B) neglected to construct an irrigation system
(C) invoked the mandate of heaven to justify their rule
(D) surprisingly ensured an equality of gender roles
(E) were unconcerned with the arts since military matters took up most of their energy

428. Zhu Xi is associated with
(A) neo-Confucianism
(B) Zen Buddhism
(C) Pure Land Buddhism
(D) the Quanzhen school of Taoism
(E) the White Cloud Sect

429. All of the following are associated with Tibet EXCEPT
(A) rice farming
(B) Vajrayana (Tantric) Buddhism
(C) *The Epic of King Gesar*
(D) the Potala Palace
(E) wrathful deities

430. All of the following are true of Vietnam between 800 and 1400 CE
EXCEPT that the
(A) Li Dynasty established a capital at Hanoi
(B) women in Vietnam generally had more privileges than the women
in China
(C) Vietnamese won their independence in 939 after a thousand years
of Chinese rule
(D) Vietnamese rejected Chinese culture because it was associated
with the hated invaders
(E) Tran Dynasty was a golden age of art and culture

431. The Sui Dynasty is best known for
(A) its lengthy rule
(B) the construction of the Grand Canal
(C) the successful occupation of Korea
(D) the neglect of the Great Wall of China, which allowed the Mongols
to invade
(E) its popularity among the Chinese people of the time

432. Song improvements in maritime technology included all of the following
EXCEPT the
(A) magnetic compass
(B) watertight bulkhead
(C) astrolabe
(D) sternpost rudder
(E) paddle-wheel ship

433. The largest city of Tang China, believed to be the largest city in the world
at the time, was
(A) Bianjing (present-day Kaifeng)
(B) Lin'an (present-day Hangzhou)
(C) Beijing
(D) Guangzhou (Canton)
(E) Chang'an (present-day Xian)

434. One of the most important accomplishments of the Korean king Sejong
the Great was the
(A) conquest of Manchuria
(B) invention of the Hangul system of writing
(C) increase of the Koguryo empire to its greatest extent
(D) expulsion of all foreign merchants from Inchon
(E) destruction of the kingdom of Silla

435. The Trung sisters were famous as
    (A) founders of the largest Khmer Buddhist nunnery
    (B) national heroines of Laos
    (C) Buddhist missionaries to Japan
    (D) leaders of a rebellion against the Chinese occupation of Vietnam
    (E) the only female rulers of the Khmer Empire

436. One characteristic of early Song China was a(n)
    (A) massive increase in iron production
    (B) more inward-looking foreign policy
    (C) enormous growth of trade along the Silk Road
    (D) initial creation of an efficient system of writing based on Roman letters
    (E) burst of popular enthusiasm for Buddhism such as the Pure Land sect

437. The Srivijaya Empire achieved its power and riches by
    (A) controlling the Sunda and Malacca straits
    (B) dominating the natural resources of the Malaysian peninsula
    (C) taxing the Malay sailors who sailed from the kingdom of Maynila (Manila)
    (D) the conquest of the Ayutthaya kingdom and the occupation of Bangkok
    (E) trading with present-day Easter Island

438. All of the following are true of the unified Silla Dynasty EXCEPT that
    (A) it ruled the Korean peninsula in the eighth and ninth centuries CE
    (B) powerful aristocratic families dominated the government
    (C) it was followed by the Goryeo Dynasty
    (D) it devised a system of writing Korean with Chinese characters
    (E) to increase their power, Silla kings tried to reduce the impact of Buddhism

439. All of the following are true of Buddhism in China EXCEPT that
    (A) it affected land distribution
    (B) it blended with Chinese philosophy
    (C) it influenced Japanese Buddhism
    (D) followers rejected Mahayana Buddhism in favor of Theravada Buddhism
    (E) followers often worshipped the Buddha as a deity

440. All of the following were characteristics of Song China EXCEPT that it
(A) was vulnerable to periodic Islamic invasions
(B) was able to support numerous large cities
(C) expanded the number of candidates eligible for the civil service examination
(D) had an extremely strong navy
(E) depended on the Silk Road for trade

441. All of the following are true of Chinese wood-block printing EXCEPT that
(A) the earliest surviving wood-block book dates from the Tang Dynasty
(B) Chinese woodblocks could be maintained for centuries
(C) the technique originated in Egypt in the third century CE and then spread to the Han Dynasty
(D) it was easier for the Chinese to print using woodblocks than movable type
(E) wood-block printing made reproducing a text relatively easy

442. All of the following are true of the Khmer Empire EXCEPT that
(A) its capital was at Phnom Penh
(B) it was greatly influenced by Indian culture
(C) it peaked about 1200 CE
(D) it excelled in sculpture and architecture
(E) it dominated the mainland of southeastern Asia

443. Foot binding
(A) became widespread during the Tang Dynasty
(B) was a religious custom originally imported from India
(C) helped Chinese women work in the fields more easily
(D) did not hurt
(E) demonstrated the wealth of a family

444. The An Lushan Rebellion
(A) increased Tang prestige with neighboring states
(B) decreased the population of the Song Dynasty by about two-thirds
(C) caused the Tang to lose control of the western regions along the Silk Road
(D) led to a strengthening of the central government after the rebellion was crushed
(E) was the direct cause of the Ming Dynasty's rise to power

445. The main reason for the collapse of the Southern Song Dynasty was
- (A) food shortages that modern historians attribute to climate change
- (B) strained economic conditions caused by the disruption of trade on the Silk Road
- (C) peasant revolts brought on by high taxation
- (D) invasion by the Mongols
- (E) a massive pandemic/plague that killed one-third of the Chinese population and destabilized the country

CHAPTER 14

The Americas

446. The ancient ceremonial center of Cahokia is located in present-day
(A) United States
(B) Mexico
(C) Guatemala
(D) Belize
(E) Peru

447. All of the following were cultivated by native peoples of the Americas before 1500 EXCEPT
(A) maize
(B) wheat
(C) squash
(D) beans
(E) tomatoes

448. Which of the following cultures did NOT develop a system of writing?
(A) Mayan
(B) Aztec
(C) Incan
(D) Olmec
(E) Mixtec

449. All of the following are associated with the Ancestral Puebloan culture EXCEPT
(A) masterful stone and adobe buildings built along cliff walls
(B) enormous mounds shaped like animals and built for unknown purposes
(C) fine pottery with black painted designs
(D) a ceremonial road system
(E) the eventual abandonment of many traditional urban and ceremonial centers

450. All of the following are true of the Olmec EXCEPT that they
    (A) are known for their colossal stone heads
    (B) developed a writing system and a calendar
    (C) inhabited the Gulf Coast regions of present-day Veracruz
    (D) raised surpluses of corn, beans, and squash
    (E) developed in the large San Lorenzo and Tabasco River valleys

451. Which of the following cultures had the highest level of scientific, technological, and intellectual achievement?
    (A) Mayan
    (B) Incan
    (C) Olmec
    (D) Toltec
    (E) Aztec

452. According to recent estimates, about how many people lived in the Western Hemisphere in 1500?
    (A) 700,000
    (B) 1.7 million
    (C) 7 million
    (D) 17 million
    (E) 70 million

453. Which of the following characterized the Incan Empire?
    (A) It developed strict social class hierarchies.
    (B) It collapsed because of peasant uprisings.
    (C) Trade was its primary economic activity.
    (D) It flourished after interaction with the Spanish.
    (E) It suffered as a result of its nonexpansionist nature.

454. When the Aztecs first came to power in the 1400s, they existed as
    (A) an independent nation
    (B) a partner of the Toltecs
    (C) a member of a triple alliance
    (D) a nomadic people
    (E) an ally of the Mixtec

455. All of the following are true of the people of the Hopewell culture EXCEPT that
   (A) their culture was centered in present-day Ohio
   (B) they built giant burial mounds
   (C) they constructed elaborate trading networks across great distances
   (D) they built on the preceding Adena culture
   (E) they were noted for their amazing houses built into the cliffs of the Mississippi River valley

456. In Incan society, the *ayllu* members
   (A) usually refused to perform the *mita*
   (B) collected tribute from subject peoples
   (C) were not closely related to each other
   (D) shared a series of reciprocal obligations that they were required to honor
   (E) generated work for artisans by practicing conspicuous consumption

457. When the Aztecs (or Mexica) arrived in the valley of central Mexico, they
   (A) established their own advanced traditions
   (B) adopted many of the existing Mesoamerican traditions
   (C) were noted for their adaptability to the traditions of other regional peoples
   (D) developed independently from other Mesoamerican cultures
   (E) insisted that other societies adopt their traditions

458. All of the following are true regarding women in classic Mayan culture EXCEPT that
   (A) Mayan society was matriarchal
   (B) women played a crucial role in the processing of raw materials
   (C) wealthy and prominent families traced their lineage through parallel descent
   (D) female deities were not uncommon
   (E) women could be rulers

459. The people of the Chavin culture
   (A) dominated the Andean highlands from about 300 to 900 CE
   (B) depended primarily on maize for their food supply
   (C) developed a sophisticated culture without the benefit of metallurgy
   (D) used llamas as beasts of burden
   (E) created an advanced culture without any large-scale temples

460. All of the following are true of the Mesoamerican ball game EXCEPT that it
(A) was played by the Olmecs, Mayas, and Aztecs
(B) was played with a ball made of rubber
(C) was both a contest of athletic skill and a ritual spectacle
(D) was a frequent source of inspiration for Mesoamerican artists
(E) emphasized individual skill over team participation

461. All of the following reasons have been suggested for the decline of the Classic Maya EXCEPT
(A) foreign invasion
(B) climate change and drought
(C) moral decay and loss of civic virtue
(D) peasant revolts and social turmoil
(E) deforestation and soil depletion

462. All of the following are true of women in Eastern Woodland culture EXCEPT that
(A) they provided most of their society's food supply
(B) in some cases, they lived in a matrilineal-based clan and inheritance system
(C) they performed economic roles that were usually gender-differentiated
(D) they worked alongside men in the fields
(E) the senior women sometimes chose the clan chief

463. The Ancient Puebloans (Anasazi) relied primarily on which of the following for food?
(A) Corn
(B) Potatoes
(C) Manioc
(D) Squash
(E) Chickens

464. All of the following are true of Cahokia EXCEPT that it
(A) was an urban site larger than London in 1250 CE
(B) was unique because it was not located near any rivers
(C) maintained extensive trade links with communities 100 miles away
(D) was abandoned more than a century before Europeans invaded North America
(E) contained a workshop for the production of copper religious items

465. The Early Classic period of Mayan culture was influenced by the culture of what great Mesoamerican capital city?
(A) Chichen Itza
(B) Teotihuacan
(C) Tenochtitlan
(D) Tula
(E) Tres Zapotes

466. All of the following are true of the ancient Maya EXCEPT
(A) they based their livelihood on the cultivation of potatoes and quinoa
(B) they transmitted the legend of Quetzalcoatl
(C) the various independent Mayan city-states were linked by trade
(D) they were polytheistic
(E) they constructed large, truncated pyramids

467. The Aztec Empire expanded into a power vacuum that emerged after the collapse of which great culture?
(A) Maya
(B) Toltec
(C) Olmec
(D) Mixtec
(E) Teotihuacan

468. All of the following were Andean cultures of the pre-Inca period EXCEPT
(A) Moche
(B) Chavin
(C) Adena
(D) Wari
(E) Chimu

469. The Toltecs
(A) were a peaceful people
(B) did not practice human sacrifice
(C) were the only major Mesoamerican cultural group that denied the legend of Quetzalcoatl
(D) based their empire on efficient administration
(E) may have been involved in long-distance trade with the Ancestral Puebloans

470. All pre-Columbian people of Central and South America
   (A) were polytheistic
   (B) integrated various ethnic groups into their societies
   (C) had a system of writing
   (D) were noted as skilled administrators
   (E) limited their trade to regional networks

CHAPTER 15

Japan

471. Japanese society in 1200 was most similar to the society of which
other 13th-century country/region?
(A) India
(B) Vietnam
(C) China
(D) Western Europe
(E) Byzantium

472. The Yayoi culture introduced all of the following to Japan EXCEPT
(A) Buddhism
(B) wet rice cultivation
(C) bronze
(D) ironworking
(E) new pottery styles

473. All of the following are true of Shinto EXCEPT that it
(A) has no founder
(B) has no fully developed theology
(C) is monotheistic
(D) is based on animism
(E) has blended with Buddhism through most of Japan's history

474. All of the following are true of the *Nihon Shoki* (also known as
the *Nihongi* and *The Chronicles of Japan*) EXCEPT that it
(A) contains a creation myth
(B) was finished in the Yayoi period
(C) helped establish the concept of the divine ancestry of emperors
(D) was written in classical Chinese
(E) is an important tool for historians and archaeologists

475. Which of the following is an accurate statement about the Heian period in Japan in the ninth century CE?
    (A) Shinto was temporarily replaced by Confucianism as the state religion.
    (B) Mongol invaders ruled Japan.
    (C) The Chinese meritocracy greatly influenced Japan's government.
    (D) It was an unusual period of peace and security in Japan.
    (E) It was a time of Japanese conquest and exploration.

476. Which book is sometimes considered the world's first novel?
    (A) *Iroha*
    (B) *Kimigayo*
    (C) *Kinuginu*
    (D) *The Pillow Book*
    (E) *The Tale of Genji*

477. The riddle "What is the sound of one hand clapping?" is known as a
    (A) *bushi*
    (B) *koan*
    (C) *daimyo*
    (D) *bompu*
    (E) *bakufu*

478. One major difference between European and Japanese feudalism during the Middle Ages was that
    (A) European feudalism was far more militaristic than its Japanese counterpart
    (B) Japanese emperors maintained power during feudalism, while European kings were only symbolic leaders
    (C) there were far fewer agricultural workers in Japanese feudalism
    (D) there was no Japanese equivalent to the position of the European lord
    (E) in Japan, peasants farmed land in exchange for money instead of military protection

479. The Kamakura period was noted for
    (A) the decline of Buddhism in Japan
    (B) the transition to the Japanese medieval period
    (C) being the apex of classical Japanese culture
    (D) a temporary increase in the power of the emperor leading to victory over the Mongols
    (E) an increase in the power of the *shoen*

480. All of the following are true of Japan during its feudal period EXCEPT that
  (A) it valued military ability over bureaucratic administration
  (B) it was carved into self-sufficient estates
  (C) Bushido was expected of men but not women of the samurai and *bushi* classes
  (D) it had a decentralized government
  (E) the samurai were released from agricultural responsibilities in exchange for military service

481. A *ronin* is a
  (A) two-handed Japanese sword and the weapon of choice for a samurai
  (B) samurai with no master
  (C) type of Japanese poet who was sensitive to the sadness of impermanence
  (D) much-hated medieval government bureaucrat in charge of tax collection
  (E) field or manor in medieval Japan

482. All of the following are true regarding women in premedieval Japan EXCEPT that
  (A) women exercised considerable political influence but were barred from the position of emperor
  (B) Chinese Confucianists expressed dismay at the relative freedom of Japanese women
  (C) the introduction of Buddhism to Japan intensified gender inequality in religious life
  (D) the great literature of the Heian period was written by women
  (E) many of the women at court were devotees of the Lotus Sutra

483. Buddhism was introduced into Japan in about
  (A) 150 CE
  (B) 350 CE
  (C) 550 CE
  (D) 750 CE
  (E) 950 CE

484. *Tennoism* refers to
  (A) a form of female foot binding imported from China
  (B) the control of large estates by the daimyo
  (C) the accumulation of land and power by Buddhist monasteries
  (D) the divinity of the emperor
  (E) the rule of Emperor Hiroki Kondo

485. All of the following were associated with the end of the Heian period and the establishment of the Kamakura shogunate EXCEPT
(A) the Genpei War
(B) the people's obedience to their clan leaders rather than the government
(C) the decline of tax revenues because Buddhist monasteries were tax exempt
(D) the creation of the office of the shogun
(E) the movement of the capital from Kyoto to Edo (Tokyo)

486. The kana system first appeared in
(A) the Jomon period
(B) the Yayoi period
(C) the Yamoto period
(D) the Heian period
(E) medieval Japan

487. All of the following statements are true of male homosexuality in ancient Japan EXCEPT that
(A) older samurai often took younger boys as lovers
(B) Shinto scriptures declared homosexuality a sin
(C) early law codes penalized incest and bestiality but not homosexuality
(D) homosexuality was common in Buddhist monasteries
(E) *shunga* scrolls depict erotic scenes of every kind of sexual activity

488. The Mongol threat to Japan was defeated at
(A) Hakata Bay
(B) Kyoto
(C) Nara
(D) the Sea of Okhotsk
(E) the Kamikaze Strait

489. Before 1500, Japan
(A) was consistently governed by a powerful emperor
(B) adopted Buddhism to replace Shinto
(C) had an amazingly egalitarian system of land distribution
(D) adopted every important feature of the Chinese style of government
(E) was dominated by aristocratic classes

490. All of the following are true of Bushido EXCEPT that it
   (A) led to the popularization of seppuku
   (B) was philosophically condemned by most Japanese Buddhists as excessively warlike
   (C) developed between the 9th and 12th centuries
   (D) could be described as the "way of the warrior"
   (E) emphasized the preservation of family honor

491. The most popular schools of Japanese Buddhism, Jodo Shu and Jodo Shinsu, are closest to which form of Buddhism?
   (A) Zen
   (B) Theravada
   (C) Newar
   (D) Vajrayana
   (E) Pure Land

492. The Jomon period is best known for its
   (A) Buddhist temples
   (B) sword manufacture
   (C) coiled pottery
   (D) ikebana
   (E) development of naval engineering

493. The Taika Reforms
   (A) attempted to enhance the power of the imperial court
   (B) declared Edo (Tokyo) the new capital and ordered it built in the Chinese style
   (C) had limited impact because they failed to address inequities in land ownership
   (D) were based on the structures and precepts of Song Dynasty China
   (E) created the office of the shogun

494. All of the following are true of *The Pillow Book of Sei Shonagon* EXCEPT that it
   (A) was written in the Heian period
   (B) is the most detailed source of factual material about the life of the time
   (C) helped popularize samurai values such as Bushido
   (D) is famous for its humorous observations and caustic depictions of the author's contemporaries
   (E) uses very few Chinese words

495. *Waka* (also known as *tanka*) is a type of
  (A) sword
  (B) samurai
  (C) poetry
  (D) calligraphy
  (E) tea ceremony

496. All of the following are characteristic Japanese cultural forms EXCEPT
  (A) Noh
  (B) a *muqam*
  (C) kabuki
  (D) a tea ceremony
  (E) ikebana

497. The *shoen* system
  (A) strengthened the power of the central government
  (B) was the standard form of land ownership during the Yamoto and Yayoi periods
  (C) contributed to the rise of a local military class
  (D) survived until the Meiji Restoration
  (E) was strengthened by the Kamakura shogunate

498. The position of daimyo was roughly equivalent to the European position of
  (A) king
  (B) lord
  (C) bishop
  (D) knight
  (E) tax collector

499. The aboriginal people of Japan are known as
  (A) Kofun
  (B) Burakumin
  (C) Lao
  (D) Hmong
  (E) Ainu

500. Keyhole-shaped burial mounds are characteristic of what Japanese period?
  (A) Jomon
  (B) Yayoi
  (C) Yamoto
  (D) Heian
  (E) Medieval

ANSWERS

Chapter 1: Prehistory and the Neolithic Revolution

1. (E) The Paleolithic Age, or Old Stone Age, extended from the time the first hominids appeared until about 8000 BCE. Paleolithic humans were not settled people. They acquired their food supply through foraging, or hunting and gathering. Agriculture and the domestication of animals are hallmarks of the Neolithic Age. As far as it can be determined, Paleolithic society lacked established social classes; however, recent research has cast doubt on the theory that Paleolithic societies were matriarchal.

2. (C) About 18,000 to 7,000 years ago, many Neolithic societies around the world developed agriculture. The degree to which aboriginal Australians practiced agriculture has been a recurring subject of debate for archaeologists. In general, the Australians did not engage in agriculture until the arrival of Europeans in the late 1700s. The other answer choices include some of the earliest agricultural cultures such as the Indus Valley in southern Asia, Sumer in southwestern Asia, and Egypt in northern Africa. In the Andean highlands, natives extensively cultivated the potato.

3. (B) Cosmic microwave background (CMB) radiation is thermal radiation that fills the observable universe almost uniformly. It is thought to be radiation left over from an early stage in the development of the universe, and its discovery is considered a landmark test of the big bang model of the universe. In archaeology, typology classifies things according to their characteristics. Typology can measure the stages of one culture against another by comparing tools found at both archaeological sites. Paleontology can compare human remains with animal remains of the time, while paleobotany does the same thing with plants.

4. (E) Anthropologists have assumed that women were probably the first farmers because men were usually preoccupied with hunting. Men roamed far from camp to hunt and scavenge dead animals, but women seldom accompanied them on hunting expeditions. However, women were probably responsible for the "gathering" component of hunter-gatherer societies in the Paleolithic Age. Based on modern hunter-gatherer societies, women probably stayed closer to an established site to tend children and forage for edible plants and firewood nearby. However, comparisons to modern-day hunter-gatherer societies suggest that the sexual division of labor may have been relatively flexible. Men may have participated in gathering plants, firewood, and insects, and women may have caught small animals and assisted men in driving herds of large game animals off cliffs. Although women were probably the first farmers, it's not clear whether their status increased or decreased as a result of the momentous transformation to agriculture.

5. (E) Archaeological eras are obviously imprecise and vary wildly from place to place. For example, some Neolithic cultures continue to exist today. In addition, the sequence is not necessarily true everywhere; there are areas, such as the islands of the southern Pacific, the interior of Africa, and parts of North and South America, where the peoples passed directly from the use of stone to the use of iron without an intervening age of bronze. However, there is a general chronological progression. Here is a rough chronology and approximate starting date of each era:

Paleolithic (Old Stone Age)	Rudimentary tools	c. 2.5 million BCE
Neolithic	Polished tools	c. 10,000 BCE
Chalcolithic (Copper Age)	Stone and copper tools	c. 4400 BCE
Bronze Age	Bronze and copper tools	c. 4000 BCE
Iron Age	Iron tools	c. 2500 BCE

6. (B) Agricultural settlements arose in about 7000 BCE in many parts of the world such as eastern Asia, southwestern Asia, and Africa. Modern scholars believe these cultures probably developed agriculture independently, especially given the large distances separating early agricultural communities. Although many of these communities developed in river valleys, there are exceptions, such as the famous Neolithic settlements of Çatal Hüyük and Jericho. Agriculture tended to develop later in Mesoamerica and South America than in the eastern hemisphere.

7. (E) Somewhere between 15,000 and 30,000 years ago, humans (Paleo-Indians) crossed the Bering land bridge from Asia to North America. They followed herds of large mammals, many of which are now extinct, to hunt for food. The term *land bridge* probably gives an inaccurate image. The Bering Strait, the Chukchi Sea to the north, and the Bering Sea to the south are all shallow waters. The Bering land bridge was actually about 1,000 miles north to south at its widest point. Local conditions meant snowfall was light, so the land bridge was probably not covered by glaciers. Instead, it would have been mainly a grassland steppe. The disappearance date is unclear, but melting glacier water probably completely submerged the land bridge about 14,000 years ago.

8. (A) The Lascaux cave paintings, in present-day southwestern France, are estimated to be about 17,000 years old and reflect the culture of Paleolithic humans. The nearly 2,000 images consist mainly of large animals, most of which are known from fossil evidence to have lived in the area at the time. The cave was discovered in 1940. The Paleolithic era is distinguished by the development of the most primitive stone tools; it extends from the earliest known use of stone tools about 2.6 million years ago to the end of the Pleistocene era around 10,000 years ago.

9. (D) The Neolithic Revolution was the first agricultural revolution, when humans made the transition from hunting and gathering to agriculture and settlement. Archaeological data indicate that various forms of domesticating plants and animals arose independently in several different places in the world—including the tropical and subtropical areas of southwestern and southern Asia, northern and central Africa, and Central America—from about 10,000 to 5000 BCE. Neanderthals disappeared about 30,000 years ago; tool-making capabilities and the ability to create fire are also developments from the Paleolithic Age.

10. (C) Neolithic cultures did not measure precise hours of the day. Prior to the invention of agriculture, spring and fall were migration periods. As agriculture replaced nomadic life, spring became planting time and fall became harvest time. However, preindustrial societies are usually task oriented rather than time oriented. The earliest sundials were Egyptian obelisks (c. 3500 BCE) and Babylonian shadow clocks (c. 1500 BCE). Neolithic cultures did possess tools, religious beliefs, and artwork.

11. (B) The Piltdown hoax is arguably the most famous archeological hoax of all time. Piltdown Man comprised a collection of bone fragments from a skull and jawbone that were presented as the fossilized remains of a previously unknown early human. These fragments were said to have been collected in 1912 from a gravel pit at Piltdown, England. The specimen became the subject of immediate controversy, but it was not until 1953 that it was exposed as a forgery. Piltdown Man actually consisted of the lower jawbone of an orangutan that had been deliberately combined with the skull of a fully developed modern human. Who perpetrated the hoax is still a subject of debate.

12. (A) Humans probably first evolved in Africa in the Pleistocene era, beginning about 2 million years ago. The early hominid population lived in Africa and migrated first to the Fertile Crescent and then to Europe and Asia. The Pleistocene followed the Pliocene era; the Pleistocene era dates from about 2.5 million years ago until about 10,000 BCE. The end of this era corresponds with the retreat of the last continental glacier; this is also the unofficial end of the Paleolithic Age in archaeology.

13. (B) The earliest species to be classified in the same *Homo* species as modern humans was *Homo habilis* ("handy man"). The skeleton was discovered by Louis Leakey in the early 1960s in the Olduvai Gorge in modern-day Tanzania. The specimen was found with tools he had fashioned for hunting and butchering animals. About one million years ago, *Homo habilis* was supplanted by an upright hominid, *Homo erectus*. A skull of *Homo erectus* was found by Richard Leakey in Kenya in 1984. Java Man and Peking Man are examples of *Homo erectus*. *Homo sapiens* did not appear until about 100,000 to 500,000 years ago.

14. (C) The Neolithic era was responsible for the first developments in the domestication of animals and plants. Therefore, it is not surprising that there was an emphasis on agricultural fertility. The other answer choices did not exist in the Neolithic era. Glyphs were developed at a later date in the river valley cultures and Mesoamerica. Iron tools were developed by the Hittites, and plows came later. A codex is a Mayan book. Aqueducts were typical of Roman culture.

15. (C) Lucy is the common name for several hundred pieces of bone representing about 40 percent of an individual *Australopithecus afarensis*. This hominid specimen was discovered in 1974 in Ethiopia by Donald Johanson. Lucy, named after the Beatles song "Lucy in the Sky with Diamonds," is estimated to have lived about 3.2 million years ago. Her discovery was significant because the skeleton seems to show evidence of small skull capacity (like apes) but a bipedal upright walk (like humans). This implied that bipedalism preceded an increase in brain size in human evolution. However, other findings have suggested that perhaps *Australopithecus afarensis* was not a direct ancestor of humans. In 1994, a new hominid (Ardi) was found, pushing back the earliest known hominid date to 4.4 million years ago.

16. (B) Geochronology is a scientific technique to measure the chronology of the earth's history as determined by geologic events. Geochronology can be used to determine the age of ancient cultures by counting the layers created by melts of water from a receding ice sheet. Dendrochronology measures climatic change by viewing the thickness in the layers in branches and around tree trunks. Carbon 14 dating tests the decay of a radioactive isotope of carbon found in artifacts. Aquachronology is a made-up term.

17. (E) In 1856, laborers working in a limestone quarry in a cave in the Neander Valley in Germany dug out the first Neanderthal bones. Neanderthals were initially considered dim-witted, brutish cavemen. However, studies of their fossils show that they walked upright like modern humans; the slouched caricature was caused by an inaccurate reconstruction of Neanderthal remains in the early 1900s. The first Neanderthal traits appeared in Europe somewhere between 600,000 to 350,000 years ago. By 130,000 years ago, complete Neanderthal characteristics had appeared. These characteristics disappeared in Asia by 50,000 years ago and in Europe by about 30,000 years ago. Neanderthals and *Homo sapiens sapiens* coexisted with modern humans for at least 10,000 years; the nature of their relationship has been the subject of much scholarly debate.

18. (D) The Iron Age occurred after the Bronze Age. It was characterized by the widespread use of iron or steel, especially for cutting tools and weapons. The use of iron coincided with other changes in society, including differing agricultural practices, religious beliefs, and artistic styles. The Iron Age is dated from approximately 2500 BCE to 500 CE. This age left many artifacts, because iron erodes slowly.

19. (C) The exact time of the first appearance of a distinct species, *Homo sapiens*, is disputed. Estimates range from 500,000 to 100,000 years ago. The oldest *Homo sapiens* fossil is approximately 400,000 years old, an occipital bone from the base of a skull found in Hungary. Although the skull had a crest at the outer neckline like *Homo erectus*, the shape was otherwise essentially modern. *Homo sapiens* first migrated from their homeland in Africa into southwestern Asia and Europe about 40,000 BCE.

20. (E) The Neolithic Revolution transformed the small, mobile groups of hunter-gatherers that had dominated human history into sedentary societies based in built-up villages. This process presumed the existence of a steady food supply if not a food surplus. The Neolithic Revolution provided the basis for concentrated, high-population-density settlements and a specialized, complex division of labor.

21. (A) The domestication of sheep, pigs, and goats took place approximately between 10,000 and 8000 BCE. It is unknown who invented the wheel and when it was invented; some archaeologists believe it was about 8000 BCE in Asia. However, clear evidence of wheeled vehicles does not appear until about 3500 BCE, almost simultaneously in Mesopotamia, northern Caucasus, and central Europe. Venus figurines are prehistoric statuettes of women portrayed with similar physical attributes from the Upper Paleolithic era. They are found mainly in Europe but also in Eurasia. Most of them date from about 25,000 BCE, although some are even older.

22. (E) The date humans achieved fire-making capability is disputed. The earliest evidence suggests that fire was used in Africa 1.5 million years ago. The problem of when humans first developed the capacity to make fire instead of "capturing" natural fires is probably unsolvable; the earliest fire-making technology would have been based on friction created by perishable wood. The evidence seems to imply that between 500,000 and 1 million years ago, humans had figured out how to make and transport fire. There is considerable evidence that they used fire as a technological instrument for firing clay, heat-treating flint, and "storing" heat in stones to roast or boil food between 20,000 and 60,000 years ago. All of these examples greatly predate the Neolithic Revolution.

23. (D) Çatal Hüyük was a large Neolithic and Chalcolithic settlement in present-day southern Turkey. It existed from about 7500 to 5700 BCE and is the largest and best-preserved Neolithic site to date. The archaeological remains of Çatal Hüyük reveal how Neolithic communities built permanent housing, diverted streams for crops, and engaged in trade. The prehistoric mound settlements were abandoned before the Bronze Age. Neolithic culture may date as far back as about 10,700 to 9400 BCE in Tell Qaramel in northern Syria. However, the widely accepted beginning of the Neolithic culture is considered to be in Jericho at about 9500 BCE. Neither site is as well preserved as Çatal Hüyük.

24. (B) Jericho is a city located near the Jordan River. As of 2012, it is in the West Bank of the Palestinian territories. Situated below sea level about 10 miles north of the Dead Sea, Jericho is often cited as the oldest continuously inhabited city in the world. Plentiful springs in and around the city have made it a desirable site for human habitation for thousands of years. Archaeologists have discovered the remains of more than 20 successive settlements in Jericho, the first dating to about 9000 BCE. Around that time, the town had grown to more than 70 dwellings and was home to more than 1,000 people. The most striking aspect of this early town was a massive stone wall, probably used for defense against floods as much as people.

25. (C) Bronze is a metal alloy made mainly of copper with a little tin as the main additive. Hard and brittle, it was extremely important in ancient times. The discovery of bronze allowed people to create improved metal objects. Tools, weapons, armor, and various building materials made of bronze were harder and more durable than those made of stone and copper. The change was so dramatic that the alloy gave its name to the time period known as the Bronze Age. The earliest tin-alloy bronzes date to the late fourth millennium BCE in present-day Iran, Iraq, and China.

Chapter 2: Egypt and Mesopotamia

26. (A) The earliest cities developed in Mesopotamia during the Bronze Age from approximately 4000 to 1000 BCE. An organizational system became necessary to maintain the intricate network of canals that the Mesopotamians had built to irrigate farmlands. The people developed a political unit known as the city-state, in which the urban area exercised political and economic control over the outlying agricultural areas. Law codes, trade routes, and ceremonial centers resulted from control of irrigation. (Mediterranean polyculture is associated with Minoan Crete, c. 2200–1400 BCE.)

27. **(B)** Neo-Assyria was an ancient empire of western Asia. It developed around the city of Ashur on the upper Tigris River and south of the later capital, Nineveh. The neo-Assyrian Empire began in 934 BCE and ended in 608 BCE. Assyrians were masters of polychrome, carved stone relief used to decorate imperial monuments. The minutely detailed reliefs often concern royal affairs such as hunting and war making. Minutely detailed human figures are depicted in triumphal scenes of sieges, battles, and individual combat. The Assyrians were not good administrators and were harsh rulers of the people they conquered. They often deported subject peoples from their homelands to work on building projects in Assyria. The Assyrians established a library at Nineveh and spread Sumerian culture throughout the area.

28. **(E)** *The Epic of Gilgamesh* is an example of epic poetry from Mesopotamia and is one of the earliest known works of literature. Scholars believe that it originated as a series of Sumerian legends and poems about Gilgamesh, the king of Uruk. These were probably combined into a longer Akkadian epic at a much later date. The most complete version is preserved on 12 clay tablets from the library of the seventh century BCE Assyrian king Ashurbanipal. *The Epic of Gilgamesh* contains a Sumerian account of the flood similar to that of the Hebrews' Genesis account.

29. **(A)** At the battle of Megiddo, Pharaoh Thutmose III defeated the king of Kadesh, who ruled over Canaan-Syria and Palestine. The battle was the first to be reported by eyewitnesses in relatively reliable detail. Thutmose III's victory reestablished Egyptian dominance in Palestine and began the centuries of Egypt's greatest expansion. All details of the battle come from Egyptian sources, especially hieroglyphic writings at Karnak and Thebes. The other answer choices all incorrectly mix kings with nations, empires, or city-states.

30. **(D)** The first purely phonetic alphabet was invented by the Phoenicians sometime before 1050 BCE. This alphabet, in which a single letter stood for only one sound in the language, proved more efficient than pictographic scripts. It gradually replaced writing systems such as cuneiform, hieroglyphics, and Linear B and became the basis for the Greek, Roman, and modern alphabets.

31. **(E)** Sumer was a collection of city-states around the lower Tigris and Euphrates Rivers in present-day southern Iraq. Each of these cities had individual rulers, but as early as the middle of the fourth millennium BCE, the leader of the dominant city-state was considered the king of the region. Egypt was located on the Mediterranean; the Yellow River valley culture was found in China; the Nubian culture was located close to the Red Sea; and the Indus Valley culture was near the Arabian Sea.

32. **(C)** Religion was extremely important in ancient Mesopotamian society; the priest or priestess of a city's main deity enjoyed extremely high status. Perhaps the most important duty of a Mediterranean priest was to discover the will of the gods through divination. The priest would study natural signs by tracking the patterns of the stars, interpreting dreams, and examining animal entrails. The priest's proclamations helped the ancient Mesopotamian people decide when and how to please the gods. *Ma'at* was an Egyptian concept that can be roughly translated as "justice"; ancient Egyptians believed that it was a divine force possessed by their rulers.

33. (E) At the battle of Carchemish (c. 605 BCE), the neo-Babylonian army—led by Nebuchadnezzar II—smashed the combined forces of Egypt and neo-Assyria. As a result, neo-Assyria ceased to exist as an independent power, and Egypt retreated and was no longer a significant force in Asia. Neo-Babylonia reached its economic peak after the battle and became the dominant military power in the region until its defeat at the hands of Cyrus the Persian at the battle of Opis in 539 BCE.

34. (B) The Phoenicians settled along the Mediterranean coast in present-day Lebanon in about 2000 BCE. They did not adopt Hebrew monotheism, although they traded with the Hebrews, especially in cedar. The Phoenicians are famous for their alphabet, which came to the Romans via the Greeks. They were great traders, producing purple dye for export and making textile fabrics from wool and linen yarn. Glass was probably first created around 3000 BCE; Egyptian glass beads date back to about 2500 BCE. The Phoenicians imported glassmaking techniques from the Egyptians but added improvements of their own and helped develop it as an export item.

35. (A) Religion played an important part in the lives of Egyptians. Egyptian religion was polytheistic, except during the reign of Akhenaton. The Egyptians had as many as 2,000 gods. Some, such as Amun, were worshipped throughout the whole country, while others were worshipped only in specific locations. Religious authority was a crucial element in validating the power of the king. Elaborate tombs reveal the ancient Egyptians' strong belief in an afterlife. Egypt is now primarily Islamic, which is a strongly monotheistic religion.

36. (B) Sumerian city dwellers first invented the technology of writing in a script called *cuneiform* to record business transactions and financial accounts. Around the fourth millennium BCE, trade and administration became too complex for people to remember, and writing became a more dependable method of recording and presenting transactions in a permanent form. Although professional scribes first used writing mainly for business purposes, it also became useful for recording religious beliefs and traditional stories and for keeping genealogical records. Writing made literature an important cultural element for the first time. About 2300 BCE, the Akkadian princess Enheduanna composed the oldest known written poetry, establishing a tradition of royal Mesopotamian woman writers.

37. (E) The Hittites established a kingdom in north-central Anatolia around the 18th century BCE. They were one of the first groups to smelt iron and used many iron tools and weapons. This helped the Hittite Empire reach its height around the 14th century BCE. At that point, it covered a large part of Anatolia, northwestern Syria, and upper Mesopotamia. In warfare, the Hittites made particularly successful use of chariots. After about 1200 BCE, the Hittite Empire disintegrated into independent neo-Hittite city-states.

38. (D) Saul (c. 1079–1007 BCE) was the first king of the united kingdom of Israel. His story is told in the biblical book of Samuel. Before the united monarchy, the Hebrew tribes lived as a confederation under informal leaders known as judges. In about 1020 BCE, under threat of invasion, the Hebrew tribes united to form the kingdom of Israel. Samuel, a judge, anointed Saul as the first king, although it was David—Saul's successor—who created a powerful monarchy.

39. (D) The Code of Hammurabi, compiled about 1700 BCE, is one of the earliest known legal codifications. It recorded the king's decisions in commercial disputes and crimes. This code also tried to protect less powerful members of Babylonian society; however, it is divided into categories of free persons, commoners, and slaves. Many laws expressed the king's view of justice; in everyday life, people determined most cases by their own judgment.

40. (E) The Hebrew Bible established a new kind of religion based on a single deity who made a series of formal and informal covenants with the Hebrews. These covenants guaranteed that the Hebrews would receive protection if they worshipped only God and lived by God's laws. However, the choice to obey those laws is not deterministic; it is instead left up to the free will of society (the collective of God's people) and each person within it.

41. (A) One of the best-known 18th-Dynasty pharaohs is Amenhotep IV (d. c. 1336 BCE), who changed his name to Akhenaton in honor of the god Aten. Akhenaton's exclusive worship of Aten is often considered to be an example of monotheism. Under Akhenaton's 17-year reign, Egyptian art flourished. However, his changes to traditional religion were not accepted by most Egyptians, and after his death, traditional religious practice was restored. When later rulers founded a new dynasty, they tried to discredit Akhenaton and his immediate successors, referring to Akhenaton as "the enemy" in archival records.

42. (D) In 721 BCE, the neo-Assyrian army captured the Israelite capital at Samaria and carried the citizens of the northern kingdom away to captivity. In Jewish tradition, these people are known as the Ten Lost Tribes of Israel. The neo-Assyrian victory left Judah, the southern kingdom with its capital at Jerusalem, as the only independent Hebrew kingdom. About 688 BCE, Jerusalem was besieged by a neo-Assyrian army under Sennacherib. The results of this siege are not clear, because both sides claimed victory. However, the kingdom of Judah did not fall until Nebuchadnezzar destroyed the city and the First Temple in about 597 BCE. Approximately 15 years before, the Medes (an Iranian people) and the Chaldeans (a Semitic people who had driven the Assyrians from Babylonia) had overthrown the neo-Assyrian Empire by destroying the capital at Nineveh.

43. (E) The kingdom of Kush was an ancient Nubian state with its center at the meeting place of the Blue Nile and White Nile in present-day Sudan. Its capital was originally Napata. After King Kashta invaded Egypt in the eighth century BCE, the Kushite kings ruled as pharaohs of the 25th Dynasty of Egypt for a century, until they were expelled in 656 BCE. Around 600 BCE, the Kushite capital was moved to Meroë. This site contains more than 200 pyramids in three groups. They are identified as Nubian pyramids because of their distinctive size and proportions.

44. (C) The metallurgical technology that developed during the Bronze Age indirectly led to the creation of the first empire. The search for bronze, lead, silver, and gold led King Sargon of Akkad to use force to take over access to these ores. In 2200 BCE, Sargon initiated a series of conquests that created an Akkadian empire with secure trade routes. Supplies of wood and metals could be floated safely down the Euphrates to Akkad.

45. (A) Although ancient Egypt had a very structured social hierarchy, men and women possessed relatively equal legal rights; women in ancient Egypt had more rights than did women in other ancient cultures. For example, an Egyptian woman could not be forced into marriage. Women were free to work outside the home or run a business if they desired. They could own, buy, and sell property. They could make wills and leave their personal goods to whomever they chose, including their daughters. If a woman was unhappy with her marriage, she could get a divorce and then remarry someone else or remain single.

46. (C) *Ma'at* can be roughly translated as "truth" or "justice." Egyptians believed it was a divine force possessed by Egyptian kings or pharaohs. Their rule on earth represented the supernatural eternal force that created harmony and stability in human life. A king who ruled according to *ma'at* ensured the annual flooding of the Nile.

47. (D) One of the earliest recorded peace treaties was concluded between the Hittite and Egyptian Empires after the battle of Kadesh (c. 1274 BCE). The peace treaty was recorded in two versions: one in Egyptian hieroglyphics and the other in Akkadian, using cuneiform script; the latter version is currently in the Istanbul Archaeology Museum. Although the majority of the text is identical, the Hittite version claims that the Egyptians came suing for peace, while the Egyptian version claims the reverse. This treaty is considered so important in the field of international relations that a reproduction of it hangs in the United Nations' headquarters.

48. (C) In the 1600s BCE (18th Dynasty–New Kingdom), Queen Hatshepsut proclaimed herself a female king and became co-ruler with her stepson after her husband's death. Hatshepsut commissioned hundreds of construction projects in both Upper and Lower Egypt. Her most famous building was the lavish complex of Deir el Bahri near Thebes, where a cult was established after her death to worship her as a god. She is generally regarded as one of the most successful pharaohs, reigning longer than any other woman of an indigenous Egyptian dynasty. The other answer choices are less important historical or mythical female pharaohs.

49. (D) The neo-Babylonian Empire lasted from about 626 to 539 BCE. At the battle of Carchemish, fought in about 605 BCE, the neo-Babylonians drove the Egyptians out of Syria. Neo-Babylonian rulers pursued a very conservative cultural policy but were also famous for their advances in astronomy and mathematics. The astonishing Ishtar Gate was a gate of the inner city of Babylon, constructed about 575 BCE by order of King Nebuchadnezzar II. It was made of blue glazed tiles with alternating rows of low-relief dragons and bulls (aurochs). A reconstruction of the Ishtar Gate was built at the Pergamon Museum in Berlin, Germany.

50. (E) The empire of Akkad collapsed around 2200 BCE, within about 200 years of its founding. The cause was an invasion of people from the Zagros Mountains known as the Gutians. Scholars know little about the Gutian period; cuneiform sources suggest that the Gutians did not maintain irrigation systems, written records, or public safety. A dark period of high grain prices and famine followed. Despite their military success, the Gutians did not assimilate Sumerian lands into a large kingdom. Akkadian poetry explained both the rise and the fall of the Akkadian Empire as the will of the gods.

51. (A) King Hammurabi's law code was written about 1700 BCE because of the increase in property ownership and private commerce. The Code of Hammurabi is one of the earliest known legal codifications that has been preserved. Hammurabi's code divided society into hierarchical categories but tried to protect less powerful citizens from exploitation. Hammurabi considered this role to be part of a king's sacred duty.

52. (D) The New Kingdom of Egypt dated from about 1567 to 1070 BCE, a time period that covered the 18th, 19th, and 20th Dynasties. The New Kingdom was ancient Egypt's most prosperous time and marked the peak of its power. The warrior-pharaohs of this period rebuilt central authority and engaged in foreign wars. The 18th Dynasty included some of Egypt's most famous pharaohs including Ahmose I, Hatshepsut, Thutmose III, Amenhotep II, Akhenaton, and Tutankhamen. The later part of this period, under the 19th and 20th Dynasties (c. 1292–1069 BCE) is also known as the Ramesside period after the 11 pharaohs who took the name of Ramses. The New Kingdom was followed by the Third Intermediate Period (c. 1070–664 BCE).

53. (D) The neo-Assyrian's harshness caused rebellions from Mesopotamia to the Mediterranean. The empire, whose power had been feared for centuries, crumbled astonishingly quickly after the death of Ashurbanipal in 627 BCE. In the seventh century BCE, the Medes and the Chaldeans combined forces to invade the weakened kingdom. In 612 BCE, they destroyed Nineveh, the Assyrian capital, after a long siege followed by house-to-house fighting. There was still some resistance, but the Assyrians and Egyptians met a final defeat at Carchemish in about 605 BCE. The giddy excitement caused by the overthrow of Assyria by people long subjected to its yoke is captured brilliantly in the biblical book of Nahum. Nahum, a minor Jewish prophet, writes of the assault and sack of Nineveh in ecstatic language.

54. (D) Indo-European languages comprise a family of several hundred related languages and dialects, including most major languages of Anatolia, Europe, southern Asia, and the Iranian plateau. Indo-European has been written since the Bronze Age in the case of the Anatolian languages, especially Hittite. Indo-European languages are currently spoken by almost three billion native speakers, the largest number for any language family. Some Indo-European languages include Spanish, Hindi, Portuguese, Bengali, Russian, German, French, Italian, Punjabi, and Urdu.

55. (B) King Menes was an ancient Egyptian pharaoh of the early dynastic period and is credited with uniting Upper and Lower Egypt. He is therefore considered the founder of the first dynasty. Menes is almost never mentioned in the archaeological record. Yet there is a comparative wealth of evidence regarding Narmer, a person also credited by posterity with the unification of Upper and Lower Egypt. This has resulted in a theory identifying Menes with Narmer.

56. (D) The Hyksos were a Semitic people from the Syria-Palestine region who took over the eastern Nile delta during the 12th Dynasty. This ended the Middle Kingdom (c. 2050–1786 BCE) and began the Second Intermediate Period of ancient Egypt. The Hyksos introduced new technologies such as bronze making to Egypt, as well as horses, war chariots, and olive trees. It is not clear whether the Hyksos invaded Egypt forcibly or migrated there peacefully.

57. (A) The first five books of the Hebrew Bible are called the Pentateuch, or Torah. These books told the history of the Hebrew people, both mythical and historical. They also declared the religious and moral codes the Hebrews were supposed to follow. These codes were similar to many Mesopotamian law codes, but they applied equally to all Hebrew people, regardless of social class.

58. (D) The Euphrates and Tigris form the basis of the major river system of southwestern Asia. Both rivers have their sources within 50 miles of each other in present-day eastern Turkey, and both travel southeast through northern Syria and Iraq to the head of the Persian Gulf. The total length of the Euphrates, the more western of the two, is about 1,740 miles; the Tigris is about 1,150 miles in length. Baghdad, the capital of present-day Iraq, stands on the banks of the Tigris. In ancient times, many great Mesopotamian cities—including Nineveh, Ctesiphon, and Seleucia—stood on or very near the Tigris.

59. (C) The neo-Assyrian Empire began in 934 BCE and ended in 608 BCE, when it was conquered by the Chaldeans and other Babylonians. It was replaced by the neo-Babylonian Empire, which lasted from about 626 to 539 BCE, when this empire was destroyed by the Persians. This Persian Empire is known as the Achaemenid Empire and lasted from about 550 to 330 BCE. It would eventually control Egypt and stretch from the Indus Valley to Thrace and Macedonia on the northeastern border of Greece. The Achaemenid Empire is covered in Chapter 3.

60. (E) By 2500 BCE, the cities of Sumeria personified the end of Neolithic (New Stone Age) culture. They were the first to practice intensive, year-round agriculture, including large-scale cultivation of land, monocropping, organized irrigation, and the use of a specialized labor force. A surplus of storable food allowed people to settle in one place instead of migrating after grazing land. Sumer was also the site of early developments in writing, especially cuneiform. This script used a mixture of phonetic symbols and pictographs expressed by wedge-shaped marks. Ziggurats are the Mesopotamian equivalent of the Egyptian pyramids; large, artificial, square mountains of stone in the form of a terraced step pyramid of successively receding stories or levels. It is unclear why ziggurats were built or how they were used, but they were constructed by the Sumerians, Babylonians, Akkadians, and Assyrians until the 17th century BCE. (Ashur was the chief god of the neo-Assyrian Empire.)

Chapter 3: Persia and Greece

61. (A) Minoan Crete flourished from about 2200 to 1400 BCE. The Minoans developed sophisticated crafts, elaborate architecture, and an extensive trade system. The general population lived clustered around the palaces and sprawling homes of the rulers. The palaces were the center of civil life as well as distribution centers for goods. Minoans developed their own script, known as Linear A. They also had an advanced agricultural system, known as Mediterranean polyculture, that enabled them to produce an agricultural surplus.

62. (D) The Minoans frequently traded with the Mycenaeans and, through these interactions, passed on aspects of their culture. Both the Minoans and the Mycenaeans engaged in maritime trade, which led to economic prosperity. Both cultures produced a written language; the Mycenaeans developed pictographic scrip called Linear B that was based on the Minoan Linear A. The Mycenaean burial chamber, called a *tholos*, contains architectural patterns similar to those in Minoan tombs. However, the chief deities of Mycenae were gods of war, and men were often buried with their weapons and armor. Minoan artifacts seem to show a lack of military weapons or fortified city walls.

63. (A) The philosopher Socrates (469–399 BCE) is considered one of the most famous philosophers in world history. All information about him is secondhand, most of it from the writings of Plato, his equally famous student. In Plato's *The Apology*, he presents an account of Socrates's defense at his trial for impiety in 399 BCE. Although Socrates believed in acquiring knowledge through asking questions, he rarely took a definitive position. In fact, in *The Apology*, Socrates claims to know nothing at all except that he knows nothing. Socrates and Plato refer to this method of constant questioning as *elenchus*, which means something like "cross-examination." The elenchus is the basis of many of Plato's most famous dialogues involving Socrates. The idea developed into the dialectic, the idea that truth can only be pursued by questioning and conflict with opposing ideas. Most Athenians thought Socrates was a Sophist, because he seemed to tear down every ethical position without offering many constructive alternatives of his own.

64. (C) Zoroastrianism, once one of the world's largest religions, was founded in Persia. It is a religion and philosophy based on the teachings of the prophet Zoroaster (also known as Zarathustra), who lived sometime between 1750 and 500 BCE (most scholars place him in about the 11th or 10th century BCE). Some form of Zoroastrianism was the state religion of many Iranian people for centuries. It is a dualistic religion; good and evil are believed to have distinct sources. The most important religious texts are known as the Avesta. The religion collapsed with the triumph of Islam after 700 CE. However, small communities continue to exist; one 2004 estimate placed the number of Zoroastrians worldwide between 145,000 and 210,000.

65. (E) The Persians decisively defeated the neo-Babylonians at the battle of Opis (539 BCE). The Persian army was led by Cyrus the Great, and the Babylonians were led by Nabonidus. At the time, Babylonia was the last major power in western Asia that was not under Persian control. As a result of his victory, Cyrus was proclaimed king of Babylonia. This incorporated the Babylonian Empire into the Persian Empire, making the latter the greatest in the world.

66. (A) The Achaemenid Empire, also known as the Persian Empire, lasted from about 550 to 330 BCE. It eventually expanded to rule over almost one million square miles, the largest empire the world had yet seen. At the height of its power, the Achaemenid Empire spanned Asia, Africa, and Europe, and it included present-day Iran, Afghanistan, Pakistan, parts of central Asia, Anatolia, Thrace, Macedonia, Iraq, northern Saudi Arabia, Jordan, Israel, Lebanon, Syria, and all significant population centers of ancient Egypt. The empire was named after its first official monarch, Achaemenes.

67. (D) The most dramatic example of political equality in a Greek city-state was the practice that allowed all free, adult male citizens to share in government. They did this by attending and voting in a political assembly where the laws and policies of the community were ratified. Women in many city-states had certain protections under the law and were counted as citizens legally, socially, and religiously. However, they were barred from participation in politics because men claimed that female judgment was inferior to male judgment. Regulations governing female sexual behavior and control of property were also stricter than those for men. But women citizens had legal protection against being kidnapped and sold into slavery, and they could use the courts for property disputes, although they usually had to have a man speak for them. Women could control property in fifth-century Athens through inheritance and dowry. However, Greek society was paternalistic. Before her marriage, a woman's father served as her legal guardian; after marriage, her husband assumed the same role.

68. (B) Only Athenian citizens voted directly on all issues before the city-state, and only free men over age 20 who had completed military training were considered citizens. The Athenian courts used juries with judges whose decisions were subject to appeal. Athens had an assembly, not a chief executive.

69. (B) The groundbreaking *Histories* of Herodotus of Halicarnassus (c. 485–425 BCE) attempted to explain the Greco-Persian wars as a clash between differing worldviews and cultures. This book was unique for its wide geographical scope, relatively critical approach to evidence, and lively narrative. Herodotus was the first historian known to collect his materials systematically and to test their accuracy at least partially; by Roman times, he was called the "father of history." He is known for his digressions; for example, the whole of Book II is one enormous digression on the geography, customs, and early history of Egypt.

70. (C) Darius I (550–486 BCE) ruled the Persian Empire at its peak, when it controlled Egypt and parts of Greece. Darius greatly extended Persian power, advancing as far eastward as the Indus Valley and westward to Thrace. He organized this vast territory into provinces and then assigned taxes payable in the medium best suited to each region's economy, whether precious metals, grain, horses, or slaves. He also required each region to send soldiers to man his royal army. A network of roads and a courier system aided communication and the movement of the army among the distant provinces. Darius was a Zoroastrian, but he generally allowed his subjects to worship as they pleased as long as they remained peaceful. Darius also sponsored large construction projects in Susa (the capital of the Persian Empire), Babylon, Egypt, Pasargadae, and Persepolis.

71. (B) Solon (c. 638–558 BCE) was a politician and poet who was appointed magistrate of Athens in 594 BCE. He is remembered for his attempts at reform in archaic Athens. He canceled the debts of the poor and created a four-part ranking of citizens by wealth to balance political power between rich and poor. Solon also created the Council of 400, chosen by lottery, which would decide the issues to be discussed in the general assembly. He reformed the judicial system, allowing any male citizen to bring a charge on behalf of any victim and to appeal the case to the assembly if necessary. To balance these judicial reforms, Solon granted broader powers to the Areopagus, a council consisting of former archons that judged the most serious cases. Solon's reforms failed in the short term, yet he is often credited with laying the foundations for Athenian democracy.

72. (C) After Athens's defeat in the Peloponnesian War in 404 BCE, Sparta became the dominant power among the Greek city-states. Spartan rule was extremely dictatorial, and other city-states resented Spartan domination. At Leuctra in 371 BCE, 6,000 Theban hoplites and 1,500 cavalry defeated 10,000 Spartan hoplites. Some military historians claim that this is the first battle in which tactics, rather than mere strength or luck, played a part. The battle altered the Greek balance of power, as Sparta was reduced to a second-rate city-state. Thebes's supremacy in Greece was short-lived, and it soon fell to the Macedonians led by Philip II.

73. (D) The Greeks were Indo-European speakers whose ancestors moved into the region by 8000 BCE. Mycenaean Greece (c. 1800–1000 BCE) takes its name from the hilltop of Mycenae in the Peloponnese peninsula, which had a fortified settlement dominated by a palace and dotted with rich tombs. The Mycenaeans engaged in farming and maritime trade. Their language, art, and buildings show a close relationship with the Minoan culture of Crete. Unlike the relatively peaceful Minoans, however, Mycenaean culture was dominated by a warrior aristocracy and spread through conquest. Linear B tablets found in Cretan palaces reveal that the Mycenaeans eventually took control of Crete about 1400 BCE.

74. (D) After the fall of the Mycenaean culture (c. 1000 BCE), Greek society entered a period of poverty and population decline that is sometimes called the Dark Ages. Greeks cultivated less land, lost their knowledge of writing, and created no great works of art or architecture. However, herding animals became more common, and the population became more mobile. Trade did not disappear, and it eventually brought new iron technology as well as exposure to the Phoenician alphabet and Asian art and fine goods.

75. (A) Aristophanes (c. 450–385 BCE) was the greatest writer of the Old Comedy that flourished in Athens in the fifth century BCE. He wrote at least 36 comedies, of which 11 still exist. Aristophanes used many forms of comedy, from slapstick to satire. He was noted for making fun of snobbishness and arrogance in politics, social life, and literature. Many of his plays continue to be performed today, including *The Clouds* (423 BCE), *Lysistrata* (411 BCE), and *The Frogs* (405 BCE). In *The Clouds*, a dishonest farmer tries to convince Socrates to give him a sophistic education to avoid paying his debts. *Lysistrata* tells the story of how the women of Greece stop the Peloponnesian War by banding together and refusing to sleep with their husbands until they have made peace. In *The Frogs*, Dionysus, the patron god of Athenian drama, descends to Hades to bring Euripides back and ends up refereeing a poetic dispute between Euripides and Aeschylus. Phrynichus (fl. 500 BCE) was one of the earliest of the Greek tragedians and is sometimes regarded as the founder of Greek tragedy.

76. (C) Hesiod was a Greek poet who lived between 750 and 650 BCE. Hesiod and Homer are the earliest Greek poets whose work has survived, and they are often paired together. Hesiod's two most famous works—*Theogony* and *Works and Days*—are a major source of Greek mythology, farming techniques, early economic thought, and astronomy. In *Theogony* (*Genealogy of the Gods*), Hesiod describes the birth of the gods from the union of primeval Chaos and Earth. For Hesiod, the life of the gods, like that of humans, was filled with sorrow, struggle, and violence. *Works and Days* includes the famous description of the five "Ages of Man"; advocates a life of honest labor; and attacks idleness, unjust judges, and usury.

77. (B) Pre-Socratic philosophers developed new explanations for the human world and its relationship to the gods. Philosophers such as Thales, Anaximander, Anaxagoras, and Heraclitus were from the region of Ionia on the western coast of present-day Turkey. These Ionian philosophers theorized that the universe was not arbitrary but instead based on natural laws. Most of them believed that although matter can change from one form to another, all matter has something in common that does not change. They did not agree what it was that all things had in common. Thales thought it was water; Anaximenes, air; and Heraclitus, fire. None of them experimented to find out. They are noteworthy for using abstract reasoning rather than religion or mythology to explain themselves. In this way, the Ionian school pioneered rationalism, the idea that a person could support an argument through evidence and logic.

78. (C) Ancient Greek city-states such as Athens, Sparta, and Thebes celebrated love between men as a guarantee of military efficiency and civic freedom. Male love was a source of inspiration in art and poetry, applauded in theaters and assemblies, and praised by philosophers like Plato. Sappho, a female poet, wrote about passion and love involving both genders. The word *lesbian* derives from Lesbos, the island of her birth, while her name is the origin of the adjective *sapphic* (meaning "relating to lesbianism"). In Plato's *Symposium*, all the major characters assume that serious love will be between men, generally the love of an older man for an adolescent youth. The older man's role is to educate, protect, love, and provide a role model for his lover; the man's reward lies in his lover's beauty, youth, and promise. According to theorist Michel Foucault, the ancient Greeks did not think of sexual orientation as a form of social identity. Acts, not people, were described as homosexual. However, some scholars believe that homosexual relationships were common only among the aristocracy and not widely practiced by the common people. Nonetheless, male love in ancient Greece was often a crucial element in war and politics, and it had a major impact on art, literature, and philosophy.

79. (D) The geography of Greece made sea travel extremely convenient. When Greek men needed or wanted more land, they boarded ships for foreign lands. Soon, Greeks had settled throughout the Mediterranean, negotiating for or kidnapping wives in areas they settled. By 580 BCE, Greeks had settled in present-day Spain, southern France, southern Italy and Sicily, North Africa, and the Black Sea coast. This process is usually called Greek colonization. It increased communication and trade among Mediterranean peoples and spread Greek culture and politics. Greek settlements in southern Italy and Sicily became so large that the region was called Magna Graecia ("Great Greece"). The Greek culture of these colonists, who began arriving in the eighth century BCE, had a lasting effect on Italy, particularly on the culture of ancient Rome. Greece consisted of disparate city-states even after colonization (c. 800–400 BCE) expanded its borders and culture.

80. (B) In 490 BCE, the Persians had numerical superiority over the Athenian army at Marathon (no Spartans were present). However, the Athenian hoplites charged the Persians and engaged them in hand-to-hand fighting, neutralizing the Persian archers, the most effective part of the Persian infantry. The defeat of Persia temporarily stopped a major invasion of Europe. The Greek army was based on the heavily armed Greek hoplite—an infantryman with spear, armor, and discipline. The Greek military formation, the phalanx, would dominate the battlefield until the Roman Empire modified it to the cohort. However, the Greek victory at Marathon was not decisive; 10 years later, an even larger Persian invasion would be defeated on sea at Salamis and on land at Plataea.

81. (B) Ancient Greece was located on Aegean islands, the Peloponnesian peninsula, and the southern Balkan peninsula. Although language and religion united the Greek peoples, the mountainous terrain isolated the city-states. This resulted in competition and made it difficult to create a unified central government. Greece's geography also restricted agriculture, which limited the size of each city-state's population. Barley, grapes, and olives were the most important crops. Annual rainfall could be extremely erratic, making farming a risky business. In most areas, flat land was scarce, limiting the large-scale raising of cattle and horses.

82. (A) In male-dominated ancient Greece, bearing male children brought special honors to a woman, because sons meant security for parents. Sons could appear in court to advocate for their parents in lawsuits, and Athenian law required sons to support elderly parents. Greek men worried obsessively about the paternity of their children, because citizenship defined the political structure of the city-state and even a man's personal freedom. Male children were not automatically assumed to be legitimate, but neither were female children regularly sold into slavery. Women were counted as citizens legally, socially, and religiously; however, they were barred from participating in politics. In 451 BCE, Pericles sponsored a law making citizenship more exclusive by conferring it only on children whose mother and father were Athenian by birth. Before this, even if Athenian men had married foreign women, they could still pass citizenship on to their children.

83. (B) The Peloponnesian League is a modern name for Sparta and its allies from about the sixth century to the fourth century BCE. By about 500 BCE, Sparta had become the most powerful state in the Peloponnesian peninsula. It acquired allies such as Corinth, Elis, and Tegea; sometimes they joined with Sparta voluntarily, and other times they were threatened with military force. The league eventually included all Peloponnesian states except Argos and Achaea. Most towns in the league swore to follow Sparta's lead on foreign policy in exchange for military protection. Sparta could also call for a percentage of a town's soldiers to serve under Spartan command. The Peloponnesian League had no permanent institutions, and the member states only met when the Spartans wanted. It appears that every ally had one vote in the Congress of Allies, but the decisions of the congress had no binding power on Sparta.

84. (A) Zoroastrians worship Ahura Mazda as the highest and supreme god. They believe human beings are essentially divine in nature and share the same spiritual nature as Ahura Mazda. Human beings have a choice in the material world: they can either follow the teachings of Ahura Mazda and remain righteous, or they can follow the ways of evil and be damned. The other answer choices are all basic beliefs of Zoroastrianism, a religion founded sometime before the sixth century BCE in Persia.

85. (C) Hippocrates of Cos (c. 460–c. 370 BCE), an ancient Greek physician, influenced the Hippocratic school of medicine, which made little or no mention of a divine role in sickness and cures; nor did it depend on magic or ritual. Little is actually known about what Hippocrates thought, wrote, and did. Nevertheless, he is credited with greatly advancing the study of clinical medicine (as opposed to theory), compiling the medical knowledge of previous schools, and prescribing practices for other physicians. Many Hippocratic medical theories lasted into the 19th century; for example, the idea that four humors made up the body. Another long-lasting concept was the idea of a crisis, a point in the progression of disease at which either the patient would die or natural processes would make the patient recover. Modern medical graduates take an ethical oath before they enter practice based on the ancient Greek oath attributed to Hippocrates.

86. (A) Greek colonies were not colonial enterprises in the modern sense. They were not established and administered by their home city-states. Instead, daring men (women were rarely involved), with almost no governmental involvement, initiated most overseas Greek settlements. City-states then claimed settlements as colonies if they became economically successful.

87. (A) Pericles (c. 495–429 BCE) was an important politician and general in Athens between the Persian and Peloponnesian wars. He influenced Athenian society by turning the Delian League into an Athenian empire. He also helped turn Athens into an educational and cultural center of the ancient Greek world. He began an ambitious project that built most of the surviving structures on the Acropolis, including the Parthenon. Pericles's most important reform was to pay men who served in public office and on juries. This made it possible for poor men to serve. It was Ephialtes who reduced the court role of the Areopagus Council around 461 BCE.

88. (C) In the fifth century BCE, Athenian democracy became more inclusive than most other governments of the ancient world. Its basic principle was majority rule through the direct and widespread participation of male citizens in the assembly to make laws and policy. Only adult male Athenian citizens who had completed their military training had the right to vote in Athens. This excluded a majority of the population such as slaves, freed slaves, children, women, and foreigners. However, there were no real property requirements limiting voting and no reference to economic or social class. Once a year, all male citizens could vote to ostracize one official from the city for being a danger to democracy.

89. (C) Sappho was born on Lesbos, a large island in the Aegean near present-day Turkey. Details of her life are sketchy; she was born about 620 BCE and was probably from an aristocratic family. She may have married and had a daughter, and she may have spent some time in exile in Sicily. Her surviving work suggests that she was the center of an extremely close group of women. Her poetry seems to have comprised songs to be sung or recited to the accompaniment of a lyre. Only about 200 fragments of Sappho's poetry remain, and many of these are only one or a few words. One poem, usually called the "Hymn to Aphrodite," may be complete. Instead of addressing the gods or recounting epic tales as Homer did, Sappho's verses have one individual speaking directly to another about the bittersweet difficulties of love. She was already considered a great poet in antiquity; Plato called her "the tenth Muse," and her likeness appeared on coins.

90. (B) The Delian League is a modern name for an alliance of city-states led by Athens. Most of these city-states were in the areas most vulnerable to Persian retaliation, such as northern Greece, the islands of the Aegean, and the western coast of Anatolia. Theoretically, every member had an equal vote, but in reality, Athens made all the decisions. Each member city-state was supposed to pay dues based on its size and prosperity. However, these dues turned into compulsory tributes to Athens. Larger member states were supposed to supply entire triremes and paid crews; smaller states could share the cost or just pay cash. Over time, most members paid their dues in cash because of the difficulty of constructing and manning triremes. The decision of member states to let Athens supply warships left them no navies of their own and cleared the way for Athens to dominate the league. Athens justified its dominance by claiming it needed to keep the league strong enough to protect Greece from the Persians.

91. (C) The ancient Greek Olympic games were a celebration that included a series of athletic competitions held for representatives of various city-states in honor of Zeus. The games apparently began in 776 BCE in Olympia (Greece). They were celebrated until 393 CE, when they were suppressed by Theodosius as part of his campaign to impose Christianity as a state religion. The games were usually held every four years. The Olympics also featured religious celebrations and artistic competitions. They welcomed any socially elite, Greek male competitor and any male spectator. Although women were banned, they created their own separate Olympic festival on a different date in honor of the goddess Hera. During the games, a special truce was in effect so that athletes could travel from their countries to Olympia in safety.

92. (B) *The History of the Peloponnesian War* was written by Thucydides (c. 455–399 BCE). This book emphasized political motives rather than divine intervention as the motivating force in history. Because he served in the war as a politician and military commander, his narrative is particularly vivid. Thucydides has been called the "founder of scientific history" because of his relatively strict standards of evidence gathering and his analysis of cause and effect. The other answer choices are all famous ancient Greek historians.

93. (A) In 399 BCE, Socrates was tried and found guilty of both corrupting the minds of the youth of Athens and of "not believing in the gods of the state." He was sentenced to death by drinking a mixture containing poison hemlock. Most of what is known of the trial comes from *The Apology* by Plato. The degree of accuracy of this work has been disputed for centuries. The Greek historian Xenophon, a contemporary of Socrates, also wrote a brief account of Socrates's actions at his trial. The philosopher's death is described at the end of Plato's *Phaedo*; Socrates turns down Crito's pleas to attempt a relatively easy escape from prison and instead drinks the poison. According to Plato, Socrates's last words were, "Crito, we owe a rooster to Asclepius. Please don't forget to pay the debt." Asclepius was the Greek god for curing illness, and Socrates's words are often interpreted to mean that he was glad to be "cured" of the disease of life and that his ethereal soul would now be free of the restrictions of his corporeal body.

94. (C) Although the ancient Greeks are popularly credited with the invention of democracy, slaves were an important part of their world. The glories of the Greek city of Athens could not have existed without the slaves who worked as house servants, craftspeople, miners, farmworkers, and sailors. In Athens's golden age, slaves probably made up almost one-third of Athens's population of 300,000. Slaves had no rights and could be beaten or killed. However, some slaves did gain their freedom and mixed into the noncitizen population. No one in ancient Greece is known to have called for the abolition of slavery; Aristotle considered it a basic component of society.

95. (E) Soldiers in densely packed battle lines were common in the ancient Near East in the third millennium BCE. However, the word *phalanx* is usually used to describe Greek armies. The phalanx was a rectangular military formation composed entirely of heavy infantry (hoplites) armed with long spears, pikes, or similar weapons. The hoplites would lock their shields together, and the first few ranks of soldiers would project their 6- to 12-foot spears out over the first rank of shields. The phalanx presented a shield wall and a mass of spear points to the enemy, making frontal assaults extremely difficult. It also allowed more soldiers than just those in the front rank to engage actively in combat. It was revolutionary because it required a foot soldier to forsake the acts of individual valor so beloved by Homer and stand shoulder to shoulder with fellow soldiers in a battle square. The Spartan phalanx used a short spear, but the Macedonian phalanx that Alexander the Great commanded used a heavy *sarisa*, a 12- to 20-foot-long pike that required the use of two hands. The Greek phalanx dominated the battlefield until the Roman Empire adapted and modified it into the cohort.

96. (E) The Parthenon is a temple on the Athenian acropolis, the rocky hill at the center of the city. It is dedicated to Athena, the patron goddess of the city. Its construction began in 447 BCE and was completed in 438 BCE. Its design followed standard Greek temple architecture—a rectangular box on a raised platform. However, it was much larger (230 feet long and 100 feet wide) than the average temple. The columns were carved in the simple Doric style. The Parthenon was meant as a house for Athena, not as a gathering place for worshippers. Only priests and priestesses could enter the temple; public religious ceremonies took place in the front. The elaborate frieze portrayed Athenian men, women, and children in a parade in the presence of the gods. The decorative sculptures are considered some of the best examples of classical Greek art.

97. (A) Aeschylus (c. 524–c. 456 BCE) is often considered the "founder of tragedy." Traditionally, characters in plays interacted only with the chorus; Aeschylus expanded the number of characters to allow for conflict among them. Only 7 of his estimated 70 plays have survived. Aeschylus was a hoplite in the Persian War and wrote about his experiences in his plays. The earliest of his surviving plays is *The Persians*, performed in 472 BCE. It is based on Aeschylus's experience at the battle of Salamis and is unusual because it describes a recent historical event. *The Persians* focuses on the popular Greek theme of hubris by blaming Persia's loss on the pride of King Xerxes.

98. (A) The spread of democracy in Greece meant that persuasive speech (oratory) became a valuable skill. Sophists (wise men), skilled in public speaking and philosophical debates, taught ambitious young men from upper-class families these new skills. They thus filled the growing demand for education in Greece in the fifth century BCE. Protagoras, one of the most famous Sophists, argued that there was no absolute reality and no absolute truth. Instead, he believed that the divine was unknowable and that truth was subjective. Leucippus and other Sophists denied the power of the gods by using physics to argue that natural laws regulated the universe. These philosophers alarmed many Athenians by challenging their traditional beliefs, undermining their political traditions, and possibly angering the gods.

99. (B) At the battle of Salamis in 480 BCE, a navy from Greek city-states commanded by Themistocles defeated the Persian navy. The battle was fought in the straits between the mainland and Salamis, an island in the Saronic Gulf near Athens. Although heavily outnumbered, Themistocles persuaded the Greeks to engage the Persian fleet. As a result of a trick by Themistocles, the Persian navy sailed into the Straits of Salamis and tried to block both entrances. In the cramped conditions of the straits, the Persians' larger numbers became problematic, as ships had difficulty maneuvering and became disorganized. The Greek fleet seized the opportunity, formed in a line, and scored a decisive victory by sinking or capturing at least 300 Persian ships. The battle of Salamis was followed by the Persian military defeat at Plataea the following year. These two battles ended the Persians' attempt to expand their empire into Europe and made the Greeks the dominant population in the Mediterranean region.

100. (C) Mediterranean polyculture is an agricultural system that optimizes a farmer's labor by growing crops that require intense work at different seasons. The Minoans created this system by cultivating olives and grapes as well as grain. Polyculture provided the Minoans with a more diverse diet, which in turn stimulated population growth. This method of farming also helped maintain the fertility of the soil and offered some protection against low yields in any single crop. Minoan farmers used wooden plows bound by leather to wooden handles and pulled by pairs of donkeys or oxen. The economic surplus allowed specialized artisans to produce goods such as storage jars, lamps, or clothes that they traded for food.

101. (B) The Persians usually allowed their conquered peoples to maintain their cultural identity. This contrasted with the Assyrians, who dispersed conquered peoples throughout the empire so they would lose their identity. The Persians spoke an Indo-European language. They spread Zoroastrianism across their empire. They generally oversaw their empire well and linked most parts of it through the Royal Road.

102. (D) In its golden age, Athens grew rich from its share of spoils taken from conquered Persian outposts as well as from tributes paid by Delian League members. Each Delian League city-state paid annual dues based on its size and prosperity; however, these dues were more like tributes. Over time, most Delian League members paid their dues in cash rather than by furnishing warships. In addition, Athens became a commercial center, attracting cargo, merchants, and crafts producers from around the Mediterranean world. The increased economic activity of the mid-fifth century BCE (and the taxes on such activity) helped bring Athens to the height of its prosperity. Athens's new riches flowed mainly into public building projects, art, and festivals.

103. (D) Because of its relative durability, pottery is a large part of the archaeological record of ancient Greece. At least 100,000 vases are known to have survived. Because few Greek works in wood, textiles, or wall painting still exist, the painted decoration of the pottery has become a major source of information about life in ancient Greek cities. Between the beginning of the sixth and the end of the fourth centuries BCE, black- and red-figure techniques were used in Athens to decorate fine pottery, while simpler, undecorated wares were created for everyday household use. Athens and Corinth dominated the international market for Greek pottery from the eighth century BCE until the end of the fourth century BCE. For example, the Etruscans in central Italy imported large amounts of decorated Greek pottery for drinking wine in the Greek fashion at dinner parties. Wheel-thrown pottery dates back to about 2500 BCE, and this was the technique used for most Greek pottery. Human figures first appeared during the Archaic period and can be found on many pieces of pottery from the Classical Age.

104. (D) The Thirty Tyrants were a pro-Spartan oligarchy installed in Athens after its defeat in the Peloponnesian War in 404 BCE. The surrender stripped Athens of its walls, its fleet, and all of its overseas possessions. Corinth and Thebes demanded that Athens should be destroyed and all its citizens enslaved. However, the Spartans supposedly refused to destroy a city that had done a good service at a time of greatest danger to Greece and took Athens into their own system. They installed a pro-Spartan council headed by Critias and Theramenes, who severely reduced the rights of Athenian citizens. The Thirty Tyrants imposed a limit on the number of citizens allowed to vote. Participation in legal functions, which had previously been open to all Athenians, was restricted to a select group of 500 persons. Only 3,000 Athenians were allowed to carry weapons or receive a jury trial. The Thirty Tyrants forced many Athenians into exile and threw leaders into jail. However, their rule did not last long. The exiled Athenian general Thrasybulus seized Piraeus in the spring of 403 BCE. The Thirty Tyrants received no help from Sparta and were deposed.

105. (A) The Peloponnesian War pitted Sparta and its allies in the Peloponnesian League against Athens and its allies in the Delian League. In 415 BCE, the Athenians sent a massive expedition to try to conquer Syracuse on the island of Sicily. Their subsequent defeat there broke Athens's naval dominance in the eastern Mediterranean. Of the approximately 45,000 men that Athens sent to control Syracuse, only 7,000 survived the final battles; 200 ships and an appreciable portion of the city's total manpower were lost in a single stroke. The defeat proved to be the crucial turning point in the Peloponnesian War, though Athens struggled on for another decade. Some members of the Delian League seized the opportunity to break away, rebellions broke out in the Aegean, and Persian and Spartan morale improved. Eventually, the Athenian replacement navy was destroyed at Aegospotami in 405 BCE, and the city surrendered in the spring of 404 BCE.

106. (E) The Peloponnesian War lasted from 431 to 404 BCE and led to the defeat of Athens and the end of its golden age. Athenian aggression against Sparta's allies, Corinth and Megara, ended the uneasy peace between Sparta and Athens. Under the leadership of Pericles, the Athenian assembly refused to compromise and instead hoped to destroy Sparta. However, Pericles died in 429 BCE and an epidemic from 430 to 426 BCE killed thousands of Athenians. Without Pericles's strong leadership, the Athenians embarked on several risky military campaigns. In 415 BCE, they sent a massive force to attack Syracuse in Sicily. The attack was a total disaster, and almost the entire Athenian force was destroyed. Sparta, with the help of its former enemy, Persia, built a strong navy. The destruction of Athens's fleet at Aegospotami effectively ended the war, and Athens surrendered in 404 BCE. Sparta became the leading power of Greece, while Athens never regained its prewar prosperity.

107. (A) In the golden age of Athens, women could control property and land through inheritance and dowry. Daughters did not inherit anything from their father on his death if he had any living sons. However, about one household in five had only daughters, and they could inherit their father's property. A daughter's share in her father's estate usually came to her as part of her dowry when she married. Husband and wife then co-owned the household's common property, which was apportioned to its separate owners only if the marriage was dissolved. In most city-states, the husband was legally responsible for preserving the dowry and using it for the support and comfort of his wife and any children she bore. A man often had to put up valuable land as collateral to guarantee his wife's dowry. Upon her death, the children inherited her dowry.

108. (E) The Persian Royal Road was an ancient intercontinental highway that was reorganized and rebuilt by the Persian king Darius I in the fifth century BCE. Darius constructed the road to allow for rapid communication through the large Persian Empire. Mounted couriers could supposedly travel the 1,600 miles from Susa to Sardis (the capital of Lydia) in 7 days; the same journey took 90 days on foot. Some sections of the road are still intact at Gordion and Sardis; these cobble pavements on a low embankment are about six to seven yards in width. Supposedly, couriers could receive fresh horses at 111 way-posting stations on the Royal Road. The Greek historian Herodotus wrote, "There is nothing in the world that travels faster than these Persian couriers." He also noted, "Neither snow, nor rain, nor heat, nor darkness of night prevents these couriers from completing their designated stages with utmost speed." This is the basis for the motto of the U.S. Postal Service.

109. (B) Popular religion in Greece centered on participation in public festivals and sacrifices meant to provide divine protection from disasters. Some form of sacrifice was the focus of most cults, and there were strict rules to avoid ritual contamination of sacrifices. The feasting that followed the sacrifice provided an excuse for the community to assemble and reaffirm its ties to the divine world. Many people took part in frequent public festivals, such as the Panathenaia festival that honored Athena and featured parades, music contests, dancing, athletics, and poetry.

110. (B) Golden age sculpture was meant to be seen by the public, even if it was commissioned by private individuals. In the Archaic Age (c. 750–500 BCE), statues had a stiff posture, a straight-ahead stance, and a "goofy" smile, somewhat reminiscent of Egyptian statuary. Male statues had only one pose: striding forward with the left leg, arms held rigidly at their sides. However, in the 400s BCE, Greek sculptors began to create a variety of poses. Physiques and postures became more naturalistic. Male statues could now have bent arms and the body's weight on either leg. Musculature was anatomically correct rather than impressionistic. Female statues also had more relaxed poses. The faces of classical sculpture were self-confidently calm. Men were usually rendered in the nude as athletes or warriors. However, women were usually portrayed in fine robes or clothing. Praxiteles, the most famous Athenian sculptor of the fourth century BCE, was the first to sculpt the nude female form in a life-size statue.

Chapter 4: The Hellenistic World

111. (B) During the Hellenistic era, Jews fought over the amount of Greek influence that was compatible with Judaism. About 167 BCE, the Seleucid king Antiochus IV converted the main Jewish temple in Jerusalem into a Greek temple and outlawed Jewish religious rites. This inspired the anti-Hellenic Jewish faction, led by Judah the Maccabee, to revolt. After 25 years of war, the Seleucids recognized Jewish autonomy. The Jews were ruled by the Hasmonean Dynasty (until 63 BCE), while Seleucid kings had formal control. The reclamation of the Second Temple was commemorated in the Jewish holiday of Hanukkah.

112. (D) Alexander the Great (356–323 BCE) was the son of King Phillip II of Macedon. He was tutored by the philosopher Aristotle and first led troops at age 18. After his father's assassination, Alexander commanded the Macedonian army and crushed the Persians. At its peak, his empire stretched from the western edge of modern-day India to Egypt (where he founded the city of Alexandria). He ruled over this empire as an absolute monarch and eventually declared himself a god. Many conquered populations liked Alexander because he included non-Macedonians in his peacekeeping outposts. However, he could be bloodthirsty and brutal when he wanted to intimidate populations. His soldiers adored him, but even their loyalty reached a limit when Alexander tried to conquer India. Exhausted by years of campaigning, his army mutinied at the Hyphasis River in western India and refused to march farther east. Alexander died unexpectedly at age 33; the cause of his death is still disputed.

113. (A) The battle of Gaugamela (Arbela) is considered one of the world's decisive battles. Historians estimate that the Persian king Darius III had about a two-to-one manpower advantage over Alexander the Great. However, most of Darius's troops were of a lower quality than Alexander's. The battle of Gaugamela was a massive victory for the Macedonians and led to the fall of the Achaemenid Empire. In addition to suffering fewer casualties than the Persians, Alexander's army captured the crucial Persian cities of Babylon, Susa, and Persepolis before continuing to the east. The battle resulted in the largest empire the world had seen to that date and allowed for the spread of Greek language, philosophy, and art in the lands from the Mediterranean to India.

114. (C) *The Republic* is Plato's most famous work and has had an enormous influence on philosophy and political science. It is a Socratic dialogue written about 380 BCE; its main concerns are the definition of justice and the character of the just city and the just person. Book VII contains Plato's famous "Allegory of the Cave," which is an attempt to solve the problem of universals. In his ideal republic, Plato envisions a city ruled by philosopher-kings. At the end of *The Republic* (Book X), Plato banishes the poets from his ideal state, claiming they are unwholesome and dangerous.

115. (C) The Diadochi ("successors") were the first generation of military and political leaders following the death of Alexander the Great in 323 BCE. The wars of the Diadochi framed the beginning of the Hellenistic era. Three of Alexander's military commanders—Antigonus (382–310 BCE), Seleucus (c. 358–281 BCE), and Ptolemy (c. 367–282 BCE)—all wanted to rule the empire themselves. They killed Alexander's son, wife, and mother and, for at least the next 25 years, struggled to determine whether Alexander's empire should survive intact or disintegrate. The result, reached after the battle of Isus in 301 BCE, was a division into three large parts which basically coincided with Alexander's possessions in Europe, Asia, and Egypt.

116. (C) After the Peloponnesian War ended the Athenian golden age, Athens began a slow economic recovery. People living in the devastated countryside began moving to the city. Although productivity in the silver mines declined, private business owners boosted the economy by trading and selling goods in their homes and small shops. Because so many men had died in the war, many women found work outside the home selling bread or clothing. In 393 BCE, Athens rebuilt the Long Walls that connected the port and the city's center. The daily lives of most Athenians slowly approached the patterns they had followed before the Peloponnesian War.

117. (A) Urban populations in Egypt and southwestern Asia were the economic and social hubs of the Hellenistic kingdoms. Seleucid and Ptolemaic rulers encouraged Greeks and Macedonians to move to old cities and to found new ones. The kings adorned the new cities with the traditional features of classical Greek city-states, such as gymnasiums and theaters. However, Greek influence rarely penetrated too far into the countryside.

118. (C) Aristotle (384–322 BCE) went to study at Plato's academy at age 17. After Plato's death, Aristotle became a traveling scholar and served as tutor to the young Alexander the Great in Macedonia. He returned to Athens in about 335 BCE to found his own school, the Lyceum. The school originally derived its name, Peripatos, from the *peripatoi* (colonnades) of the Lyceum gymnasium in Athens where the members met. A similar Greek word, *peripatetikos*, refers to the act of walking. As an adjective in English, *peripatetic* means "itinerant," "wandering," or "walking about." Most scholars believe that after Aristotle's death, a legend arose that he was a peripatetic lecturer (that he walked about as he taught) and the designation Peripatetikos replaced the original Peripatos.

119. (B) Stoicism was founded by Zeno of Citium (c. 334–262 BCE). Stoics believed that fate determined everything but that human actions still had meaning through the pursuit of virtue. The term *stoicism* derives from the Painted Stoa in Athens where philosophers gathered to discuss their doctrines. According to Stoic philosophy, virtue can be achieved by cultivating good sense, justice, courage, temperance, and traditional participation in politics. However, it broke with tradition by supporting equal citizenship for women. Later Stoics, such as Seneca and Epictetus, emphasized that virtue was completely sufficient for happiness. Stoicism was a long-lasting philosophy, flourishing from the Hellenistic period to the Roman era. It did not disappear until the closing of all philosophy schools in 529 CE by Emperor Justinian I, who thought their pagan character contradicted the Christian faith.

120. (C) Menander is the best-known representative of Athenian New Comedy. After the Macedonian conquest, Greek comedy moved away from the personal and political satire common in Aristophanes's plays to safer subject matter. New Comedy characters were inspired by the cooks, merchants, farmers, and slaves of the city. Menander wrote more than 100 plays. He was known for his characterizations, and his poetic style was often compared to Homer's. Instead of writing about the great myths, Menander's plots involved young people in love, parents concerned with misbehaving children, unwanted pregnancies, long-lost relatives, and a variety of sexual misadventures. His plays were well known for several centuries but disappeared in the Middle Ages. He is known today through a few manuscripts that have been recovered in the last hundred years and through Latin adaptations by the famous playwrights Plautus and Terence.

121. (D) Arsinoë II (316–270 BCE) was the ambitious queen of Thrace, Asia Minor, and Macedonia. She was the oldest child of Ptolemy I, the wife of King Lysimachus, and later coruler of Egypt with her brother and husband Ptolemy II Philadelphus ("the sibling-loving"). Arsinoë played a major role in the politics of the western empire after the death of Alexander the Great. When she was 16, Ptolemy I married her to King Lysimachus. They had three sons together, and Arsinoë constantly schemed to secure her own children's inheritance at the expense of Lysimachus's children by earlier marriages. She accused Lysimachus's oldest son (Agathocles) of plotting to murder his father and convinced the old king to execute him in 282 BCE. The scandal led directly to Lysimachus's death and Seleucus's conquest of his kingdom in 281 BCE. Yet Arsinoë was not defeated. She found refuge with her brother, Ptolemy II, and then convinced him to divorce his wife (her dead husband's daughter) and make her his wife and coruler of Egypt. This began the Ptolemaic dynastic tradition of marriages between sibling corulers.

122. (D) In the Hellenistic era, most political and economic power lay in the cities, even though most of the population lived in small villages in the countryside. Poor people and slaves performed the vast majority of the labor required to support the urban economies of this period. It is estimated that as much as 80 percent of the adult population, free and slave, had to work the land to produce enough food to feed the population.

123. (B) Euclid was a Greek mathematician best known for his treatise on geometry, *The Elements*. This book influenced the development of Western mathematics for more than 2,000 years; it was the main textbook used for teaching geometry from its publication until the late 19th century. Little is known of Euclid's life, except that he taught at Alexandria in Egypt during the reign of Ptolemy I. In *The Elements*, Euclid deduced the principles of what is now called Euclidean geometry from a small set of axioms. It is not clear if he originated the proofs in *The Elements*, but the organization of the material is thought to be his work.

124. (B) Plato (c. 429–347 BCE) was interested in metaphysics, the philosophical consideration of reality that lies beyond the human senses. Around 386 BCE, he established the Academy, a philosophical school in Athens that attracted numerous students, including Aristotle. Plato believed that moral qualities in their ultimate reality are universal and absolute, not relative. He defined forms—which included goodness, justice, beauty, and equality—as the only true reality, which existed in a higher realm beyond the daily world. In the "Allegory of the Cave," Plato suggested that everyday experiences of the senses consisted of only dim and imperfect representations of these realities.

125. (C) Hellenistic art, architecture, and sculpture differed from Greek art of the golden age. The latter emphasized balance and restraint, while the former tended to emphasize private and personal emotions. The simple Doric and Ionic temples gave way to luxurious palaces, costly mansions, elaborate public buildings, and monuments to power and wealth. Many of the Hellenistic statues and figures carved in relief were huge. Exaggerated realism and violent emotionalism were common, such as in *Laocoön and His Sons*. The frieze of the great altar of Zeus at Pergamum mingles giant gods, ferocious animals, and hybrid monsters in desperate combat. Because many artists and writers were paid by kings, they avoided political topics or subjects that criticized public policy.

126. (A) Hellenistic kings spent huge amounts of money to support scholarship and the arts. They believed it increased their court's reputation to have famous thinkers, poets, and artists work for them. The Ptolemaic kings established the first scholarly research institute, along with a massive library, called the Museum ("place of the Muses") in Alexandria. Linked to the Museum was a building in which hired scholars could dine together and produced encyclopedias of knowledge. Callimachus (c. 310–240 BCE) wrote the *Pinakes* (Lists), a bibliographical survey of all the authors of the works held in the library of Alexandria. The *Pinakes* was one of the first known documents to list, identify, and categorize a library's holdings.

127. (C) After Alexander the Great's death in 323 BCE, a 25-year war raged to control his massive empire. The rivals were known as the Diadochi ("successors"): Antigonus, Seleucus, Cassander, and Ptolemy. Of the four, Antigonus, based in Anatolia, probably had the necessary military skill, wealth, troops, and ambition to unify the empire. However, at Ipsus in 301 BCE, he was defeated by a coalition of his three rivals. The battle ended the struggle among the Diadochi to create one unified Hellenistic empire. Instead, Alexander's vast holdings were carved up between the victors. In this way, the battle decided the character of the Hellenistic Age.

128. (A) Archimedes of Syracuse (c. 287–212 BCE) was a Greek mathematician, engineer, inventor, and astronomer. He is considered to be one of the greatest scientists of antiquity. His advances in physics include Archimedes's principle, which states that a body immersed in a fluid experiences a buoyant force equal to the weight of the fluid it displaces. He also explained the principle of the lever; according to legend he stated, "Give me a place to stand on, and I will move the earth." Archimedes is credited with designing innovative machines, including siege engines and the screw pump that bears his name. He's also considered the greatest mathematician of antiquity; his accomplishments include developing a formula to calculate the area under the arc of a parabola and accurately approximating pi. Archimedes died during the Roman siege of Syracuse, when he was killed by a Roman soldier despite orders that he should not be harmed. Greek fire was an incendiary weapon used by the Byzantine Empire, usually in naval battles; it was not invented until the seventh century CE. Archimedes may have used mirrors collectively as a parabolic reflector to burn ships attacking Syracuse.

129. (C) None of the women poets from the Hellenistic period seem to have enjoyed royal patronage. They excelled in writing epigrams, a style of short poem originally used for funeral epitaphs. Many elegant poems written by women from varying regions of the Hellenistic world still survive. Some female poets from around 300 BCE include Anyte of Tegea in the Peloponnese, Nossis of Locri in southern Italy, and Moero of Byzantium. They frequently wrote about women in their poems and expressed a wide variety of personal feelings.

130. (A) Unlike the Greek city-states, Macedonia had a powerful hereditary monarchy. However, the monarchy was checked by the landed aristocracy and often disturbed by power struggles within the royal family. Macedonian kings could govern effectively as long as they retained the support of the most powerful nobles. Monarchs demonstrated their skill by participating in some of the favorite activities of male nobles, such as fighting, hunting, and drinking. Queens achieved influence because they came from powerful noble families of the realm. Macedonians had great ethnic pride. They thought of themselves as Greek by blood but superior to the Greeks, whom they viewed as too soft to endure the difficulties of life in the north.

131. (A) Alexandria was founded about 331 BCE by Alexander the Great. The new city was intended to be the Hellenistic center of Egypt and the link between Greece and the rich Nile River valley. Alexandria remained Egypt's capital for nearly a thousand years until the Muslim conquest of Egypt in 641 CE, when a new capital was founded at Fustat (later absorbed into Cairo). Ancient Alexandria was known for its lighthouse and for possessing the largest library in the ancient world. The city was home to the largest Jewish community in the world; the Septuagint, a Greek translation of the Hebrew Bible, was produced there. In 2012, Alexandria was the second-largest city in Egypt, with a population of about 4.1 million.

132. (D) To collect taxes, urban administrations in Hellenistic kingdoms were staffed by immigrant Greeks and Macedonians. However, the Seleucids and Ptolemies also employed non-Greeks in mid- and low-level administrative positions that called for more interaction with native peoples. Local men who wanted to work in a government position improved their chances if they learned Greek. This brought the worlds of Greece and southwestern Asia into closer contact. However, Greeks and Macedonians viewed themselves as too superior to mix with locals, and non-Greeks were rarely admitted to the highest ranks of royal society.

133. (B) *Laocoön and His Sons* is a large marble sculpture from the Hellenistic period. The Roman author Pliny the Elder attributed the work to three sculptors from Rhodes (Athrenodoros, Agesander, and Polydorus) and described it as "a work to be preferred to all that the arts of painting and sculpture have produced." It shows the Trojan priest Laocoön and two of his sons at the moment they are strangled by sea serpents. Laocoön was killed after attempting to expose the Trojan Horse by striking it with a spear. Athena sent the serpents, which were interpreted by the Trojans as proof that the horse was sacred. The most famous account of this story is in Virgil's *Aeneid*. The work was probably sculpted between 42 and 20 BCE. Its rediscovery in the 1500s made a great impression on Italian sculptors and dramatically influenced sculpture during the Italian Renaissance. The original is now in the Vatican Museums in Rome.

134. (D) Hellenistic religious practices were quite diverse. Cults that had once held only local significance spread with the Greek language across the Mediterranean world. Worshippers in ruler cults tried to control chance by expressing gratitude or flattery to the rulers. For example, the Athenians created a cult to the Macedonian king Antigonus after he liberated the city. Other cults sought cures for physical ills from mythical healing divinities; Asclepius supposedly offered remedies to worshippers who visited his shrine. The mystery cult of the Egyptian god Isis achieved enormous popularity among Greeks and later Romans. However, Caracalla was a Roman emperor from 209 to 217 CE and not related to the Hellenistic Age.

135. (E) Aristarchus (310–230 BCE) was a Greek astronomer and mathematician who determined how to measure the distances to and sizes of the sun and moon. Because he deduced that the sun was so much bigger than the moon, he concluded that the earth must revolve around the sun. Therefore, he is famous for suggesting the first known heliocentric model of the solar system. He also put the other planets in their correct order of distance around the sun. However, his ideas were rejected in favor of the geocentric theories of Aristotle and Ptolemy.

136. (E) Epicurus (341–270 BCE) founded a school of philosophy built around philosophical materialism, the belief that all human knowledge is based on experience and perception. Epicureans believed that pleasure and pain were the sole measures of what is good and evil. They taught that death is the end of the body and the soul, and therefore it should not be feared. They broke with Greek tradition by teaching that humans have nothing to fear from the gods, because the gods do not reward or punish humans. Instead, the universe is infinite and eternal, and events in the world are ultimately based on the motions and interactions of atoms moving in empty space. For Epicureans, the purpose of philosophy was to attain a happy, tranquil life characterized by freedom from fear and the absence of pain. Peace of mind came from a self-sufficient life surrounded by friends apart from the common world rather than through active citizenship. Epicureans were also unusual in admitting women and slaves as regular members of their school.

137. (C) The armies and navies of the Hellenistic kingdoms were manned by professional soldiers. The Seleucid and Ptolemaic kings enthusiastically promoted immigration by Greeks and Macedonians, who received land grants in return for military service. When this source of loyal manpower ran out, the kings had to use local men as troops. Military expenses became a huge problem for the Hellenistic kingdoms, and this led to a rise in taxation.

138. (B) By the third century BCE, the successor kings had reached a balance of power. The Antigonids ruled Macedonia and mainland Greece, the Seleucids ruled Syria and Mesopotamia, and the Ptolemies retained control of Egypt. There were frequent struggles over border areas, which left room for the establishment of smaller, independent kingdoms. One example is the kingdom of the Attalids in western Anatolia, with the wealthy city of Pergamum as its capital. In Bactria (in present-day Afghanistan), the descendants of the Greek colonies settled by Alexander broke off from the Seleucid kingdom and founded their own regional kingdom.

139. (C) Aristotle's *Politics* as it exists today is probably a copy of his lecture notes. Many scholars believe it was meant to be combined with *Nicomachean Ethics* as part of a larger work dealing with the philosophy of human affairs. The Greek title of *Politics* means "the things concerning the polis." According to Aristotle, the polis is the highest form of political association. Only citizens of a polis can fully pursue a life of good quality, which is the end goal of human existence. *Politics* defends private property, condemns capitalism, justifies slavery, and regards women as inferior to men. Like Plato, Aristotle criticizes democracy because it places power in the hands of the uneducated masses. After reviewing and criticizing constitutions and constitutional theories, he categorized six different kinds of cities: three good and three bad. The three good kinds are constitutional government, aristocracy, and kingship; the three bad kinds are democracy, oligarchy, and tyranny.

140. (C) The battle of Chaeronea in 338 BCE was one of the most decisive of the ancient world, in which Philip II of Macedon completely destroyed the forces of Athens and Thebes that had united against him. The Greek city-states could no longer resist Macedonia, and Philip was free to impose a settlement on Greece. He formed the League of Corinth, which made the Greek city-states allies of Macedonia and each other, with Philip as the guarantor of the peace. Although it ended Greek independence for decades, the battle of Chaeronea laid the groundwork for Alexander the Great's attack on Persia and his support for Hellenic culture in his conquests.

141. (D) Philip II of Macedon (382–336 BCE) was king of Macedonia from 359 BCE until his assassination. He was the father of Alexander the Great and Philip III. He initially promoted peace with his neighbors, using the time to build his forces and introduce military innovations. Philip effectively used lines of soldiers armed with long spears, combined with a cavalry strike force, to crush the neighboring Illyrians and defeat his local rivals for the kingship. Then he launched an ambitious campaign of diplomacy, bribery, and military action to achieve his goal of leading a united Macedonian/Greek army against the hated Persians. By 340 BCE, he had convinced most of northern Greece to follow his lead on foreign policy. However, his ambitions provoked Athens and Thebes into forming a coalition against him. He defeated them at the battle of Chaeronea (338 BCE) and became leader of all Greece. He formed the Greek states into the League of Corinth to attack Persia but was assassinated by a Macedonian nobleman for reasons that are still disputed.

142. (D) Diogenes (c. 412–323 BCE) is considered one of the founders of Cynicism. None of his writings have survived, even though he is reported to have written more than 10 books. However, there are many anecdotes concerning his life and sayings attributed to him. Diogenes used his behavior to critique the social values and institutions of what he saw as a corrupt society. He declared himself a "citizen of the world" and made a virtue of poverty. He begged for a living and slept in a tub in the marketplace. He became notorious for his philosophical stunts, such as carrying a lamp in the daytime, claiming to be looking for an honest man. He publicly mocked Alexander the Great and lived to tell about it. He also embarrassed Plato by disputing his interpretation of Socrates and sabotaging his lectures.

143. (A) Pergamum was an ancient Greek city in modern-day Turkey that became the capital of the kingdom of Pergamum under the Attalid Dynasty (281–133 BCE). Bactra, also called Bactra-Zariaspa (present-day Balkh, Afghanistan), was Bactria's capital. Antioch (on the Orontes River) was an ancient city near the modern city of Antakya, Turkey. It was founded near the end of the fourth century BCE by Seleucus I and eventually rivaled Alexandria as the chief city in the area. It may once have had a population of half a million people, but it declined to insignificance during the Middle Ages. Cyrene was an ancient Greek city in the Ptolemaic kingdom, located in present-day Libya. Tyre was an ancient city conquered by Alexander the Great after a famous siege in 332 BCE; it was part of the Seleucid kingdom.

144. (D) Macedonian is a south Slavic language related to Bulgarian and Serbo-Croatian; it was not the language of Hellenism. The spread of the Greek language in a form called Koine ("shared" or "common") reflected an international culture based on Greek models. Local languages did not disappear, but Greek became the common language of politics, culture, and trade.

145. (E) Praxiteles of Athens was one of the most famous sculptors of the fourth century BCE. Ctesibius (fl. 285–222 BCE) created the scientific field of pneumatics by inventing machines operated by air pressure. He also built a working water pump and the first accurate water clock. Erasistratus (304–250 BCE) founded a school of anatomy in Alexandria where anatomical research was carried out. He distinguished between veins and arteries, described the valves of the heart, and concluded that the heart functioned as a pump. Praxagoras, of the Greek island of Cos (b. c. 340 BCE), discovered the value of measuring the pulse in diagnosing illness. Herophilos of Chalcedon (335–280 BCE), working in Alexandria, was the first scientist to systematically perform scientific dissections of human cadavers and is therefore considered the first anatomist.

Chapter 5: The Roman Republic and Empire

146. (A) Christianity only became the official state religion of Rome when Theodosius proclaimed it so in 391 CE. The missionary journeys of Paul throughout the Mediterranean basin helped spread the new religion, as did the ease of travel on Roman roads and the Silk Road.

147. (C) Philip V, king of Macedon (the Antigonid kingdom), sided with Hannibal against the growing Roman power in the Second Punic War in 215 BCE. Their defeat in 201 BCE allowed Rome to dominate Macedonia and Greece. The Seleucid and Ptolemaic kingdoms remained independent until the first century BCE; the Seleucid kingdom fell to Rome in 64 BCE. The Ptolemaic kingdom followed in 30 BCE, when the Egyptian queen Cleopatra chose the losing side in the Roman civil war between Marc Anthony and the future emperor Augustus. Thus, Rome became the heir of all the Hellenistic kingdoms.

148. (A) The battle of the Teutoburg Forest took place in 9 CE, when an alliance of Germanic tribes led by Arminius (also known as Hermann) ambushed and destroyed three Roman legions led by Publius Quinctilius Varus. This was a major Roman setback that, in hindsight, represented the high-water mark of the empire in the north. In general, after Teutoburg Forest, the Romans gave up trying to occupy the land east of the Rhine. The lack of obvious strongholds and a passable road network, the rugged countryside, the difficulties in living off the land, and the warlike nature of the Germans all contributed to Rome's decision to leave Germany alone. As a result, north-central and northeastern Europe remained free of Latin law and culture for several hundred more years, which allowed the Germanic languages to survive. According to Suetonius, on hearing the news of the Teutoburg defeat, Augustus tore his clothes, refused to cut his hair for months, and for years afterward was heard to moan, "Quinctilius Varus, give me back my legions!"

149. (B) The First Triumvirate was the political alliance of Julius Caesar, Crassus (the wealthiest man in Rome), and Pompey. It formed in 60 BCE and lasted until Crassus's death in 53 BCE. The name of First Triumvirate is misleading; it was never called this by contemporary Romans, and it had no official status. It was actually a secret agreement, although many leading families were involved. The alliance between Pompey and Caesar was cemented by the marriage of Caesar's daughter, Julia, to Pompey. In 59 BCE, Caesar was elected consul and began to build a client army in Gaul. The alliance ended following the deaths of Crassus in battle (at Carrhae) and Julia in childbirth; after that, Caesar and Pompey drifted toward civil war.

150. (B) The Visigoths were a Germanic people who originally lived near the Balkans. In the fourth century CE, they fled from the Huns and asked Valens, the eastern emperor, for asylum in exchange for military service. Although Valens agreed, a famine broke out, and the empire would not supply them with the promised food or land. The Visigoths rebelled, and at the battle of Adrianople in 378 CE, they destroyed the Roman army; Valens was killed during the fighting. The results forced the Romans to negotiate with the Visigoths and settle them within the empire. Valens's successor, Theodosius, granted them permission to establish an independent kingdom. The Visigoths eventually moved west into Gaul and had a tense relationship with the western empire between 395 and 410. Alaric, the Visigoth leader, declared war on Rome after the western general Stilicho was executed by Honorius in 408, and the Roman legions massacred the families of thousands of German soldiers serving in the Roman army. In 410, Alaric's troops entered Rome and sacked the city. While Rome was no longer the official capital of the western empire (the capital had been moved to Ravenna in 404 for strategic reasons), its fall shocked the Roman world.

151. (A) Hypatia (c. 370–415 CE) was a Greek scholar from Alexandria; she is considered the first notable woman mathematician. Her father was the last librarian of the library at Alexandria, and she was educated in Athens and Italy. It appears she also studied and taught Neoplatonist philosophy and astronomy in Alexandria around 400 CE. Little is known of her writings; many works attributed to Hypatia may have been collaborative works with her father. Her contributions to science are reputed to include the charting of planets and the invention of the hydrometer (to determine the relative density and gravity of liquids). The Christians of Alexandria believed Hypatia was the cause of strained relations between the imperial Roman prefect and the patriarch Cyril. A group of Christian monks wanted the politician and the priest to reconcile, so they assassinated her. According to one version, the monks "took her to the church called Caesareum, where they completely stripped her and then murdered her by scraping her skin off with tiles and bits of shell. After tearing her body in pieces, they took her mangled limbs to a place called Cinaron and there burnt them."

152. (A) Little direct evidence exists about the founding of Rome, but citizens of the republic believed the year 753 BCE was the mythical date. Romans at first believed that their city was founded by Aeneas, a refugee from the Trojan War. However, this legend was supplanted over the centuries by the attribution of the founding to twin brothers, Romulus and Remus (who, in some versions, become ancestors of Aeneas). According to the later legend, Romulus and Remus nearly died in infancy when Aeneas abandoned them by the Tiber River. A she-wolf discovered them and restored them to health. In 753 BCE, Romulus founded Rome and became its first king. Virgil's *Aeneid* is the usual source for information about these myths. In modern times, scholars have continued to debate the date of Rome's founding.

153. (E) Augustus (63 BCE–14 CE) is considered the first emperor of the Roman Empire, which he ruled for 41 years from 27 BCE until his death. In 27 BCE, he created the principate, a new political system. Augustus did not want to abandon the idea of the republic completely, so he constructed a government in which the old institutions and offices remained intact but he held ultimate power. His rule through widespread patronage, military power and coercion, and the accumulation of the offices of the defunct republic was the model for most later imperial governments. Augustus's reign marked a period of relative peace that lasted for two centuries in the Mediterranean world; it was known as the Pax Romana (Roman Peace). Augustus dramatically enlarged the empire. He annexed Egypt and Dalmatia, expanded Roman possessions in Africa, and completed the conquest of Spain. However, he was emperor when the Germans crushed the Roman legions at Teutoburg Forest. Augustus reformed the Roman system of taxation, developed networks of roads, and established a standing army and the Praetorian Guard. Much of Rome was rebuilt under his rule, and he was a patron of Virgil, Ovid, Livy, and Horace. When he died in 14 CE, the Senate declared Augustus a god.

154. (C) Ovid (43 BCE–18 CE) was a Roman poet who is well known for *The Metamorphoses* as well as three collections of erotic poetry. He is usually ranked with Virgil and Horace as one of the three greatest poets of Latin literature. His poetry was extremely influential in Europe during the Middle Ages (more than 400 manuscripts survive). *The Metamorphoses*, completed in 8 CE, remains an important source of classical mythology. The recurring theme of the book, as with nearly all of Ovid's work, is the nature and power of love, personified in the figure of Cupid. The other Roman gods, especially Apollo, are repeatedly confused, humiliated, and made ridiculous by Cupid. In a sense, *The Metamorphoses* inverted the accepted order by elevating humans while making the gods and their desires the objects of low humor.

155. (C) In ancient Roman society, people regarded homosexual interest and practice as an ordinary part of the range of human experience. Nearly every famous Roman poet wrote love poems to boys. However, male love did not have the same high cultural import for Romans as it did for the Greeks. It was not usually the subject of deep, inspiring personal devotion, although 14 of the first 15 emperors took male lovers, and the emperor Hadrian (reigned 117–138 CE) is famous for his relationship with Antinous. In some forms, homosexuality was criticized. Romans perceived homosexual relations mainly as a form of dominance and linked sexual passivity with the political impotence of boys, slaves, and women. Roman men viewed women as people who were there to serve them in sexual intercourse. Real sex meant penetration, and women cannot do that naturally with each other. When a man penetrated another man in anal intercourse, he used that man in the function of a woman and blurred the line between masculinity and femininity. Romans divided people into those who did sex (adult male citizens) and those to whom sex was done (women, boys, and slaves). This is one of the reasons the male writers of books and legal codes were less concerned with lesbianism; it did not seem as threatening to their gender stereotypes and the power structure. In fact, references to love between women in Roman literature are rare. As Christianity became more powerful in the Roman Empire, homosexuality came under greater attack and harsher legislation.

156. (E) The Etruscans, who may have migrated from Anatolia, moved to the Italian peninsula about 800 BCE. They remained influential for the next three centuries, especially northwest of the Tiber River (present-day Tuscany and part of Umbria). They were famed artisans and traders who were knowledgeable about ironwork. They were ruled by kings who controlled organized armies that used horses and war chariots (which the Etruscans introduced in Italy). Etruscan gold work was among the finest in the ancient world, and they were also famous for their glossy black pottery. Many Roman religious beliefs and architectural forms (such as the arch) were probably borrowed from Etruscan culture. The Romans also used a modified version of the Etruscan alphabet, which the Etruscans had learned from the Greeks. The last Etruscan king was expelled and the Roman Republic established in 509 BCE.

157. (B) Although slaves occupied the lowest place in the Roman social hierarchy, they provided the basis of the imperial workforce. Unlike Greece, Rome gave citizenship to freed slaves. This arrangement gave slaves a reason to persevere and cooperate with their masters and reduced the incentive to revolt. Conditions of Roman slavery varied widely according to occupation. In general, slaves in agriculture and manufacturing had a grueling existence and were often worked to death; household slaves (which included many women) had it somewhat easier.

158. (A) The highest officials in the Roman Republic were called consuls. Two consuls were elected each year in a symbolic show of the principle of sharing power. The consul's most important duty was to command in battle. Winning a consulship was the highest political honor a Roman man could achieve. To gain this position, a man traditionally had to work his way up a "ladder" of offices. After 10 years of military service from about age 20 to 30, a man would begin by seeking election as a quaestor, a financial administrator. He would then move up to a position as one of the aediles who cared for the city's streets, sewers, markets, aqueducts, and temples. Each move to a higher rung on the ladder was more competitive, and few men reached the level of the office of praetor. The board of praetors performed judicial and military duties.

159. (E) The Gracchi brothers, Tiberius and Gaius, were Roman tribunes in the second century BCE. Although they were from the upper class, they supported land reform legislation that would redistribute to the plebeians the latifundia (large estates) acquired in Rome's many wars in Italy, Sicily, Egypt, North Africa, and Spain. People captured during these wars were often enslaved and forced to work on the latifundia raising export crops such as grain, olives, or grapes. Small landowners, unable to compete with the large estates, sold their lands. In 133 BCE, Tiberius Gracchus attempted to limit the size of the latifundia and move landless citizens to work on redistributed land. This offended the Senate, so they had Tiberius and 300 of his followers clubbed to death. In 123 BCE, Gaius used public funds to purchase grain to resell to the poor at low prices. The Senate assassinated his supporters, and Gaius committed suicide before he could be killed. The violent deaths of the Gracchi and their followers introduced factions into Roman politics for the next century. Members of the elite positioned themselves either as supporters of the people (*populares*) or "the best" (*optimates*). *Insulae* were Roman apartment houses or tenements, usually cheaply constructed, and sometimes as high as seven stories. (For *curiales*, see the answer to question 182.)

160. (C) The eastern and western sections of the Roman Empire had their own capital cities. Byzantium had been reconstructed and eponymously renamed by Constantine in 324 CE as his "new Rome." In the west, Honorius (reigned 395–423) wanted to keep the Alps between his territory and the marauding Germanic bands to the north. However, he also wanted the capital in a more defensible location than Rome. In 404, he moved the capital to Ravenna, a port on Italy's northeastern coast. Ravenna was an excellent choice; city walls and marshes protected it from attack by land, while access to the sea (and to the eastern empire) kept it from being starved out in a siege. Honorius's decision turned out to be wise because Rome was sacked by the Visigoths only six years later. But Ravenna never rivaled Constantinople in size or splendor. It does, however, have a unique collection of early Christian mosaics and monuments; eight fifth- and sixth-century buildings there are listed as UNESCO World Heritage sites.

161. (D) The Edict of Milan was a letter issued in 313 CE and signed by emperors Constantine I and Licinius. The letter proclaimed religious tolerance in the Roman Empire and ordered the return of property confiscated from Christians in Diocletian's Great Persecution of 303. The edict did not outlaw polytheism or make Christianity the official state religion. Instead, it proclaimed free choice of religion for everyone. It carefully referred to the empire's protection by "the highest divinity"—an ambiguous term intended to please both polytheists and Christians. Constantine, although a converted Christian, wanted to avoid angering traditional believers, because they still greatly outnumbered Christians. However, he also tried to promote his newly chosen religion. In 321, he made the Lord's Day a holy occasion each week on which no official business or manufacturing work could be performed, but he called it Sunday to blend Christian and traditional notions by honoring two divinities.

162. (E) Christianity only slowly became the majority religion in the Roman Empire. Although it benefited from the patronage of Christian emperors in the fourth century, it offered other advantages as well. In its earliest history, Christianity was more popular with the poor and underprivileged; its appeal included a strong sense of community in this world and the promise of salvation in the next. There is no indication that Roman soldiers were particularly enthusiastic about Christianity. The New Testament does mention several occasions when Roman soldiers were convinced by Jesus. However, the number of Christian soldiers in the Roman army was relatively small; Christian soldiers had sometimes created disciplinary problems by renouncing their military oath. In addition, the army placed a strong emphasis on pagan ritual (such as Mithraism), which devout Christians abhorred. Finally, Christians would have been reluctant to join an organization sometimes used to persecute their coreligionists. However, once Christianity gained official status in the fourth century, it attracted new believers in the military. Soldiers finally found it comfortable to convert and serve in the army, justifying military duty as serving Christ.

163. (D) In the earliest periods of Roman history, a married woman would be subjugated to the legal control of her husband (*cum manu*). The custom basically died out by the first century BCE in favor of free marriage (*sine manu*), which did not grant a husband any rights over his wife. Instead, it relied on the tradition of *patria potestas* (power of the father), which gave a father legal power over his children. In a free marriage, the wife remained under *patria potestas* until her father died. In the ancient world, few fathers lived long enough to supervise the lives of their married children; four out of five parents died before their offspring reached the age of 30. In a free marriage, a woman became independent on her father's death, retaining her family rights of inheritance (although she did not gain any with her new family). Free marriage was not a traditional form of marriage, and because property was not involved, the husband could annul it simply by telling his wife that the marriage was at an end. However, free marriage was popular in noble households, so it was unlikely that one side would so openly insult the other.

164. (B) Cicero (106–43 BCE) was a Roman philosopher, politician, and writer; he is usually considered the greatest of Roman orators and Latin prose stylists. He was famous for his witty letter-writing style. Cicero tried to adapt the ideas of Greek philosophy to Roman life by creating a doctrine known as *humanitas*. Its principles based the value of human life on generous and honest treatment of other people and an almost Stoic commitment to morality. Cicero's speeches and letters are important sources for descriptions of the last days of the Roman Republic. Unfortunately for Cicero, he made an enemy of Marc Anthony by attacking him in a series of speeches. Cicero was proscribed as an enemy of the state by the Second Triumvirate and murdered in 43 BCE. Medieval philosophers loved Cicero's writings on natural law, and Petrarch's rediscovery of Cicero's letters helped spark the so-called European Renaissance.

165. (E) Arianism was a heterodox Christian religious belief founded by Arius (c. 250–336 CE), a priest from Alexandria. The doctrine arose over questions regarding the precise nature of the Trinity. Arius maintained that Jesus, as God's son, did not exist eternally. Instead, he believed that God had created his son from nothing and given him special powers. This view implied that Jesus was not identical in nature to God and that Christian monotheism was not absolute. The Council of Nicaea (present-day Iznik, Turkey) was convened by the Roman emperor Constantine in 325 CE to deal with the issue. The council made the first effort to create a consensus in the Christian church through an assembly of bishops. It settled the Christological issue by condemning Arius and his doctrine. However, Arianism had many followers during the fourth and fifth centuries, especially among the Germanic tribes who had trouble understanding the concept of God's son being identical in nature to God.

166. (E) Nero (37–68 CE) was the last Roman emperor of the Julio-Claudian Dynasty. His reign from 54 to 68 CE is notoriously controversial because of the unreliability and prejudice of most ancient sources against his actions. He had a passion for music and acting, and he built theaters and promoted athletic games. The spectacular public festivals he sponsored and the money he distributed to the masses in Rome kept him popular with the poor. His generals defeated the Parthian Empire and crushed a revolt in Britain. In 64 CE, most of Rome was destroyed in a great fire; many Romans believed Nero himself had started it to clear land for his planned palatial complex. After the fire, Nero sponsored a public relief effort as well as significant reconstruction that helped drain the treasury. As a result, he devalued the Roman currency for the first time in the empire's history. Nero's rule is often associated with many executions, including those of his mother and wife and the probable poisoning of his stepbrother, Britannicus. He was also an early persecutor of Christians. In 68 CE, a series of revolts drove Nero from the throne, and he committed suicide. His death ended the Julio-Claudian line, and chaos followed in the so-called Year of the Four Emperors.

167. (C) Almost no one had a stronger impact on western Christian orthodoxy than Augustine (354–430 CE); for a thousand years, his writings were the most influential texts except for the Bible. He was particularly concerned with the question of how to understand and regulate sexual desire. Augustine promoted the influential doctrine that sex automatically trapped human beings in evil, and they should therefore strive for asceticism or even celibacy. This was perhaps not surprising for a religion whose founder was supposed to have no biological father, who was believed to have no siblings, and who never married. Augustine advocated sexual abstinence as the highest course for Christians, because he believed Adam and Eve's disobedience in the Garden of Eden had forever ruined the original perfect harmony God created between the human will and human passions. Augustine reluctantly supported the value of marriage in God's plan, but he noted that even sexual intercourse between loving spouses carried the taint of humanity's fall from grace. For him, sexual pleasure could never be a human good. By the end of the fourth century, the importance of sexual renunciation and virginity as a Christian virtue had grown so strong that congregations began to call for virgin priests and bishops.

168. (B) The fall of the Roman Empire remains one of the greatest historical questions; there are more than 200 theories on why Rome declined and fell (or even if it fell), and new theories are proposed all the time. However, many modern scholars emphasize that most political institutions are not assassinated and do not collapse. They believe the words *transformation* and *evolution* are more accurate to express the complex changes in the Roman Empire. Having said that, the decline of Rome has been attributed to all the answer choices given except an increase in population. Most historians believe the empire's population gradually decreased, especially in the western provinces. In addition, the Roman Empire suffered from the so-called Antonine Plague (also known as the Plague of Galen) that began about 165 CE. For the next 20 years, recurring waves of diseases, possibly the first epidemics of smallpox or measles, swept through the empire. According to one estimate, the plague killed five million people—as much as one-third of the population in some areas—and decimated the Roman army. Similar epidemics, such as the Plague of Cyprian, also occurred in the third century.

169. (D) Emperor Diocletian (244–311 CE) rescued the Roman Empire from its third-century crisis by replacing the principate with a more openly authoritative system of rule called the *dominate*. Diocletian was an uneducated soldier who rose through the ranks to become emperor in 284 after the battle of the Margus. As a soldier and an emperor, he was courageous and intelligent, and he showed a talent for leadership. Because he relied on the large army for support, he had to raise taxes to support it. Diocletian's government tried to control the people liable for taxes by imposing oppressive restrictions. The government made many occupations compulsory and hereditary, thereby eliminating the possibility of social mobility. Coloni (tenant farmers), who had traditionally been free to move from farm to farm, were increasingly tied to a particular plot of land, and their wives and children were also restricted. The system was a precursor of medieval feudalism.

170. (A) The Anglo-Saxons were composed of Angles from present-day Denmark and Saxons from northwestern Germany. This mixed group invaded Britain in the 440s after the Roman army had been recalled from the province to defend Italy against the Visigoths. The Anglo-Saxons established their kingdoms by taking territory away from the indigenous

Celtic peoples and the remaining Roman inhabitants. However, they never conquered Scotland, Wales, or Cornwall. The historian Bede, who lived in the eighth century, wrote that the Angles settled in East Anglia, the East Midlands, and Northumbria, while the Saxons moved into Sussex, Essex, Middlesex, and Wessex. The third mysterious group, the Jutes, settled mainly in Kent, Hampshire, and the Isle of Wight.

171. (C) The family formed the bedrock of Roman society, because it taught values and determined the ownership of property. The tradition of *patria potestas* ("power of the father") gave a father ownership of all property accumulated by his children or slaves as long as he lived. Fathers also technically held the legal power of life and death over their children and their household. However, the power of fathers did not give husbands legal power over their wives; the wife remained under her father's *patria potestas* until he died.

172. (E) Marcus Aurelius (121–180 CE) was emperor from 161 to 180; he was the last of the so-called Five Good Emperors. He is also considered an important Stoic philosopher. During his reign, he defeated the Parthian Empire but had to defend the Roman Empire from Germans and Briton invaders from the north. He wrote *The Meditations* in Greek while on campaign between 170 and 180. This book is still read as a paean to service and duty. It describes how to achieve self-control in the midst of conflict by following nature as a source of guidance and inspiration. Marcus Aurelius was concerned with improving the living conditions of the poor and tried to decrease the brutality of the gladiatorial shows. He also persecuted Christians as natural enemies of the Roman Empire. Marcus's choice of his only surviving son (Commodus) as his successor turned out to be a disaster. (It was the emperor Diocletian who made the *curiales* spend their own money to pay for the shortfall in tax collection.)

173. (E) The battles of Lake Trasimeno (217 BCE) and Cannae (216 BCE) were brilliant victories by Hannibal over the Romans in the Second Punic War. Cannae is sometimes considered the greatest tactical victory in military history. The Carthaginian defeat at the Metaurus River in 207 BCE ended the attempt by Hasdrubal (Hannibal's brother) to reinforce Hannibal in Italy. The Roman victory at Zama (202 BCE) brought an end to the Second Punic War and made Rome the dominant power in the western Mediterranean. Actium, on the other hand, was the battle that ended the Roman Republic in 31 BCE.

174. (D) For three or four centuries after Jesus's death, the overwhelming majority of the population of the Roman Empire still practiced polytheism. Its deities ranged from those of the state's cults (such as Jupiter and Minerva) to spirits believed to inhabit local groves and springs. Famous old cults, such as those that practiced the initiation rituals of Demeter and Persephone at Eleusis outside Athens, remained popular. Hundreds of shrines to the mysterious god Mithras have been found, but the cult is poorly understood because almost no texts survive to explain it. In some way, the slaying of a bull was a central part of the cult's identity; only men could be worshippers and many seem to have been soldiers. Many upper-class Romans guided their lives by the ancient Greek philosophy of Stoicism. It was based on self-discipline; its most famous Roman adherents were the playwright Seneca (4 BCE–65 CE) and the emperor Marcus Aurelius. The Hellenized cult of the Egyptian goddess Isis was also popular; Isis was portrayed as a compassionate goddess who cared for the suffering of each of her followers. Her image was that of a loving mother, and a central doctrine of her cult concerned the death and resurrection of her husband, Osiris. Waldensianism was a medieval Christian social movement and heresy.

175. (B) The Roman currency throughout most of the Roman Republic and the western half of the Roman Empire consisted of coins. These included the aureus (gold), the denarius (silver), the sestertius (bronze), the dupondius (bronze), and the as (copper). These coins were generally used from the middle of the third century BCE until the middle of the third century CE. The silver denarius became the backbone of the Roman economy almost as soon as it was introduced in 211 BCE. It was valuable because it contained silver; the less silver in a coin, the less the coin was worth. When taxes and other revenues could not cover government or military expenses, Roman emperors debased the coinage by reducing the amount of silver and increasing the amount of cheaper metals. Nero was the first Roman emperor to devalue the coinage. Roman coins were 94 percent silver in 27 BCE, 89 percent in 100 CE, 64 percent in 200 CE, and 4 percent in 300 CE.

176. (A) Spartacus (c. 109–71 BCE) was the famous leader of a major slave uprising against the Roman Republic. In 73 BCE, he broke out of a gladiatorial school at Capua and fled to Mount Vesuvius, where he was joined by thousands of fugitive slaves. Spartacus was an accomplished military leader, and his slave army defeated several Roman forces. He may have wanted to escape from Italy, but many of his followers preferred plundering the south. He was finally killed in battle by Crassus's forces in Lucania; Pompey helped annihilate the survivors. Of the captured slaves, 6,000 were crucified along the Capua-Rome highway. In modern times, Spartacus's struggle has often been portrayed as the story of oppressed people fighting for their freedom against a slave-owning aristocracy.

177. (B) Constantine the Great (272–337 CE) was Roman emperor from 306 to 337. He was the best general of his time, defeating his rival for power, Maxentius, at the battle of Milvian Bridge (near Rome) in 312. He also fought successfully against the Franks, Alamanni, and Visigoths during his reign. By 336, Constantine had reoccupied most of Dacia, which the emperor Aurelian had abandoned in 271. Constantine transformed the ancient Greek city of Byzantium into a new imperial residence named after himself; Constantinople would be the capital of the eastern Roman Empire for more than a thousand years. He was the first Roman emperor to convert to Christianity (he was baptized on his deathbed) and also issued the Edict of Milan in 313, which proclaimed tolerance of all religions throughout the empire. During his reign, he convened the Council of Nicaea (325) to deal with the Christological issues raised by Arianism. (It was Diocletian who subdivided the Roman Empire into the tetrarchy.)

178. (A) The Essenes were a Jewish sect that flourished from the second century BCE to the first century CE. They were much smaller in number than the Pharisees and the Sadducees. The Essenes gathered together in communal settings to practice asceticism and voluntary poverty. They seem to have been obsessed with ceremonial purity, including scrupulous cleanliness, the wearing of only white clothing, and extremely strict observance of the Sabbath. Josephus recorded that thousands of Essenes lived in Roman Judea. They are commonly believed, although without direct evidence, to have written the religious documents known as the Dead Sea Scrolls. The Essenes' beliefs may have influenced the development of early Christianity. The sect ceased to exist after Bar Kohba's failed rebellion in 132–135 CE.

179. **(C)** In the Roman Republic, the passage of laws, government policies, elections, and certain trials took place in a complicated system of differing assemblies. An assembly was an outdoor meeting of adult male citizens; they were only for voting, not discussion. Every assembly concerning laws and policies was preceded by a public gathering when speeches were made about the issues. Everyone, including women and noncitizens, could listen to those speeches. Each assembly was divided into different groups whose size was determined by status and wealth. Voting took place by group, with each group—rather than each individual—having a vote.

180. **(D)** Christians had always been subject to local discrimination in the Roman Empire, but early emperors did not issue general laws against them. It was not until the 250s CE, under the reigns of Decius and Valerian, that laws were passed compelling Christians to sacrifice to Roman gods or face imprisonment and execution. Diocletian was a religious conservative who attributed the empire's problems to the hostility of Christians to Rome's traditional religion. As a result, he launched a massive attack on Christianity in 303 that is sometimes called the Great Persecution. He expelled Christians from the government, seized their property, tore down their churches, and executed them for refusing to participate in religious rituals. In the western empire, the violence stopped after about a year; in the east, it continued for a decade. According to one estimate, about 3,500 Christians were executed, and many more were tortured or imprisoned. However, most managed to avoid punishment. The public executions of Christian martyrs were so gruesome that they aroused the sympathy of some polytheists. The Great Persecution failed to stop the spread of Christianity or placate the anger of the old Roman gods. Constantine, in the Edict of Milan, restored Christians to full legal equality and returned property that had been confiscated during the persecution.

181. **(D)** In the Roman Republic, the shrine of the goddess Vesta (known as Hestia by the Greeks) housed the official eternal flame of Rome. Vesta was the goddess of the hearth and a protector of the family; in a larger sense, the flame guaranteed the state's permanent existence. The shrine was tended by the Vestals (or Vestal Virgins), six unmarried women sworn to chastity before puberty for a term of 30 years. As Rome's only female priesthood, the Vestals were exempt from the usual social obligations to marry and bear children; they were not subject to the *patria potestas* and were free to own property or make wills. They were supposed to devote themselves to the study and correct observance of state rituals that were off-limits to the male priests. Their most important duty was to make sure the eternal flame did not go out. If it did, the Romans assumed that one of the women had broken her vow of chastity; the punishment was to be buried alive. Over many centuries, there were only 10 recorded convictions for breaking the vows of chastity. The Vestals were a powerful force in Rome. When Sulla proscribed the young Julius Caesar, the Vestals interceded on Caesar's behalf and gained him a pardon. The Vestals were disbanded and the sacred fire extinguished in 394 CE by order of the Christian emperor Theodosius.

182. **(B)** In the late Roman Empire, the word *curiales* referred to the merchants, business owners, and medium-sized landowners who served in their local curia as magistrates and decurions. The unsalaried *curiales* were expected to collect the funds necessary for public building projects, temples, festivities, and local welfare systems. They were also responsible for providing food and board for the army and for maintaining the water supply. They were supposed to pay for any shortfalls out of their own pocket. As the economy of the empire worsened in the third and fourth centuries CE, membership among the curial class became financially ruinous to all but the wealthiest people. For centuries, the Roman Empire had counted on a regular supply of public-spirited members of the elite who would happily fill these crucial local posts to win the admiration of their neighbors. In the late days of the empire, this tradition broke down as wealthier people avoided public service to escape bankruptcy, many by taking positions that canceled curial responsibilities, such as in the army, the imperial government, or the church. At one point, compulsory service on a municipal council became a punishment for a minor crime. Efforts to remedy the situation failed, and the councils dwindled in importance through the late Roman Empire.

183. (A) Proscription was a procedure created by Sulla in the first century BCE. A list would be posted of people who were supposedly guilty of treason against Rome. Anyone could then legally hunt down and execute these proscribed people, and their property was confiscated by the state. This procedure led men on the winning side of the civil war to fraudulently add the names of anyone whose wealth they desired to the list. The Second Triumvirate was the official political alliance of Octavius, Lepidus, and Marc Anthony. It was an official, legal arrangement that was actually written into the constitution by the Lex Titia in 43 BCE. This new government was a joint dictatorship, in which the three members were essentially permitted to completely ignore republican and senatorial tradition. The Second Triumvirate revived proscription as a way to get money as well as eliminate political opposition. About 130 to 300 senators and possibly as many as 2,000 equites were proscribed. (Equites were prosperous hereditary landowners, second in wealth and status only to patricians.) Lepidus's own brother was proscribed, as was Anthony's cousin and one of Octavian's distant relatives through adoption. The most notable victim of the proscriptions was Cicero, who was executed for antagonizing Marc Anthony.

184. (E) The movement of the Germanic tribes into the Roman Empire was the factor that caused the actual fall of the empire. Alaric I, king of the Visigoths, sacked Rome in 410 CE. In 476 CE, Romulus Augustus, the last emperor of the western Roman Empire, was deposed by Odoacer. This event is traditionally regarded as the end of the Roman Empire and the beginning of the European Middle Ages. The other answer choices are underlying causes, not immediate causes, of the empire's decline.

185. (E) A postal service is an arrangement to send letters, packages, and magazines from one place to another. Hieroglyphics make reference to a postal service in Egypt about 2000 BCE. A postal system using mounted relay messengers was organized in China in about 1000 BCE and in the Persian Empire in about 500 BCE. Riders on horses would stop at regularly placed post houses either to get a fresh horse or to give their mail to another messenger for the rest of the trip. The same kind of relay system existed in the Roman Empire. The postal service made it possible for the government in Rome to communicate with officials and generals in distant provinces.

186. (A) Julius Caesar (100–44 BCE) was a Roman general who played the crucial role in the transformation of the Roman Republic into the Roman Empire. Caesar was a brilliant general; his victory over Gallic forces under Vercingetorix in the battle of Alesia (52 BCE) established Roman dominance in Gaul for the next 500 years. Caesar was adored by his soldiers, and his victories created a rivalry with the Roman government. In 60 BCE, he entered into a secret agreement with Crassus and Pompey known as the First Triumvirate, which dominated Roman politics until 53 BCE. They were opposed in the Senate by a conservative elite that included Cato the Younger and Cicero. The Senate ordered Caesar to stand trial in Rome, but instead he marched from Gaul to Italy and crossed the Rubicon in 49 BCE; his soldiers followed him without hesitation. This sparked a civil war. Caesar and his outnumbered army gained a stunning victory over Pompey at the battle of Pharsalus in 48 BCE. After assuming control of the government, Caesar was proclaimed dictator for life. His office and honors pleased many Romans but outraged a narrow circle of *optimates* who resented their exclusion from power. A group of senators, led by Brutus, assassinated him on the Ides of March (March 15), 44 BCE, in the hope of restoring the republic. Instead, the result was a series of civil wars that ultimately led to Augustus's establishment of the permanent Roman Empire.

187. (A) Hero of Alexandria (c. 10–70 CE) was a Greek mathematician and engineer, often considered the greatest experimenter of antiquity. He published a description of a steam-powered device called an *aeolipile*. He also invented a windwheel, one of the earliest examples of harnessing wind on land. Ptolemy (90–168 CE) was a famous Roman scientist living in Egypt. His works on astronomy and geography were standard textbooks in the field until the time of Copernicus in the 16th century. The so-called Ptolemaic system placed the motionless earth at the center of the universe, with all other heavenly bodies revolving around it. Galen (c. 130–c. 200 CE) was a physician who discovered that arteries carry blood instead of air. Based on his own experimentation, he added to the medical field's knowledge about the brain, nerves, spinal cord, and pulse. Until the 16th century, his authority was virtually undisputed. Pliny the Elder (23–79 CE) wrote the encyclopedic *Naturalis Historia*, an extensive compilation of facts about the natural world that became a model for all future works on that subject. Gerard of Cremona (c. 1114–1187 CE) was a medieval translator of Arabic scientific works in Toledo, Spain.

188. (C) Plautus (254–184 BCE) was a Roman playwright specializing in comedies. His plays, adapted from the Greek New Comedy, were popular representations of middle- and lower-class life. He wrote in colloquial Latin and was famous for his coarse humor. Plautus's plays used many characters who would become standard comic figures: the braggart soldier, the resourceful slave, the young lover and his mistress, and the courtesan. About 20 of his plays survive, and their plots and characters have had an enormous influence on the history of comedic traditions. Terence (c. 195–159 BCE) was the other great Latin comedian during the Roman Republic. He was a slave who received his freedom because of his wit and manners. Six of his plays survive; all seem to be adapted to a greater or lesser degree from Greek plays by Menander and his school. Terence was more refined than Plautus, but Plautus was usually funnier.

189. (C) The baths were part of day-to-day life in ancient Rome. *Thermae* were large bath complexes such as those built by the emperors Caracalla and Diocletian. *Balneae* were smaller facilities, either public or private, that could be found everywhere in the empire. Ancient Rome had as many as 900 public baths; small baths held about 300 people, while the largest might hold 1,500. Because admission fees were low, almost everyone could afford to go daily. Roman baths were similar to modern health clubs in that they were centers for exercising and socializing as well as washing. A visitor could spend some time in a cold bath (the *frigidarium*), then a warm bath (the *tepidarium*), and finally a hot bath (the *caldarium*). A large complex would also contain an exercise area (the *palaestra*) and a swimming pool. The building of a bath complex required complex heating systems to carry the water around the establishment. Bathers usually swam naked, and women had full access to the baths, but men and women usually bathed separately. Since bathing was thought to be particularly valuable for sick people, communal baths contributed to the spread of communicable diseases. Baths fell out of style with the growth of Christianity.

190. (C) These are the opening lines of *The Aeneid*, the Latin epic written by the Roman poet Virgil (70–19 BCE). Virgil is usually considered the greatest writer in Latin literature. He is known for three incredibly influential works: *The Eclogues* (or *Bucolics*), *The Georgics*, and *The Aeneid*. In *The Eclogues* (completed about 37 BCE), he idealized rural life and set the standard for pastoral poetry for the next 2,000 years. His work had a major impact on the Middle Ages, when the fourth eclogue, concerning the birth of a boy, was often interpreted as a prediction of the coming of Christ. *The Georgics* (completed in 30 BCE) imitated the Greek poet Hesiod by describing the charms of real life and work on the farm. For the rest of his life, Virgil worked on *The Aeneid*, a national epic honoring Rome and foretelling prosperity to come. In 12 books, he told how Aeneas escaped from Troy to Carthage and became Queen Dido's lover. At Jupiter's command, he left Carthage, went to Sicily, visited his father's spirit in Hades, and landed in Italy. There he founded the Roman state and waged successful war against the natives. *The Aeneid* was the main classical Latin literary text of the European Middle Ages; most famously, Dante made Virgil his guide in *The Divine Comedy*.

191. (D) Origen (c. 184–c. 255 CE) was an early Christian scholar and theologian. He argued that Christianity was both true and superior to Greek philosophy as a guide to correct living. He particularly wrestled with the idea of the preexistence of souls. Philo (20 BCE–50 CE) was a Jewish philosopher who claimed the Bible could only be understood through the use of allegory. He tried to harmonize Greek philosophy and Jewish traditions. Although he had a negligible impact on Judaism, he influenced several early Christian thinkers. Plotinus (c. 205–270 CE) developed new ideas based on Plato's philosophy. Neoplatonism's religious doctrines focused on the human longing to return to the universal Good from which human existence derives. By turning away from the life of the body through the intellectual pursuit of philosophy, individual souls could ascend to the level of the universal soul. Porphyry (234–c. 305 CE) was also a Neoplatonic philosopher who studied under Plotinus. His *Isagoge* was an introduction to logic and philosophy, and in Latin translation, it was the standard textbook on logic in the Middle Ages. Neoplatonism's stress on spiritual purity appealed to Christian intellectuals and had a massive impact during the Middle Ages. John Scotus Eriugena (c. 815–c. 877 CE) was a medieval Irish theologian and Neoplatonist philosopher.

192. (C) The city of Pompeii was a flourishing port as well as a prosperous resort with many villas near present-day Naples. Pompeii and the smaller Herculaneum were completely destroyed during a catastrophic two-day eruption of Mount Vesuvius in 79 CE. The eruption buried Pompeii under 15 to 20 feet of ash and pumice. The town was forgotten for nearly 1,700 years before its accidental rediscovery in 1748. The cinders and ash had the fortunate effect of preserving the city with incredible completeness. Its excavation provided an extraordinarily detailed insight into the life of a city during the Roman Empire. As of 2011, it was one of the most popular tourist attractions in Italy, drawing about 2.5 million visitors every year.

193. (D) Historians often refer to the period of the Roman Republic from about 500 BCE to 287 BCE as the Struggle of the Orders. The republic's two orders were a closed circle of elite families (patricians) and the rest of Rome's citizen population (plebeians). Patricians made up only a tiny percentage of the population (about 130 families in the early republic), but they monopolized Roman political offices. Bitter fighting between the two orders recurred for more than 200 years following the foundation of the republic. Eventually, the plebeians united to resist patrician power. To pressure the elite order, the plebeians sometimes resorted to withdrawing physically from a city or settlement. The men then refused to do their military service. In 287 BCE, the plebeians finally won the right to make laws in their own assembly.

194. (C) Sulla (138–78 BCE) was a Roman general. He served under Marius in Africa and became consul in 88 BCE when Mithradates VI of Pontus was attacking Roman territory in the east. Sulla (the senatorial favorite) and Marius (the popular favorite) both wanted the command against Mithradates; Sulla received it by marching with his soldiers on Rome and killing or exiling his opponents. Mithradates was defeated in 84 BCE, and Sulla came back to Italy the following year with 40,000 men. He had himself named dictator in 82 BCE without any limitation of term. He then began to murder his enemies through the use of proscription. He cleverly reorganized the Roman government, making senators the only group allowed to judge a case against their colleagues and forbidding tribunes the right to offer legislation on their own. Sulla's dictatorship was notoriously cruel; it demonstrated how the patron-client system led poor soldiers to feel stronger ties of obligation to their generals than to their republic.

195. (B) Rome's society was based on the patron-client system. This was an interlocking network of personal relationships that morally and legally obligated people to help and serve one another. A patron (*patronus*) was a man of superior status and usually higher birth. He would provide his clients with benefits such as legal or political support, gifts, or loans. In return, the client (*cliens*) repaid the patron by owing duties, such as working for votes in the patron's campaigns for public office or lending the patron money to support public works. The patron-client relationship was a major instrument for the public display of status. Patrons expected clients to accompany them to the forum on a daily basis to see and be seen. Most Romans believed that stability was achieved through the faithful maintenance of patron-client relationships.

Chapter 6: China: Hsia to Han

196. (C) The Silk Road comprised the most famous network of trading routes in ancient China. It connected Asia with the Mediterranean world, as well as northern Africa and Europe. The Silk Road connected both land and water routes to Eurasia. The 4,000-mile route crossed China, central Asia, northern India, and the Parthian and Roman Empires. It connected the Yellow River valley to the Mediterranean Sea, passing through Chinese cities such as Kansu and Sinkiang and through present-day countries Iran, Iraq, and Syria. Caravans carried many goods, including silk, as far as the Roman Empire. Trade in silk especially grew under the Han Dynasty in the first and second centuries CE. In some areas, caravans were protected by pastoral nomads.

197. (A) The Han Dynasty was established in the third century BCE after the Qin Dynasty's harsh laws sparked a series of civil wars. Under Han rule, feudalism was revived in China but partially combined with a centralized autocracy. There was an emperor and a centralized bureaucracy, but the government did distribute hereditary fiefs in parts of the empire. In the third century CE, the central government of the Han Dynasty degenerated into the three kingdoms ruled by warlords (the Three Kingdoms period).

198. (B) The quotation is from Chapter 78 of the Tao Te Ching, a small book supposedly written by Lao-tzu in the sixth century BCE. The book is the main document of Taoism, an important Chinese philosophy and religion. Water is one of Lao-tzu's favorite metaphors to explain the ultimately unknowable Tao. Water is seemingly soft and weak, yet it has the power to penetrate, dissolve, and wash away rocks. Water's ability to yield is exactly what makes it strong. Dripping water hollows out stone. Water embraces instead of confronts and caresses instead of beats, but in the end, it subdues. Lao-tzu applies this analogy to human behavior. The wise person gains by yielding. Humility is superior to pride, which feeds temper and triggers impatience.

199. (B) For nearly as long as humans have known how to use iron, they have used it for agricultural tools. Scholars believe that the first iron plows were used in China during the Warring States period (c. 475–221 BCE). These plows were pushed by hand, not by animals. However, before the Han Dynasty (202 BCE), Chinese plows were made almost entirely of wood, except for the iron blade of the plowshare. By the Han Dynasty, the entire plowshare was made of cast iron; these were the first known heavy moldboard plows.

200. (E) Confucius, or Kung Fu-tzu (c. 551–479 BCE) was born into a poor noble family. His sayings and teachings were collected by his students in *The Analects*. Confucian philosophy stressed the development of virtue (*jen*), and the four other answer choices are basic components of the virtuous life. Confucianism, unlike Christianity, believes that human nature is essentially good. Confucius proposed that people could be taught to be virtuous, primarily through the study of literature, history, and philosophy. Therefore, education should be open to anyone, regardless of social class. When society became educated and virtuous, stability would return and the turmoil of the late Zhou Dynasty would end.

201. (D) The prosperity of the Han Dynasty produced significant population growth, as well as a great deal of advanced technology. Among the inventions and advances attributed to the Han are paper, the rudder, the compass, porcelain, the seismograph, acoustical studies, and a calendar of 365 days. The Grand Canal, a 1,200-mile-long canal that links northern and southern China, was built under the Sui Dynasty (589–618 CE).

202. (E) The Warring States period covers the time of the later Zhou Dynasty from about 475 BCE to the unification of China under the Qin Dynasty in 221 BCE. During this period, a number of local warlords claimed independence for their regions and became involved in seemingly interminable wars. Ironworking spread in China, and iron replaced bronze as the dominant metal used in warfare. Scholars developed different philosophies, including Confucianism, Taoism, Legalism, and Mohism, to try to deal with the anarchy of unending war. In 256 BCE, Qin Shi Huang came to the throne of Ch'in, the westernmost state. Between 230 and 221, he conquered his seven rivals and unified China into an empire. The development of wood-block printing is usually associated with the Tang Dynasty.

203. (A) Mencius (c. 372–289 BCE) was arguably the most famous teacher of Confucian thought. He lived during the Warring States period and defended the teachings of Confucius against other influential schools of thought, especially Mohism. One of his basic principles was that human nature is good, and he declared that morality cannot be taught to the last possible detail. That explains why external controls and governments always fail in improving society. According to Mencius, only education can awaken the innate abilities of the human mind. He denounced memorization and instead supported actively questioning the text. In politics, Mencius argued that it is acceptable for subjects to overthrow or even kill a ruler who ignores the people's needs and rules harshly, because an unjust ruler is no longer a true ruler. His teachings have been very influential on the development of Confucianism.

204. (D) According to traditional sources, the Shang (Yin) Dynasty (c. 1600–1000 BCE) was the second Chinese dynasty (after the Hsia, or Xia). The Shang ruled in the northeastern regions in the Yellow River valley. It was during their rule that the pictographic and ideographic writing system that the Chinese still use was invented. The oldest form of Chinese writings were questions written on animal bones (oracle bones). These questions were deciphered and answered by ancient Chinese priests. Ideographs consist of two pictures placed next to each other to form an abstract concept. Phonograms, the equivalent of homonyms, were used to represent words that sound alike but mean different things. By 500 BCE, this writing system defined Chinese society; it was so complex that only the wealthiest Chinese could take the time needed to master its alphabet. Paper was invented in the second century CE and gunpowder in the ninth century CE.

205. (A) Of the five answer choices, the Hsia Dynasty (c. 2200–1600 BCE) was the first and the Han (c. 206 BCE–220 CE) was the last. The three dynastic periods in the middle were the Shang (c. 1600–1000 BCE), the Zhou (c. 1046–256 BCE), and the brief yet crucial Qin (221–207 BCE).

206. (D) The Qin Dynasty (221–207 BCE), unlike the Zhou Dynasty that preceded it, was extremely short. Yet it remains a noteworthy period in Chinese history. It was the Qin Dynasty that connected separate fortification walls into what eventually became the Great Wall of China. This demonstrates that the empire was centralized, well organized, and territorial. The Qin Dynasty also increased trade, improved agriculture, and enhanced military security. By weakening the landowning lords, the central government directly controlled the peasants, giving the Qin access to a large workforce. This dynasty also introduced several reforms: for example, currency, weights, and measures were standardized, and a better system of writing was established. The strength of the Qin state was increased by Legalist reforms, but the rulers believed that all opposing opinions were treason. This led to book burnings and the execution of scholars.

207. (C) The Shang economy had a fairly advanced system of agriculture, with plows pulled by domesticated water buffalo or humans. Peasants grew mainly rice in the hot and swampy south, where growing conditions were ideal, and millet in the arid north. Animal husbandry (pigs, dogs, sheep, chickens, horses, and oxen) was relatively insignificant compared to farming, and although trade was important, it was not the backbone of the economy. Neither hunting and foraging nor tribute played much of an economic role. However, the Shang Dynasty was advanced in metallurgy; bronze weapons and tools were common in that era.

208. (C) Legalism was a Chinese political philosophy based on the idea that a highly efficient and powerful government is the key to social order. It was developed by Shang Yang (390–338 BCE) during the Warring States period. This philosophy disagreed with the Taoist and Confucian beliefs that humans could improve through meditation or education. Instead, Legalists believed that stability depended on better police and army administrators, more efficient tax collectors, and a less corrupt legal system. They also believed that humans were essentially evil and lazy, and this made constant vigilance necessary for stability. They wanted to make laws covering many areas of everyday life and clearly state the punishment for violating each law. Legalists were convinced that a government that allowed its subjects freedom was promoting disorder.

209. (D) The Shang Dynasty lasted from about 1600 to 1000 BCE. The Shang spoke a Sino-Tibetan language, fought on horseback and in chariots, and used bronze weapons. During this dynasty, the government expanded irrigation systems on the Yellow (Huang He) River. Wheat and millet became staple crops in the area, leading to a rapid rise in population. Shang artists were noted for their skill in bronze. Silkworm cultivation also began in China during this time. However, Shang society was deeply divided between peasants and nobles.

210. (A) The concept of the mandate of heaven originated with the Zhou Dynasty's desire to rationalize the overthrow of the Shang. The concept is first found in the written records of the words of the duke of Zhou, younger brother of King Wu. The notion was later supported by Mencius, an influential Confucian philosopher. The mandate of heaven supposedly granted a dynasty the authority to rule and explained the success and failure of emperors and dynasties until the end of the empire in 1912 CE. Whenever a dynasty fell, Chinese sages declared that it had lost the moral right to rule, which is given by heaven alone. In this sense, *heaven* did not mean a personal god but a universal all-encompassing power. However, unlike the European concept of the divine right of kings, the mandate of heaven depended on the conduct of the ruler in question. The idea was adopted by succeeding Chinese dynasties as a rationalization for their assumption of power from a previous weakened dynasty.

211. (B) The Han Dynasty lasted from 206 BCE to 220 CE. Its collapse was caused by many factors. Land was distributed unequally between the rich and the poor, and several peasant revolts occurred after natural disasters wrecked the agricultural economy. The late Han emperors relied on small groups of the elite and particular families to make policy; this alienated the peasantry from the government. The weak central government made military leaders and local warlords more powerful. The imperial court of Han was plagued with corruption. Gradually, central authority disintegrated. The Xiongnu were ancient nomadic peoples living along the Han borders, and the Han government paid them heavy tributes. However, the Xiongnu never successfully invaded the Han Empire to cause its collapse, which was primarily internal in nature.

212. (B) In the Shang and Zhou Dynasties, China had been dominated by aristocrats in chariots. However, chariots were not easy to produce; participation in battle was therefore limited to a small percentage of the population, mostly the ruling elite of the city-states. In the Warring States period (c. 475–221 BCE), changes in military technology gave the advantage to states with greater resources and larger populations. The casting of individual weapons allowed the states to arm masses of foot soldiers. The weapons of soldiers gradually changed from bronze to iron. Dagger-axes were an extremely popular weapon in various kingdoms, especially the later Qin, which produced 18-foot-long pikes. Leaders began using infantry and cavalry, and chariots gradually fell out of favor. From this period on, the nobles in China became a literate class rather than warrior class, as the kingdoms competed by throwing masses of soldiers at each other. This was also the period when the military strategist Sun Tzu wrote *The Art of War*, which is recognized today as the most influential and oldest military strategy guide.

213. (E) Sun Tzu (also known as Sun Wu or Sunzi) was an ancient Chinese military general, strategist, and philosopher. He is traditionally believed to have written *The Art of War*, an influential ancient Chinese book on military strategy, during the Warring States period. The book is composed of 13 chapters; each chapter is devoted to one aspect of warfare such as planning offensives (Chapter 3), incendiary attacks (Chapter 12), and employing spies (Chapter 13). *The Art of War* remains the most famous of the so-called Seven Military Classics of ancient China. It grew in popularity in the 20th century, and Sun Tzu's work has continued to influence both Asian and Western culture and politics. However, some historians have questioned whether Sun Tzu was an authentic historical figure.

214. (A) The Zhou Dynasty was established in the 11th century BCE and, in its eastern form, lasted almost 800 years. Zhou rule is divided into two distinct eras: the early (Western) Zhou Dynasty (c. 1027–771 BCE) and the later (Eastern) Zhou Dynasty (771–256 BCE). The move of the capital east from Haojing to Chengzhou in 771 BCE marks the historical boundary between the Western Zhou and Eastern Zhou. Although the use of iron was introduced to China during the Zhou Dynasty, this period is also considered the high point for the creation of Chinese bronzeware. At the same time, the Chinese written script evolved into its modern form. The Zhou Dynasty officially ended in 256 BCE; Qin Shi Huang's unification of China in 221 BCE led to the establishment of the Qin Dynasty.

215. (A) Empress Lu Zhi (also known as Empress Dowager Lu or Empress Gao) was the wife of Emperor Gaozu (Liu Bang) of Han, the founder of the Han Dynasty. They had two known children—the eventual Emperor Hui and Princess Luyan. After her husband's death, Empress Lu seized control by naming her infant son emperor. She was ruthless and skilled enough in political manipulation to rule for 16 years. Although she was an able administrator, she made sure to remove members of her late husband's family from positions of power and replace them with members of her own family. During her reign, the people of the empire enjoyed a respite from the turmoil that followed the end of Qin Dynasty. After her death in 180 CE, generals who had helped her husband rise to power overthrew the government.

216. (C) Some of the earliest examples of Chinese writing have been found on oracle bones from Bronze Age China. To ascertain the will of the gods, the Chinese would write questions to them on animal bones or shells. The oracle would then heat these bones and read the cracks, thereby divining the gods' answers. Inscriptions on oracle bones suggest that Chinese writing evolved from pictographs. Later, several pictographs were combined to form an ideograph, or symbol that represents an abstract concept. Most oracle bones date from the late Shang Dynasty, somewhere between the 14th and 11th centuries BCE.

217. (D) The first Chinese civil service exam was given during the Han Dynasty. Officially, anyone who qualified could study to take the exam and join the Chinese bureaucracy. However, studying the Chinese alphabet and the intricacies of Confucian doctrine took years to complete and was expensive. Sometimes a town might pool its resources and pay for one of its brightest children to enter school. In practice, however, only well-to-do Chinese could take the time for the necessary training to work as civil servants.

218. (B) The Terracotta Army is a collection of terra-cotta sculptures depicting the armies of Qin Shi Huang's reign (c. 210 BCE); it was intended to protect the emperor in the afterlife. The army was unknown because of its underground location and because it was never mentioned in historical records. It was discovered in 1974 in Shaanxi province by local Chinese farmers drilling a well. The figures include warriors, generals, chariots, horses, acrobats, strongmen, and musicians. In the three pits containing the Terracotta Army, there were more than 8,000 soldiers, 130 chariots with 520 horses, and 150 cavalry horses. Most sculptures remain buried. Both the scale of the project and the craftsmanship of each statue is astonishing. In 2005, the Terracotta Warriors and Horses Museum received more than two million visitors.

219. (B) According to traditional sources, the Hsia was the first Chinese dynasty, lasting from about 2200 to 1600 BCE. Reliable information on the Hsia is archaeological, as China's first written system—oracle bone script—did not exist until the Shang Dynasty. The Hsia Dynasty was the first to irrigate land, cast bronze, and mobilize a strong army.

220. (D) Mohism (or Moism) was a Chinese philosophy developed by the followers of Mozi (470–c. 391 BCE), also called Mo Tzu. Mohism evolved at about the same time as Confucianism, Taoism, and Legalism and was one of the four main philosophical schools of ancient China. At the time, it was considered a major rival to Confucianism. In contrast to the Confucianists, who taught that devotion was particularly due to one's family, Mohism prescribed equal love for all people. Unlike Confucius, Mozi did not accept the concept of the mandate of heaven; instead, he believed that the position of the emperor should be based solely on merit. Mohism's rejection of offensive warfare was one of its basic doctrines. Adherents argued that "good" was whatever produced the greatest well-being among all people. Mohist doctrines also advocated the elimination of extraneous ritual and music. Mohists held that religious belief was essential to a well-ordered society and were enthusiastic believers in ghosts and spirits. Mohism declined after the Qin Dynasty adopted Legalism as the official government philosophy and persecuted all other philosophical schools.

The Han and most successive dynasties adopted Confucianism as the official state philosophy, and Mohism essentially disappeared as an independent school of thought.

221. (B) Confucius believed that stability resulted from hierarchy. Thus, instead of "sibling to sibling," Confucius paired younger brother to older brother. Women were considered inferior to men and sisters inferior to brothers. Confucianists envisioned a society of families led by virtuous males. Each family member should graciously accept his or her role and submit to the hierarchy for the sake of order. The brightest, most virtuous men would form a bureaucracy and assist the emperor in administering stable rule. For Confucianists, all members of society have specific roles, or *li*. The roles change as children grow to adulthood. Knowing and scrupulously adhering to one's *li* ensures stability by eliminating role stress. Confucianists believe that families and groups are more important than individual self-expression.

222. (E) Liu Pang (c. 256–195 BCE) was of peasant origin and became a minor official before joining the free-for-all struggle that followed the collapse of the Qin Dynasty. His victory at the battle of Kai-Hsia (Giaxia) in 203 BCE removed his last rival for power in China and allowed him to establish the Han Dynasty. The battle took place in modern Anhui province. His rival, Xiang Yu, was killed, and most of his supporters surrendered. Liu Pang took the title of emperor (*Huang-ti*), and this began the Han Dynasty. He took the throne name Gaozu (spelled a variety of ways) and ruled until 195 BCE.

223. (C) The Three Kingdoms period was part of a period of disunity in Chinese history called the Six Dynasties (c. 200–600 CE). It began with the decline of the Han Dynasty in about 200 CE and lasted until about 280 CE, when it was replaced by the Jin Dynasty. The three kingdoms were Cao Wei, Shu Han, and Dong Wu (or Eastern Wu). Each state was headed not by a king, but by an emperor who claimed to be the legitimate heir of the Han Dynasty. Technology advanced significantly during this period, including advances in hydraulics and the invention of a proto-wheelbarrow, a repeating crossbow, and a nonmagnetic directional compass. The Three Kingdoms period was extremely bloody and the population decreased, although the size of the decline is a subject for dispute. The period has been romanticized in the cultures of China, Japan, Korea, Taiwan, and Vietnam, even though it lasted for less than a century.

224. (A) According to Lao Tzu, the universe depended on a set of complementary opposites—balances between the *yin* (feminine forces) and the *yang* (masculine forces). Yang characteristics were activity, heat, and light, while those of the yin were passivity, cold, and dark. For the universe to maintain equilibrium, yin and yang needed to be equally balanced. For Taoists, these balances apply to everything from weather to meal preparation. Yin and yang explain how polar opposites are interdependent in the natural world and how each one gives rise to the other in turn. The concept that opposites only exist in relation to each other is the heart of many branches of classical Chinese science and philosophy, a guideline of traditional Chinese medicine, and a basic principle of many Chinese martial arts.

225. (E) Emperor Wu of Han (156–87 BCE), also known as Wu Ti, ruled for 54 years, from 141 to 87 BCE. He is considered the greatest emperor of the Han Dynasty, and his empire surpassed that of the Romans in size. As a military campaigner, Emperor Wu did *not* follow Mohism's rejection of offensive warfare. Instead, he led Han China to its greatest expansion, from present-day Kyrgyzstan in the west to Korea in the northeast and northern Vietnam in the south. He also successfully repelled the nomadic Xiongnu who tried to raid northern China. His diplomatic missions to central Asia led to the development of the Silk Road both eastward and westward. The Silk Road trade not only introduced different cultures to China, but it also spread China's influence to other parts of the world. Emperor Wu strongly adopted the principles of Confucianism as the state philosophy; he even founded a school to teach bureaucrats the Confucian classics. He created a strong, centralized state and appointed provincial administrators to promote government efficiency. These policies had a lasting effect for centuries and an enormous influence on neighboring civilizations.

Chapter 7: India Through the Gupta Empire

226. (D) Although Buddhism never developed a missionary movement, Buddha's teachings nevertheless spread across the Indian subcontinent and from there throughout Asia. In each culture, Buddhist methods and styles were modified to fit the local mentality without compromising the essential points of wisdom and compassion. When Buddhist traders and merchants visited and settled in different lands, some members of the local population naturally developed an interest in the foreigners' beliefs. This occurred in the oasis states along the Silk Road in central Asia from about 200 BCE to 200 CE. As local rulers and people learned more about this Indian religion, they invited monks from the merchants' native regions as advisers or teachers. In this manner, many Asians eventually adopted the Buddhist faith. However, Shinto, Jainism, and Zoroastrianism remained confined mainly to Japan, India, and Persia, respectively. Judaism spread through the various Jewish diasporas.

227. (D) Broomyard millet is a kind of grain that grows wild in Asia. Hunters and gatherers in Neolithic China probably ate millet, and the first signs of its cultivation date to 7500 BCE in northern China. The domestication of rice in the Yangtze River valley may have taken place at the same time, but the first signs of agriculture date to about 5000 BCE. Wet-field cultivation of rice in paddies probably became popular in the first millennium BCE. In India, rice is first mentioned in the Yajurveda, probably written between 1400 and 1000 BCE. Rice paddies are perfectly suited for the seasonal monsoons of the Indian subcontinent. Spices grew wild but were soon cultivated as preservatives and curatives. Bananas and plantains were first domesticated in southeast Asia, while yams may have originated in both Asia and Africa. (Poi is not a plant, but a Polynesian staple food made from the bulbous root of the taro plant.)

228. (A) Chandragupta Maurya (c. 340–298 BCE) was the founder of the Maurya Empire (321–c. 180 BCE). He conquered most of the Indian subcontinent and is considered the first genuine emperor of India. After his conquests, the Maurya Empire extended from Bengal to Assam in the east to Afghanistan in the west and from Kashmir and Nepal in the north to the Deccan Plateau in the south. Chandragupta Maurya's government was supported by taxes on agriculture, while standardized coinage throughout the empire helped trade. The government's control of manufacturing, mining, and shipbuilding strengthened the state. Chandragupta Maurya's powerful army consisted of infantry, cavalry, chariots, and war elephants. He did not, however, favor one religion over another. He gave up his throne toward the end of his life and became a follower of a Jain saint.

229. (A) A *monsoon* is traditionally defined as a seasonal reversing wind accompanied by corresponding changes in precipitation. Usually, the term refers to the rainy phase of a changing seasonal pattern, but there is also a dry phase. The prevailing summer winds of the Indian subcontinent—summer monsoons—blow northeastward off the Indian Ocean and deposit considerable rain. The mountain barriers capture the rain and drain it into three major river systems: the Brahmaputra, Ganges, and Indus. The winter monsoons, on the other hand, blow southward across the dry Asian interior. These winds are cooler and very dry. Because India's rainfall is uneven, it has had a decisive influence on life in the region. Agriculture in the three river valleys revolves around the summer monsoons, which may account for as much as 80 percent of the rainfall in India. An insufficient seasonal accumulation of rain can cause drought and famine, while too much rain can cause flooding and destruction.

230. (A) The position of women declined under the Gupta. Under the increasingly strict Hindu law, women were considered minors, subject first to their fathers, then to their husbands, and finally to their sons. They were not allowed to own or inherit property, and they could not participate in sacred rituals or study religion. Marriages were usually arranged, and child marriage became more common during this era. Female infants were often seen as economic liabilities, and female infanticide was occasionally practiced. Widows with sons were not permitted to remarry. Finally, the custom of sati—a widow's self-immolation after her husband's death—began to grow in popularity in the Gupta Empire.

231. (B) The *Manusmriti* (laws of Manu) provides detailed rules, presumably directed to Brahman priests, governing ritual and daily life. The text consists of a speech given by Manu, a mythical "first man" who was transformed into a king by Brahma because of his ability to protect the people. A group of seers begs Manu to tell them the law of all the social classes. The rest is an encyclopedic representation of human life and how it should be lived, made up of 2,684 verses divided into 12 chapters. The text covers such wide-ranging topics as the social obligations and duties of the various castes, the proper way for a righteous king to rule, relations between men and women, birth, death, taxes, karma, rebirth, and ritual. The *Manusmriti* especially tries to validate and preserve the high caste position of the Brahmans. It forbids the lowest castes to participate in the Brahmin rituals and subjects them to severe punishments. Women are considered inept and sensual, and they are restrained from learning the Vedic texts or participating in important functions. Although it was probably written by many Brahmin priests, Hindu tradition claims that the *Manusmriti* records the words of Brahma, giving the text supernatural authority. It was probably composed between 200 BCE and 200 CE, after the Mauryan Empire (and its Buddhist influence) but before the Gupta Empire.

232. (E) The Gupta Empire was noted for its achievements in mathematics and science. Gupta mathematicians accurately calculated the value of pi and the circumference of the earth. Indian numerals also seem to have originated in Gupta India. The mathematician-astronomer Aryabhata (476–550 CE) correctly insisted that the earth rotates about its axis daily and that the apparent movement of the stars is actually caused by the rotation of the earth. He also discovered that the moon and planets shine by reflected sunlight. The *Sushruta Samhita* (c. 650 CE) is a famous Sanskrit medical text that includes chapters on surgery; the ancient Sanskrit *Kama Sutra*, written by Vatsyayana, is a standard work on human sexual behavior. It is also likely that the game of chess originated during this time. Many of the discoveries made by Indians during this period diffused throughout the world via trade. (The earliest clear illustrations of the spinning wheel come from 13th-century Baghdad, China, and Europe.)

233. (C) The quotation is from the Bhagavad Gita, a classic book of Hinduism since it was first composed in about the first century CE. In the second teaching, the god Krishna (sometimes considered an avatar of Vishnu) explains the doctrine of reincarnation to the warrior Arjuna. In many Indian religious traditions (Hinduism, Buddhism, Jainism), the soul (*atman*) is immortal, while the body is subject to birth and death. Reincarnation occurs when, after the death of the body, the soul comes back to life in a new form such as another animal or any other living thing. According to the Hindu sage Adi Shankara (c. 800 CE), the world as it is ordinarily understood is like a dream. People are trapped in *samsara* (the cycle of birth and death), because they are ignorant of the true nature of existence. After many births, some people experience dissatisfaction and begin to seek higher forms of happiness through spiritual experience. Eventually, they realize that the true self is the immortal soul rather than the body or the ego. When this happens, all desires for the pleasures of the world vanish. When all desire is gone, they will not be born again; they will have attained liberation (*moksha*).

234. (A) The composition of the *Mahabharata* and the *Ramayana* took place between about the sixth and first centuries BCE. Although it is disputed, the two epics were probably first transmitted orally and evolved through several centuries before achieving their final form in the Gupta period (about the fourth century CE). The *Mahabharata* is one of the longest poems in the world; it has about 100,000 verses and many long prose passages—about 1.8 million total words. It is roughly 10 times the length of *The Iliad* and *The Odyssey* combined, and about 4 times the length of the *Ramayana* (which is about 50,000 lines). The *Mahabharata* concerns the conflict between two families for control of an Indian city, but it also contains long digressions into Hindu mythology and philosophy; the Bhagavad Gita is only a small part of the *Mahabharata*. The *Ramayana* deals with the exile of Prince Rama, the abduction of his wife by the demon-king Ravana, and the Lankan war. Like the *Mahabharata*, the *Ramayana* has several layers of substories, including tales of Hanuman, the monkeylike general/god.

235. (C) The classifications mentioned in the passage are terms for the various Hindu castes. The Indian caste system is a method of social stratification and restriction in which communities are defined by their hereditary groups. These are grouped under four well-known categories: Brahmins (scholars, teachers, and fire priests); Vaishyas (farmers, cattle raisers, traders, and bankers); Kshatriyas (kings, warriors, law enforcers, and administrators); and Sudras (artisans, craftsmen, and service providers). Each of these categories contains the actual *jatis* (castes) within which people are born, marry, and die. Theoretically, everyone has a place in society and accepts that place to keep society from disintegrating into chaos. Certain groups of people such as foreigners, nomads, and the *chandalas* (who disposed of the dead) were excluded and treated as untouchables (*harijan*). This meant that orthodox upper-caste families would not even touch them or invite them to their homes. The Rigveda mantras (hymns) are the oldest and most philosophical of the Vedas and one of the oldest surviving texts in any Indo-European language. They were probably composed in the northwestern region of the Indian subcontinent between 1700 and 1100 BCE. The Rigveda also contains several mythological and poetical accounts of the origin of the world, as well as ancient prayers for life and prosperity.

236. (D) Jainism is a religion that teaches pacifism and nonviolence toward all living things. Its practice emphasizes the importance of self-effort to move the soul to divine consciousness and liberation. Any soul that has conquered its own inner enemies and achieved the state of supreme being is called a *jina* (conqueror). Jains trace their origins to a succession of 24 *jinas* in ancient eastern India. The last *jina* was Vardhamana, also known as Mahavira ("The Great Hero"). Around 550 BCE, Mahavira established what are today considered to be the central beliefs of the religion. Jains hold that every living thing has a soul that is potentially divine; therefore, they try not to harm any living beings. They follow a strictly vegetarian diet. At the heart of right conduct lie the five great vows: nonviolence (*ahimsa*), truthfulness (*satya*), avoidance of stealing (*asteya*), celibacy (*brahmacharya*), and nonattachment (*aparigraha*). Every day most Jains bow and say their universal prayer, the Namokara Mantra. In the modern world, Jains are a small but influential religious minority with more than four million followers in India. There are growing immigrant communities all over the world.

237. (B) The Gupta Empire was an ancient Indian empire from about 320 to 550 CE that covered much of the Indian subcontinent. Like the Han and Roman Empires, it suffered from repeated foreign attacks along its border areas. Perhaps the last great Gupta king was Skanda Gupta, who ascended the throne about 455 CE. After that, inefficient leaders led to the weakening of the central government, and a number of feudal chiefs in the northwestern region became independent rulers. The Guptas successfully resisted the northwestern kingdoms until the arrival of the Huns, who led raids across the Himalayas into northern India. The Huns excelled in horsemanship and may have used iron stirrups. They were established in Afghanistan, with their capital at Bamiyan by the first half of the fifth century CE. Efforts by the Gupta to repel the Huns led to a serious drain on the treasury. Hun inroads destroyed the ports and markets of western India and ruined the Guptas' rich trade with Rome. By 530, the empire was overrun by further invasions and broke up into many smaller local governments; however, much of the Deccan Plateau and southern India seem to have been unaffected by these events in the north.

238. (B) The Tamil people are an ethnic group native to Tamil Nadu (a state in southern India) and the northeastern region of present-day Sri Lanka (Ceylon). One estimate in 2010 placed the number of Tamils at about 77 million, with more than 60 million living in southern India. Most Tamils speak Tamil; like the other languages of southern India, it is Dravidian and unrelated to the Indo-European languages of northern India. Tamil culture developed in about the third century BCE, when increased trade led to urbanization along the western and eastern coast of present-day Kerala and Tamil Nadu. Three large Tamil states (Chera, Chola, and Pandya) developed, as did several small, warring principalities. Large quantities of Roman coins have been discovered at the sites of several ancient Tamil cities. Tamil art is famous for its unique temple architecture and images of deities in stone and bronze; Chola bronzes have become a virtual symbol of Hinduism. Many present-day Tamils practice a sort of folk Hinduism, venerating an assortment of local village deities. A sizeable minority of Tamils are Christians, Muslims, and Jains.

239. (E) It is ironic that Buddhism dominated southeastern Asia but died out in the land of its origin. In India, Buddhist monks had become more preoccupied with philosophy than with serving the needs of the common people. In addition, changes in Hinduism favored a personal relationship with major deities like Shiva and Vishnu. More temples were built to house statues of the gods, and even untouchables and women were allowed to practice this new form of Hinduism. At first, the Buddhist disapproval of the caste system benefited many artisans and merchants who supported Indian monasteries. However, the fall of the Han Dynasty in China caused a decline in trade and weakened merchant support and endowments for Buddhist monasteries. The Upanishads acquired new prominence, as they were partially interpreted to mirror Buddhist beliefs that the ultimate purpose of the soul was to merge with the divine essence and that the world itself was an illusion. By the time of the Gupta Dynasty, Hinduism had again become the main religion in India, and its reinforcement of the caste system meant that Indian social structures became very rigid.

240. (A) Kalidasa was a famous classical writer who is usually considered the greatest poet and dramatist in the Sanskrit language. Nothing certain is known about him other than his works, but scholars believe he lived during the third century CE. His plays and poetry are primarily based on Hindu Puranas and philosophy. Kalidasa wrote three plays, of which *Abhijnanasakuntalam* (Of Shakuntala Recognized by a Token) is considered his masterpiece. It tells the story of King Dushyanta; his wife, Shakuntala; and a magic ring. The play was the first Indian drama to be translated into a Western language (1789), and by 1900, there were at least 46 translations in 12 European languages.

241. (E) Ashoka the Great (c. 304–232 BCE) was an Indian emperor of the Mauryan Dynasty who conquered and ruled most of the Indian subcontinent from about 269 to 232 BCE. Ashoka converted from Hinduism to Buddhism after witnessing the slaughter resulting from one of his wars of conquest in eastern India. He helped spread Buddhism to present-day Sri Lanka, the Himalayan regions, and the grasslands of central Asia. He also established monuments marking several significant sites in the life of the Buddha. Because of his religious beliefs, Ashoka promoted vegetarianism to reduce the slaughter of animals, especially cattle. His attempts to build a centralized state with an efficient government led to frequent clashes with the Brahmins whose power he threatened. Ashoka publicized his Buddhist program by engraving his decisions on large rocks and sandstone pillars that he had scattered throughout his empire. He is considered one of India's greatest rulers; the emblem of modern India is an adaptation of the Lion Capital of Ashoka. (The dissemination of Indian numerals is associated with the Gupta Empire.)

242. (D) Ashoka ruled for about 40 years. After his death in 232 BCE, the Mauryan Dynasty lasted only 50 years more. Its decline was caused by economic problems and pressure from attacks in the northeast. By 180 BCE, India had fragmented into small warring states. The situation continued for almost 600 years as waves of invaders—Bactrians, Scythians, Kushians, and Parthians—entered the region. India's history during this period was chaotic until the rise of the Gupta Empire in the fourth century CE. Animal sacrifices, musical festivals, and dances that had been prohibited under Ashoka and his heirs then returned. The Guptas performed Vedic sacrifices to legitimize their rule, but they also patronized Buddhism, which continued to provide an alternative to Hindu orthodoxy. Buddhism did not disappear in India until after the 13th century CE.

243. (D) Theravada (the Ancient Teaching) is the oldest surviving Buddhist school of thought. It is relatively conservative compared to Mahayana Buddhism and considered closer to early Buddhism. For many centuries, it has been the main religion of Sri Lanka and most of continental southeastern Asia (Cambodia, Laos, Myanmar, and Thailand). Today, Theravada Buddhists number more than 100 million worldwide. Theravada's main scriptures are in Pali, a Middle Indo-Aryan language. Mahayana (Great Vehicle) is the other (and larger) main branch of Buddhism. It emerged in the first century CE as a more liberal and accessible interpretation of Buddhism. It spread quickly to China, Japan, Vietnam, Korea, Singapore, Nepal, Tibet, and Mongolia. Mahayana is a path available to people from all walks of life, not just monks and ascetics. Various subdivisions of the Mahayana tradition—Zen, Nichiren, and Pure Land—promote different ways of achieving enlightenment, but all agree that it can be attained in a single lifetime by a dedicated layperson. Theravada discourages the use of ritual, while Mahayana often includes the veneration of celestial beings, buddhas, and bodhisattvas; religious rituals and magical rites; and the use of icons, images, and other sacred objects.

244. (D) Sati (also called suttee) was a traditional Indian religious funeral practice in which a recently widowed woman, either voluntarily or by coercion, would immolate herself on her husband's funeral pyre. There are numerous hypotheses for the origins of this custom. Although it was theoretically voluntary, there was extreme community pressure in some places to perform the act. Aristobulus of Cassandreia, a Greek historian who traveled to India with Alexander the Great, recorded the practice of sati in the city of Taxila. However, the practice was little known before the Gupta Empire and appears to be part of the general decline in the position of women during that period. In the later years of the empire, memorial stones known as *devli* were erected to honor instances of sati. In some cases, they became shrines to the dead women, who were treated as objects of reverence. By about the 10th century CE, sati was known across much of the subcontinent, although it was never common. The practice has been outlawed in India since 1829; nonetheless, there have still been several known cases in the 21st century.

245. (E) The Four Noble Truths are an important principle of Buddhism. They are derived directly from teachings of the Buddha, although the exact wording may differ depending on the source. They are as follows: (1) suffering exists; (2) suffering comes from attachment to desires; (3) suffering ceases when attachment to desires ceases; and (4) the attachment to desires only ceases by practicing the Buddha's Eightfold Path.

246. (D) The Indus, Brahmaputra, and Ganges are all among the top 30 longest rivers in the world. The Indus River, from which the name India is derived, is now almost entirely within Pakistan. Both the Ganges and Brahmaputra flow through northwestern India and empty into the Bay of Bengal. The Ganges is the most sacred river to Hindus; millions of Indians live along its banks. As of 2011, it is also one of the most polluted rivers in the world. The Syr Dar'ya is a river in central Asia, sometimes known as the Jaxartes or Yaxartes from its ancient Greek name. It's almost 2,000 miles long and flows through Kazakhstan, Kyrgyzstan, Uzbekistan, and Tajikistan.

247. (C) The classical empires of the Han, Romans, and Gupta all experienced economic weakness and internal political weakness before their downfall. All three empires had to deal with foreign tribes threatening the stability of their borders. After their fall, all three empires broke up into smaller local governments. However, political conflicts with religious authorities were not significant in any of these empires. Although all three endured religious controversies (Christian versus pagan, Buddhist versus Hindu, Confucian versus Taoist), they could not be considered major conflicts between political and religious authorities.

248. (E) The Indus Valley culture was a Bronze Age culture that thrived from about 2600 to 1700 BCE. It was located in northwestern India around the Indus River and was one of the world's earliest urban cultures. Inhabitants developed new techniques in handicraft and metallurgy, producing copper, bronze, lead, and tin. The culture is noted for its cities built of brick, roadside drainage system, and multistoried houses. The main phase of this culture is known as the Harappan; it was named after Harappa, one of its first cities to be excavated (in the 1920s in what was at the time the Punjab province of British India, now Pakistan). The city is believed to have been quite large for its time, perhaps with more than 20,000 residents. More than 1,000 cities and settlements of Indus Valley culture have been found, including Lothal, Kalibanga, and Mohenjo-daro (a UNESCO World Heritage site).

249. (D) The Aryan invasion myth first developed in the late 1800s. The original version viewed the Indo-Aryan migration as the invasion of a highly developed, light-skinned culture that conquered a primitive, dark-skinned aboriginal culture. However, the discovery in the 1920s of urban ruins and a sophisticated culture in the Indus Valley stood the theory on its head. In the more recent version, the Aryans became a tribe of Indo-European-speaking, horse-riding nomads living on the Eurasian steppes. About 1700 BCE (the date can vary considerably), they invaded the ancient urban cultures of the Indus Valley and destroyed that more advanced Dravidian culture. However, the Aryans borrowed from (or plundered, depending on one's viewpoint) the older culture to create what later became Hinduism. The war between the powers of light and darkness, a recurring theme in Vedic scriptures, was interpreted to refer to a war between light- and dark-skinned peoples. In the late 20th century, historians basically refuted this theory. Archaeological evidence suggests that the Indus Valley culture broke down because of droughts and floods, not warfare. There are no references to an invasion in the Vedas and no biological or archaeological evidence of a massive intrusion of people of a different race. DNA samples imply that there was no "demographic disruption" in northwestern India at any time between 4500 and 800 BCE. This would eliminate the possibility of any massive invasion during that period. Nonetheless, the old theory still has many defenders.

250. (D) The Puranas, Sanskrit for "of ancient times," are a type of religious writing not included in the Vedas. They usually tell the story of the births and deeds of Hindu gods and the creation, destruction, or re-creation of the universe. Puranas also include encyclopedic genealogies of kings, heroes, sages, and demigods, as well as descriptions of Hindu cosmology, philosophy, and geography. They were written almost entirely in the same flowing style as the *Mahabharata* and *Ramayana*. There are traditionally 18 Puranas, but there are several different lists of the 18. The earliest Puranas were written between 350 and 750 CE and the latest between 1000 and 1500. The stories usually feature one particular god, and many teach that submission to the whim of the gods is the best choice. There are also Puranas in Jainism and Buddhism.

Chapter 8: Byzantium

251. **(E)** Constantinople's location on the European side of the Bosporus Strait placed it at the junction of trade routes from several different cultures. The site lay along the land route from Europe to Asia and the sea route from the Black Sea to the Mediterranean. Constantinople's harbor, the Golden Horn, was deep, spacious, and easy to defend. The city was (re)founded by the Roman emperor Constantine on the site of an existing city—Byzantium—settled in the early days of Greek colonial expansion. Constantine himself may have laid out the general plan of the city in 324 CE, and the construction was quick; the dedication was in 330. Throughout most of the Middle Ages, Constantinople was Europe's largest and wealthiest city. It was conquered by the Ottoman Turks in 1453 and renamed Istanbul.

252. **(E)** *Iconoclasm* is the term for opposition to religious images known as icons. It derives from the Greek words for "image breaking." From 726 to 843 CE, arguments between supporters (iconodules) and opponents (iconoclasts) of icons dominated the politics of the Byzantine Empire and the theology of the Christian church. Christian icons are sacred images representing Jesus Christ, the Virgin Mary, saints, and Bible scenes. By the seventh century, icons had become an accepted part of Christian belief and church decoration. They were respected, admired, adored, venerated, and even worshipped. The difference between *veneration* (a feeling of deep respect or reverence for a person or thing) and *worship* (religious reverence for a divine being or power) troubled some Byzantine Christians. They feared that people might worship the icon rather than God, leading to a restoration of Greek and Roman paganism. Leo III, a valiant soldier who had become emperor in 717, decided that the military misfortunes of the Byzantine Empire were divine punishment for the improper worship of icons. He was probably influenced by Islamic views that forbade the representation of the human form for religious use. Because the main opponents of the iconoclasts were monks, Leo III joined iconoclasm with an attack on the power of the monasteries. After a century of quarreling, the iconodule position was victorious in 843. Today, anyone who attacks a cherished idea or respected institution is called an iconoclast.

253. **(C)** The Sassanid Empire of Persia was the major force on the border of the eastern Byzantine Empire in the late sixth century CE. The Sassanids collected land taxes from the prosperous farmers of Mesopotamia (present-day Iraq) and turned Persia into a center of trade. At Ctesiphon, the capital of Sassanid Persia, the rulers set up a bureaucracy of scribes and patronized the arts. The Sassanids also reformed the army by paying and arming new warriors drawn from the lower nobility known as *dekkans*. *Dekkans* were heavily armored soldiers on horseback, forerunners of the medieval knights. The Sassanid king Chosores II (reigned 591–628) wanted to re-create the Persian Empire of Xerxes and Darius. He invaded the Byzantine Empire in 603, took Damascus and Jerusalem in 613, and conquered Egypt in 619. The Byzantine emperor Heraclius reorganized his army, and by 627, the Byzantines had regained all their lost territory. The 24-year war exhausted both empires and left them open to invasion by the Arabs. The Byzantines also suffered territorial losses in the 600s to the Lombards in Italy and to the Slavs, Avars, and Bulgars in the Balkans.

254. (C) In 1054, the Eastern and Western branches of Christianity split, and they remain split to the present day. The schism occurred over both practical and doctrinal differences. Prior to the schism, five bishops (or patriarchs) representing Alexandria, Antioch, Constantinople, Jerusalem, and Rome were technically supposed to act as an executive committee on church matters. However, the patriarch of Constantinople gained power in the east, because he controlled church matters in the emperor's seat of residence. Western Europeans, on the other hand, increasingly followed the dictates of the pope in Rome. Western Europeans became uncomfortable with the Bible written in Greek (and Greeks with the Vulgate), a language they did not understand. The use and meaning of icons was also a sore point between the two branches, as was the pope's insistence on the celibacy of the clergy (which was disputed in Eastern Christianity).

255. (D) The Macedonian renaissance, from about 870 to 1025 CE, takes its name from the Macedonian dynasty that began with Basil I. It is sometimes called the first Byzantine renaissance to differentiate it from the second Byzantine renaissance of the 13th century under the Palaeologan Dynasty. Photios I (c. 810–c. 893) was patriarch of Constantinople and the most important intellectual of the Macedonian renaissance. He helped convert the Slavs to Christianity and also widened the split between the Eastern Orthodox Church and the Roman Catholic Church (although the formal schism did not occur until 1054). Constantine VII (905–959), also known as Porphyrogenitos (the purple-born), was the fourth emperor of the Macedonian dynasty. He was a scholarly emperor, a generous patron of the arts, and a hardworking administrator. Emperor Basil II (958–1025), the "Bulgar Slayer," launched methodical attacks against Bulgarian territory from 1001 to 1018. His victories resulted in the Byzantine control of Bulgaria and the Bulgars' adoption of the Byzantine form of Christianity.

256. (E) The word *monasticism* comes from the Greek word *monos*, meaning "single" or "solitary." Coenobitic monasticism is a tradition that stresses community life over isolated asceticism. Christian monasticism began in Egypt during the fourth century CE, when communities of men and women withdrew from everyday society to lead lives of self-denial. They wanted to imitate Jesus's suffering to demonstrate their complete devotion to God. Monks initially lived alone but then began to form communities to provide mutual support in their quest for holiness and piety. The first community of monks, or coenobitic monastery, was organized by Pachomius in Egypt in about 323. The most isolationist and ascetic monasticism also developed in the eastern part of the empire.

257. (C) The Byzantine emperors, like their predecessors in Rome, sponsored entertainments on a grand scale to rally public support. A hippodrome was a Greek stadium for horse and chariot racing, similar to the Roman circus. The most famous hippodrome was in Constantinople; it is estimated to have been about 400 feet wide and 1,500 feet long, with stands that held 100,000 spectators. The hippodrome was the center of the city's social life, and huge amounts were bet on chariot races. Constantinople's residents divided themselves into competitive factions called Blues and Greens after the racing colors of their favorite charioteers. The team associations became a focus for social and political issues for which most Byzantine people lacked any other form of outlet. The teams combined aspects of street gangs and political parties, often taking positions on theological problems or supporting rival claimants to the throne. The groups frequently brawled with each other over politics and theology, as well as race results. The most severe riot was the Nika revolt of 532 (against the rule of Justinian), in which an estimated 30,000 people were killed. By 1453, the hippodrome had fallen into ruin.

258. (B) Because Christian theologians generally went beyond Roman tradition in restricting sexuality, some limitations on women increased. Women in the Byzantine Empire had few legal rights and limited contact with men outside their family group. As in many pre-industrial cultures, they were subject to the authority of their fathers and husbands, divorce became more difficult to obtain, remarriage was discouraged (even for widows), and stricter legal penalties for sexual offenses became common. Women veiled their heads, but not their faces, to show modesty. Female prostitution remained legal, but Byzantine emperors raised the penalties for those who forcibly made prostitutes of women under their control, such as children or slaves.

259. (D) *Pronoia* refers to a system of land grants in the Byzantine Empire. Emperor Alexius I gave his soldiers *pronoia* in return for military service. The distribution of such grants to nobles gradually brought an end to the *theme* system, under which peasant soldiers had settled on imperial lands. The *pronoia* system partially converted the Byzantine Empire into a feudal kingdom, where great lords received fiefs in return for loyalty. However, the land could not initially be inherited or divided up among the holders. This way, the Byzantine emperor had more direct authority over society than most rulers in western Europe. The *pronoia* system had the added benefit (from the emperor's viewpoint) of removing nobles from Constantinople, making it harder for them to challenge the emperor's authority directly or usurp the throne.

260. (D) Hagia Sophia is the masterpiece of Byzantine architecture, famous for its massive dome and stunning mosaics. It was the largest cathedral in the world for almost a thousand years; the diameter of its central dome remained unsurpassed until the Italian Renaissance. The building was originally constructed as a church between 532 and 537 CE on the orders of Justinian and designed by the Greek scientists Isidore of Miletus and Anthemius of Tralles. The enormous central dome, 102 feet in diameter and 184 feet high, is carried on pendentives, an architectural feature that had never been used on this scale before. The pendentives support the dome on a square framework of four huge, equal arches that rest on huge piers. Forty windows underneath the dome flood the building with a sort of mystical light that makes the dome seem very light. The interior is completely free of any sense of the enormous weight of the structure, and the dome seems to hover weightlessly over the nave. All the interior surfaces, including the pillars, were originally covered with polychrome marbles and gold mosaic. Hagia Sophia was so richly decorated that Justinian famously proclaimed, "Solomon, I have outdone thee!" The building was sacked in the Fourth Crusade but not destroyed. When the Ottoman Turks conquered Constantinople in 1453, Hagia Sophia became a mosque; the former church served as model for several great Turkish mosques in the city. The building is now a Turkish museum.

261. (B) The Byzantine Empire was ruled by the Palaeologan Dynasty from the restoration of Greek rule in Constantinople (1261 CE) to the fall of Constantinople at the hands of the Ottoman Empire (1453). The Palaeologoi were the last ruling dynasty of the Byzantine Empire. The first of the line, Michael VIII Palaeologus (reigned 1261–1282), was probably the most successful. He rebuilt Constantinople to some extent after its destruction in the Fourth Crusade, although these attempts were costly and resulted in high taxes. He also partially restored Byzantine prestige through the clever use of diplomacy. However, the power of Byzantium's enemies and constant civil wars undermined the state. Nonetheless, the Palaeologan period saw art and literature flourish, in what has sometimes been called the Palaeologan renaissance. Gregory Choniades and Theodore Metochites studied astronomy, mathematics, and philosophy, and they also became officials in the Greek Orthodox Church. The migration of Byzantine scholars to the West, even before 1453, helped spark the rebirth of classical learning in Italy.

262. (B) Between 570 and 750 CE, the Byzantine Empire fought against invaders on almost all fronts. In the seventh century, either Emperor Heraclius (reigned 610–641) or Constans II (reigned 641–668) divided the empire into military districts called *themes*. In each *theme*, control over all civil matters was given to one general (a *strategos*). Men joined the army because they were promised land with low taxes. They often fought alongside local farmers who provided their own weapons and horses. The *strategoi* led the local troops into battle, served as the emperor's regional tax collectors, and became the leaders of a new rural elite. In general, the reorganization of the military worked to the local peasant's advantage. It also strengthened the Byzantine Empire against invaders, especially Muslims, in the ninth and tenth centuries. The old Byzantine army had relied heavily on foreign mercenaries; the new army depended on native farmer-soldiers living on state-leased military estates. However, some scholars dispute this interpretation, claiming that the *themes* were not a major break with the past and that they had only a small direct social impact.

263. (A) Justinian I (sometimes known as Justinian the Great) was the most famous early Byzantine emperor, ruling from 527 to 565 CE. During his reign, he nearly bankrupted the treasury in order to reconquer the lost western half of the classical Roman Empire. His desire to project imperial glory led him to embellish Constantinople with magnificent architecture, including the construction of Hagia Sophia. Justinian took his Christianity very seriously and zealously enforced laws against polytheists, compelling them to be baptized or forfeit their lands and official positions. In pursuit of sexual purity, his laws made male homosexual relations illegal for the first time in Roman history; previous emperors had only taxed male prostitutes. Justinian's wife, Empress Theodora (c. 500–548), was arguably the most influential woman in the history of the Byzantine Empire. When Justinian prepared to flee Constantinople during the Nika revolt, Theodora shamed him into remaining and fighting.

264. (E) Justinian compelled polytheists to be baptized or forfeit their lands and official positions. To guarantee the empire's religious purity, he closed the famous Athenian Academy that had been founded 900 years earlier by Plato; it never reopened. Many of its scholars had already fled to Persia to escape harsher restrictions on polytheists. The Academy lacked supporters because the Athenian elite, its traditional patrons, were increasingly Christian. Justinian's closing of the Academy has become one of the symbols of the end of antiquity and the beginning of the Middle Ages.

265. (C) Ravenna is a city in northern Italy on the Adriatic Sea. In 404 CE, Emperor Honorius transferred the capital of the Western Roman Empire from Milan to Ravenna for defensive purposes; Ravenna was surrounded by swamps and marshes, and Byzantine forces could easily reach it by sea. It was later the capital of the Ostrogothic kingdom in the fifth century. In 535, Justinian's general Belisarius invaded Italy and conquered Ravenna (540). It then became the seat of Byzantine government in Italy until 751, when the last exarch was killed by the Lombards. Ravenna has a unique collection of early Christian mosaics and monuments that brilliantly blend Greco-Roman tradition, Christian iconography, Byzantine influence, and European styles. Ravenna is sometimes called the "mosaic city" for the stunning examples adorning the walls of its churches and monuments.

266. (C) The Fourth Crusade (1202–1204) was led by the Venetians, already an economic power in the Mediterranean. The crusade was originally intended to conquer Muslim-controlled Jerusalem through an invasion of Egypt. However, the Venetians were less interested in reconquering the Holy Land than they were in weakening the economic power of the Byzantine Empire. A complicated dispute over politics and payments led the Crusaders to attack Constantinople in 1204. The western Europeans burned down a great part of the city; slaughtered many inhabitants; and wantonly destroyed monuments, statues, paintings, and manuscripts accumulated over a thousand years. The Crusaders never went on to Jerusalem. However, they did take piles of captured jewels, gold, and relics back to western Europe. The Byzantines did not regain control of the empire until 1261.

267. (E) The so-called "Plague of Justinian" was a pandemic that affected the Byzantine Empire (among other places) from 541 to 542 CE during Justinian's reign. It was one of the greatest plagues in history. It may have been some form of outbreak of bubonic plague, which was later linked to the Black Death of 1348. The epidemic probably killed about one-third of the empire's inhabitants; the actual number of deaths is uncertain. The loss of so many people created a shortage of army recruits in Byzantium and required the hiring of expensive mercenaries. Many farms were left vacant, and this greatly reduced tax revenues. Some scholars estimate that the plague killed more than 200,000 people in Constantinople alone, 40 to 50 percent of the city's population. New waves of the plague continued to strike until the eighth century. One estimate places the worldwide death toll from the Plague of Justinian as high as 25 million people.

268. (D) Justinian was the first Byzantine emperor to try to codify Roman law. The result was a law code known as the *Corpus Iuris Civilis*, or Justinian's Code. The *Corpus Iuris Civilis* was issued between 529 and 534 CE, and it reduced the confusing number of legal decisions made by earlier emperors. The work as planned had three parts: the Code was a compilation of imperial enactments to that date; the Digest was an encyclopedia of mostly short extracts from the writings of Roman jurists; and the Institutes was a student textbook introducing the Code. All three parts, even the textbook, were supposed to have the force of law and be the only law. However, Justinian soon had to make more laws, and these New Laws are considered a fourth part of the *Corpus*. Justinian's Code, written in Latin, shaped church and commercial law and influenced legal scholars for centuries.

269. (A) *Monophysite* means "single-nature believer." The term refers to a Christian theological position that disputed the orthodox doctrine that Jesus's divine and human natures were equal but distinct. Monophysites believed that Jesus's divine nature took precedence over his human side, giving him essentially a single nature. The position was first popularly presented by Eutyches (380–c. 456 CE), who declared that Christ was "a fusion of human and divine elements." Eutyches and his doctrine were condemned at the Council of Chalcedon in 451. However, the Monophysites split off from the orthodox church to found independent churches in Egypt, Ethiopia, Armenia, and Syria. The theological debate between Monophysitism and the orthodox church was a continuous problem in achieving religious unity in the early Byzantine Empire. Varying degrees of the Monophysite position can still be found in the Syriac Orthodox Church, the Coptic Orthodox Church, and the Armenian Apostolic Church.

270. (A) Emperor Leo III put an end to a period of instability, successfully defended the empire against the invading Umayyads, and forbade the veneration of icons. He was a valiant soldier who, in 717 CE, led the Byzantine armies to victory in the Muslim siege of Constantinople. The emperor then seems to have decided that the misfortunes of the Byzantine Empire were punishments from God for the improper worship of icons. Leo was probably influenced by the Muslim view that forbids the representation of the human form for religious use. His civil law code, the *Ecloga* (Selection), written in Greek rather than Latin, was a handbook that influenced Byzantine law. Leo left a revived empire to his son, Constantine V. The Isaurian Dynasty ruled the Byzantine Empire until 802. (After the battle of Kleidion in 1014, the Byzantine emperor Basil II divided the defeated Bulgarian prisoners into groups of 100, blinded 99 men in each group, and left one man in each group with one eye to lead the others home.)

271. (A) Foreign merchants traded in the Byzantine Empire either at Constantinople or in border cities. The Byzantine government issued special privileges to certain nations and people—such as Venetians, Russians, Jews, and Syrians—regulating the fees they had to pay and the services they had to give. Foreign merchants from each nation lived in the city at state expense for about three months to complete their trading activities. The Venetians especially helped Byzantine trade with Latin Europe, and they received several specific benefits. For example, at the end of the 10th century, they bargained to reduce their customs duties per ship from 30 *solidi* to 2 *solidi* in exchange for the promise to transport Byzantine soldiers to Italy whenever the emperor commanded. Venetian traders were common after the First Crusade (1099) and had "factories" on the north side of the Golden Horn. Large numbers of western Europeans lived in Constantinople in the 12th century; one estimate placed the number of foreigners in the city in the 1170s at about 70,000 out of a total population of about 400,000.

272. (D) John Chrysostom (c. 349–407) was archbishop of Constantinople and an important early Christian theologian. He was famous for his eloquence, his attacks on the abuse of authority by church and political leaders, and his support of asceticism. He is often considered the greatest preacher in the early church, and after his death, he was given the Greek name Chrysostomos, meaning "golden mouthed." One of his regular topics was continued paganism in the Byzantine culture, and he often thundered against the theater, horse races, and the revelry surrounding holidays. He frequently attacked the "pitiable and miserable" Jewish people; some consider him a founder of Christian anti-Semitism. John Chrysostom is considered a "doctor of the church" and among the greatest of the Greek fathers.

273. (A) Kievan Rus was a medieval Slavic state, based in the city of Kiev, that included most of present-day Ukraine and Belarus and part of northwestern Russia. The state was situated at the center of interactions between the Vikings, Byzantines, Slavs, and Islamic Turks. Kievan power and influence grew steadily through the 10th and 11th centuries CE, but it was later weakened by civil wars and the state fell to the Mongols in 1237–1240. Vladimir I (reigned 980–1015) introduced Christianity to Kievan Rus, and the people adopted Greek Orthodoxy from the Byzantines. The reign of Vladimir's son, Yaroslav the Wise, represented the high point of Kievan Rus (1019–1054). The economy of the state was based on agriculture and on extensive trade with Byzantium, Asia, and Scandinavia. The Kievan people traded fur, animal hides, slaves, burlap, hemp, and hops for Byzantine wine, silk, steel blades, religious art, and horses. Kievan Rus also was connected to Byzantium through culture (especially architecture) and a shared religion.

274. (E) Stylites (from the Greek *stylos* meaning "pillar") were a type of Christian ascetics. In the early days of the Byzantine Empire, stylites stood on pillars preaching, fasting, and praying. They believed that the extraordinary privation and punishment they inflicted on their bodies was a form of self-crucifixion that would help ensure the salvation of their souls. The first stylite was probably Simeon Stylites the Elder, who climbed onto a pillar in Syria in 423 CE and remained there until his death 37 years later. Two other extremely famous stylites were Daniel the Stylite (409–493) and Saint Alypius (d. 640). There were stylites in the Byzantine Empire until the 12th century and in the Russian Orthodox Church until 1461. Some pillar hermits softened the extreme austerity by building a tiny hut on top of the column as a shelter against the sun and rain.

275. (C) Anna Comnena (1083–1153) was a Byzantine princess and scholar and one of the world's first female historians. She was the daughter of the Byzantine emperor Alexius I Comnena and Irene Doukaina. Although there is some dispute, it appears she plotted against her brother John II in order to make her husband (Nicephorus Bryennius) emperor. She was unsuccessful, and when her husband died, she retired to a convent, where she wrote *The Alexiad* (finished 1148). It is a historical account of her father's reign, including the First Crusade. In it, Anna criticized the western European Crusaders, who she thought were barbarians.

276. (D) Eunuchs were castrated men who held privileged positions in the Byzantine imperial court. They worked as civil servants, palace officials, or high-ranking army officials. Popular Byzantine opinion held that eunuchs were unfit for imperial power. Because eunuchs could not have children of their own, Byzantine emperors did not consider them a threat. By surrounding themselves with eunuchs, emperors tried to limit the possibility of revolutions and usurpations. The *parakoimomenos* (the one who sleeps beside the emperor's chamber) was an important Byzantine ministerial position usually reserved for eunuchs. Under Justinian in the sixth century CE, the eunuch Narses was a successful general in several campaigns. Basil Lekapenos, the out-of-wedlock son of the emperor Romanos I, was castrated when young. He served as chief administrator of the Byzantine Empire from 945 to 985, wielding great power and patronizing the arts. Romanos I also had his son Theophylact (917–956) castrated and made him patriarch of Constantinople in 933, a position he held until his death in 956.

277. (E) The battle of Manzikert was fought between the Byzantine Empire and Seljuk Turks in 1071 CE near present-day Malazgirt in eastern Turkey. The Seljuk Turks, under Alp Arslan, decisively defeated the Byzantines and captured Emperor Romanos IV Diogenes. This defeat essentially ended Byzantine authority in Anatolia and Armenia and allowed the Turks to populate Anatolia. The emperor had been unable to muster Byzantine troops because the *strategoi* were too busy defending their own districts. Instead, he relied on a mercenary army of Normans, Franks, Slavs, and even Turks. The result was a disaster for the empire; the Byzantines lost control over Anatolia, the heart of the empire and the major recruiting ground for soldiers. This weakened the empire's ability to defend its borders. As a result, it was limited to the area immediately around Constantinople and was never again a major military force. Historians are unanimous in dating the decline of Byzantine fortunes to this battle.

278. (B) Byzantine literature and art is almost entirely concerned with religious expression. According to one estimate, of the approximately 2,000 to 3,000 volumes of Byzantine literature that survive, only 330 consist of secular poetry, history, and science. The remaining volumes are sermons, liturgical books, theology, and devotional treatises. While some secular literature was produced between the ninth and twelfth centuries CE, the output is generally small. The only genuine heroic Byzantine epic is the *Digenis Acritas*, the most famous of the Acritic songs. These were heroic or epic poetry that emerged in about the ninth century to celebrate the exploits of the Acrites, the guards defending the eastern frontier of the Byzantine Empire.

279. (A) Procopius of Caesarea (c. 500–c. 565 CE) was a famous Byzantine historian from the time of Justinian. He accompanied the general Belisarius as his secretary in Justinian's wars and is considered the main historian of the sixth century. He wrote *The Wars of Justinian*, *The Buildings of Justinian*, and *The Secret History*. *The Secret History* covers the same years as the first seven books of *The Wars of Justinian* but was written later and never published. Procopius filled the scandalous *Secret History* with anecdotes and gossip regarding the private lives of Justinian and Theodora. The other answer choices are all Byzantine historians of a later date and lesser fame.

280. (D) Manuel I Comnenus (1118–1180 CE) was a Byzantine emperor who was eager to restore the empire to its past glories and so followed an extremely ambitious foreign policy. At one time or another, he made alliances with the pope, invaded Italy, and meddled in European diplomacy. Manuel allied Byzantium with the Second Crusade, supported and then controlled the Crusader states, and invaded Fatimid Egypt. He also placed the kingdom of Hungary under Byzantine control and attacked his neighbors in the west and the east. However, toward the end of his reign, Manuel suffered a serious defeat when the Seljuk Turks crushed his army at Myriocephalon. He liked western Europeans and gave them high positions in the Byzantine Empire. During his reign, the Genoese, Pisan, and Venetian merchant colonies in Constantinople grew dramatically. Byzantine power catastrophically declined after Manuel's death; some historians believe the causes can be found in his reign.

Chapter 9: Islam

281. (E) The Jews deny that Jesus is the promised Messiah. In the Koran, Jesus is a respected prophet, but Muslims are fiercely monotheistic. They base their faith on the worship of Allah, the one God. Muhammad (c. 570–632) saw himself as God's last prophet and the person charged with receiving and preaching God's final words to humans. Islam grew out of the traditions of Bedouin tribal society. It has different worship practices from Judaism, such as the feast of Ramadan, the *salat* (formal prayer), and the *hajj* (a pilgrimage to the holy city of Mecca). The other answer choices are basic principles of both Judaism and Islam.

282. (A) *Islam* is the Arabic word for submission. It was a religious movement begun by Muhammad during the seventh century on the Arabian peninsula. The religion depends entirely on individual faith and adherence to the Koran, because Muslims do not have priests, liturgies, or any intermediaries between God and humans. *Muslim*, the word for a follower of Islam, is the active participle of the same verb of which *Islam* is the infinitive. *Islam* means "voluntary submission to God"; believers demonstrate submission by worshipping God, following his commands, and rejecting polytheism. The word appears numerous times in the Koran (which means "recitation" in Arabic).

283. (A) Baghdad is located along the Tigris River; the city was commissioned by Caliph Al Mansur (714–775) in 762 to be the capital of the Abbasid Caliphate. The city's location gave it control over strategic and trade routes along the Tigris. Baghdad quickly eclipsed Ctesiphon (the capital of the Persian Empire), located about 20 miles to the southeast, and became an important cultural and commercial center of the Islamic world. The so-called House of Wisdom was a library and translation institution that played a crucial role in preserving and translating texts from the ancient Greek into Arabic. From the ninth to the thirteenth centuries, the Abbasids encouraged scholars to come to Baghdad and share information, ideas, and culture. In the Middle Ages, Baghdad may have been the largest city in the world, with an estimated population of a million people. The city is reflected at the height of its glory in the *Thousand and One Nights*. The Mongols destroyed Baghdad and massacred the population in 1258, beginning a long decline.

284. (D) Islam grew out of the loosely organized tribal society of the Arabian peninsula. Bedouin society formed few cities and had little political organization. Its members herded sheep or camels and traded or raided for other goods. Traditions and values were transmitted primarily through oral poetry and storytelling. The clan was the main social institution, and clans grouped together in tribes. Outsiders were typically viewed as rivals, and tribes constantly fought with one another. Bedouin male culture emphasized bravery in battle and generosity afterward; warriors often gave away the booty they acquired in combat. Women were sometimes part of this booty, and men frequently had more than one wife (polygyny). Mecca, a major desert oasis near the Red Sea, was an important commercial center. Meccan caravans sold Bedouin products, such as leather goods and raisins, to more urbanized areas in the north. Mecca also played an important religious role, because it contained a polytheistic shrine known as the Kaaba. The Quraysh tribe controlled the shrine and benefited by taxing pilgrims as well as selling them food and drink.

285. (D) The Fatimid Caliphate Dynasty was a Shiite dynasty that ruled North Africa and Egypt from 909 to 1171. It was the only major Shiite caliphate in Islam. The Fatimids named themselves after Fatima, the wife of Ali and Muhammad's only surviving daughter. They initially allied themselves with North African Berbers and established a state in 909 in present-day Tunisia. The founder of the dynasty, Ubayd Allah, controversially claimed to be the Mahdi (divinely guided messiah). In 969, the Fatimids conquered Egypt and, for the next hundred years, tried to take Damascus from the Abbasids. The Fatimids generally tolerated non-Shiite sects of Islam as well as Jews and Christians. The caliphate reached its apex in the 11th century, controlling northern Africa, Arabia, and even parts of Syria. However, internal anarchy, economic crises, and famines led to a decline. Saladin abolished the dynasty in 1171.

286. (B) The Seljuk Turks ruled parts of central Asia and the Middle East from the 11th to the 14th centuries. The Seljuks were originally one of a number of bands of Turkish nomads from the central Asian steppes. Tughril Beg (c. 993–1063), the grandson of the semi-legendary Seljuk, is usually considered the founder of the Seljuk Dynasty. He entered Baghdad in 1055 and was proclaimed sultan. The Seljuks, led by Alp Arslan, crushed the Byzantine army at Manzikert (1071) and occupied Anatolia. They also captured Jerusalem in 1071 and Antioch in 1085; this Seljuk expansion was the direct cause of the First Crusade (1096–1099). Alp Arslan's son, Malik Shah (reigned 1072–1092), ably administered this huge empire. In Persia, the Seljuks adopted the culture and made Persian the official language of the government. Around 1100, the Seljuk Empire began to fall apart; the attacks of the Turco-Mongols led to the final collapse in 1157.

287. (C) The Mughal Empire ruled much of the subcontinent of India from 1526 to 1827. The dynasty was founded by Babur (1483–1530), a Turkish chieftain who was a descendant of Tamerlane (Timur). In 1504, Babur captured Kabul and established a kingdom in Afghanistan. After failing to conquer Samarkand in 1512, he began southward raids into India. In 1526, he defeated the sultan of Delhi at a crucial battle at Panipat. He then captured Agra and Delhi and eventually nearly all of northern India. At its height, from about 1650 to 1725, the Mughal Empire extended from Bengal in the east to Baluchistan in the west and from Kashmir in the north to the Kaveri basin in the south—more than a million square miles in total. (Badr al-Jamali was an Armenian general under the Fatimids; Baibars was a Mamluk sultan of Egypt; Bayezid I was an Ottoman sultan; and Barkyaruq was a Seljuk sultan.)

288. (C) Sufism is a general term for several ascetic and mystical movements within Islam. Two central Sufi concepts are *tawakkul* (total reliance on God) and *dhikr* (perpetual remembrance of God). Sufism originally gained followers in opposition to the worldliness of the Umayyad Caliphate; the word *Sufi* first appears in the eighth century. An important early figure was Rabia al-Adawiyya (717–801), a woman who rejected heaven and hell and insisted instead that the love of God was the only valid form of worship. Sufi devotional practices vary widely. Many early Sufis lived in a cell in a mosque and taught a small band of disciples. Sufis believed that by self-discipline, asceticism, and concentration on God, it was possible to achieve a union with the divine. They often served as missionaries for Islam and helped spread the religion in Africa and Asia. Sufism particularly thrived between the 13th and 16th centuries; Rumi (1207–1273) was a noted Islamic poet and Sufi mystic. His followers founded the Mevlevi Order in 1273 in present-day Turkey and are known as whirling dervishes because of their famous practice of whirling as a form of *dhikr*. (*Dervish* is a common term for an initiate of the Sufi path.) Sufism has often faced opposition from orthodox clerics. However, a statement by leading Islamic scholars in 2005 specifically recognized Sufism as a part of Islam.

289. (E) The relative early freedom for women in Islam was severely curtailed by the Abbasid Caliphate. The male elite in Abbasid society believed that women possessed insatiable lust; therefore, men needed to be segregated from all women except those of their family. The Abbasids introduced the custom of the harem and the veil. A harem (from the Arabic for "forbidden place") refers to the sphere of women in a polygynous household. Wives and concubines (who were often slaves) of the Abbasid caliphs were confined to secluded quarters in the palaces that were forbidden to men. Women gradually disappeared from public records and events, as the ideal of secluding women became important for men who wanted to demonstrate their power. Urban women who appeared in public went accompanied by servants or chaperones and used a veil to discourage the attention of men. The use of the veil by Muslim women was customary only after the exposure of Islamic culture to Persian and Byzantine culture. Eventually, the practice of veiling (*hijab*) spread from upper-class women to urban and rural women of all classes. (Women in Islam were subject to their husbands, but they were not considered chattels.)

290. (D) A madrasa was a Muslim school for professors and their students, often attached to a mosque and funded by donations from the ruling elite. All-male classes interpreted the Koran and studied other literary and legal texts. Although most students paid fees to attend classes, some received scholarships. Visiting scholars attracted audiences by engaging in intellectual sparring with the professors. These institutions of higher learning in the Islamic world predated the creation of universities in Europe by several hundred years and are still common today.

291. (B) After Muhammad's victory at the battle of Badr (624), he gained new followers and consolidated his position in Medina. He had originally seen the Jews of Medina as allies. He referred to Jews (as well as Christians) as "people of the Book" who shared the core principles of his teachings. Muhammad anticipated the support of the Jews, but they did not convert to Islam as he expected. After the battle, he accused them of supporting hostile tribes. He eventually expelled, executed, or enslaved the Jewish population of Medina. However, the Koran states that the Jews were specially chosen by God, who raised many prophets among them, blessed them, granted them favors, and held them over all other nations.

292. (D) In seventh-century Arabia before Islam, women were traditionally viewed as the property of men. In some ways, women benefited from the expansion of Islam. In the early days of Islamic rule, women could receive an education, engage in business activities, and participate in public life. The Koran provided for the care of widows and orphans, outlawed female infanticide, gave women the right of inheritance, and proclaimed that as believers, men and women were equal. At first, Muslim women even joined men during the five prayer periods. However, both the Koran and the sharia (Islamic law) established a patriarchal society. Islamic law recognized patriarchal inheritance; to ensure the legitimacy of heirs, women were subjected to control by male members of their household. Both the Koran and the sharia allowed Muslim men to follow the example of Muhammad and acquire up to four wives (although a man was obliged to support them and treat them equally); women were permitted only one husband. A woman's testimony in court was given only half the weight of a man's. Beginning in the eighth century, women began to pray separately from men. Islam, like Judaism and Christianity, retained the practices of a patriarchal society in which women's participation was extremely circumscribed.

293. (A) Janissaries were elite infantry soldiers in the Ottoman Empire. The corps was formed in the 14th century and consisted mostly of war captives and Christian boys levied through the *devshirme* system. All recruits were converted to Islam and trained under the strictest discipline. They became the first Ottoman standing army, partially replacing tribal warriors (*ghazis*) whose loyalty and morale were not always guaranteed. The Janissary corps was distinctive because the soldiers wore unique uniforms, received salaries for their service, marched to music, and lived in barracks. In return for their loyalty, they received booty during wartime and enjoyed a high living standard and respected social status. Ottoman military bands, primarily composed of Janissaries, are some of the oldest military marching bands in the world. Ottoman *mehter* music, which for centuries accompanied the Ottoman army into battle, is noted for its powerful percussion and shrill winds combining *kos* (giant timpani), *davul* (bass drum), *zurna* (a loud shawm), trumpets, bells, and cymbals. The Janissaries constituted the backbone of the Ottoman army and soon acquired the power to make and unmake sultans.

294. (A) *Koran* means "recitation" in Arabic and is the name of the holy book of Islam. In 610, Muhammad began hearing a voice that he identified as that of God, or Allah. The voice ordered him to preach and live by God's words and to convert other people. Muslims believe the Koran is God's verbatim revelation as told to Muhammad by the angel Gabriel and then recited by Muhammad to others until his death in 632. Shortly after his death, the Koran was compiled into a single book by order of Abu Bakr, the first caliph. The earliest revelations emphasize the mercy and goodness of God, but eventually, the revelations covered all of human existence. The Koran is divided into 114 chapters of unequal length called *suras*. The suras are usually classified as either Meccan or Medinan, depending on the place and time of revelation. The chapter arrangement is not connected to the sequence of revelation; longer chapters appear earlier in the Koran while shorter ones appear later. For Muslims, the Koran contains the legal and moral code by which they should live. The Koran's revelations stress the importance of a personal relationship with God, the obligations of the rich to the poor, and the certainty of either reward or punishment on Judgment Day. The Koran assumes familiarity with the stories in Jewish and Christian scriptures. It summarizes some of these stories, covers others at length, and presents entirely different accounts and interpretations of others.

295. (C) The Umayyad Caliphate was the second of the four major Arab caliphates (the first was the Rashidun from 632 to 661). Under Abd al-Malik (646–705), the Umayyad Caliphate reached its peak, and Damascus became the capital of the Muslim world. Muslim armies overran most of Spain, invaded parts of India, and expanded to Samarkand and Tashkent in central Asia. At its greatest extent, the caliphate covered more than five million square miles, making it one of the largest empires in world history. Arabic became the official state language, and documents and currency were issued in that language. Thus, the Umayyads brought together areas that had not been linguistically united. They constructed famous buildings such as the Dome of the Rock at Jerusalem and the Umayyad Mosque at Damascus. They also essentially transformed the caliphate from a religious institution to a secular, dynastic one. Decline began in the early eighth century with some military setbacks, a financial crisis, and recurring revolts and civil war. The Muslim advance into France was halted at Poitiers (732), and Arab forces in Anatolia were destroyed (740). When the Abbasids overthrew the caliphate in 750, they tried to kill all members of the Umayyad house. However, one survivor, Abd ar-Rahman, escaped and established himself as a Muslim ruler in Spain (756), founding the dynasty of the Umayyads of Cordoba, which lasted until 1031.

296. (C) The Ottomans were one of several Turkish tribal confederations in central Asia that emerged during the breakdown of the Seljuk Empire. As converts to Islam, the Ottomans raided Byzantine territory and gradually reduced the Byzantine Empire to the city of Constantinople. Bursa fell in 1326 and Adrianople (present-day Edirne) in 1361; each in turn became the capital of the expanding Ottoman Empire. In the Balkans, the Ottomans took advantage of Christian disunity, allying with the Bulgarians and even some Serbian princes to win the battle of Kosovo in 1389 and destroying the last Christian resistance in the region. They secured almost complete control of southeastern Europe in 1396 when they crushed a crusading army sent by Pope Boniface IX at Nicopolis. In 1453, they finally succeeded in conquering Constantinople. Within a century, the Ottomans had changed from an obscure nomadic tribe to the heirs of the oldest surviving European empire. Their superior military organization aided their rapid success, but they also benefited from the weakness and disunity of their foes. Ottoman expansion reached its peak in the 16th century under Selim I (1467–1520) and Suleiman I (the Magnificent), who reigned from 1520 to 1566.

297. (D) Although the regions of the Islamic world were politically and culturally diverse, they maintained a measure of unity through trade networks and language. The principle bond was Arabic, the language of the Koran and of poetry. Arabic was also the language of commerce and government from Baghdad to Cordoba. Despite political differences, borders were usually open. With few regulations and no national barriers to trade, merchants often dealt in exotic goods across widespread trade networks.

298. (E) Muslims are required to make the hajj to Mecca (not Medina) if they are healthy and have the financial resources to do so. The hajj is a demonstration of the solidarity of the Muslim people and their submission to Allah. The other answer choices are requirements of the Five Pillars of Islam that every Muslim is expected to obey.

299. (A) Omar Khayyam (1048–1131) was a multitalented Persian poet who lived at times in Nishapur (in present-day Iran), Samarkand, and Bukhara (in present-day Uzbekistan). He was one of the most famous astronomers of medieval Islam and also wrote an important book on algebra that includes a geometric method for solving cubic equations. However, he is best known for his poetry, especially through the very loose translations of Edward Fitzgerald (1809–1883). Fitzgerald made Omar Khayyam the most famous "Oriental" poet in England and the United States in the *Rubaiyat of Omar Khayyam*. This famous excerpt (quatrain 12) from Fitzgerald's third through fifth editions is the most well-known quatrain (*rubaiyaas*), but it is not a direct translation. There are many 20th-century translations, and each renders this quatrain differently.

300. (B) Despite political differences, Muslims were free to trade across the entire Muslim world with no national barriers and few regulations. Muslim merchants bought tin from England, salt and gold from Timbuktu, amber and copper from Russia, and slaves from every region. They also developed letters of credit (*sukuk* or *sakk*) that were the predecessors of modern checks. However, double-entry bookkeeping (in which every transaction or event changes at least two different ledger accounts and the entries are usually labeled *credit* and *debit*) was invented in Italy in the late Middle Ages. The earliest example is from a Florentine merchant at the end of the 13th century. It was widely used by Italian banks by the 15th century and was an important part of the commercial expansion of Europe.

301. (B) Mamluks were Turkish slaves or freedmen who were trained as professional mounted soldiers and famous for their horsemanship and courage. In the late ninth century, the Abbasid caliphs came to depend on independent military commanders who led armies of Mamluks. These soldiers were paid to maintain their mounts and arms, and many gained fame and high positions at the courts of regional rulers. The Mamluks, unlike the Byzantine *strategoi*, were highly mobile. They were not tied to specific estates but instead were paid from rents collected by the local government. They were organized into tightly knit companies bound by devotion to a specific general and by strong camaraderie. For these reasons, they easily moved from ruler to ruler for higher pay. They achieved their greatest success in Egypt in the 13th century, where they resisted the crusade launched by King Louis IX of France. In 1254, they established their own dynasty in Egypt, expanded eastward to defeat the Mongols at Ayn Jalut (1261), took control of Syria, and drove the Crusaders out of the Outremer (1302). The Mamluks retained power in Egypt into the 19th century.

302. (C) Maimonides (1135–1204), also known as Moses ben Maimon, was the most influential Jewish thinker of the Middle Ages. He was born in Cordoba but fled the city for Morocco when the Almohads began persecuting Jews. He lived briefly in Israel before settling in Cairo about 1168 and serving as the official leader (*nagid*) of Egyptian Jewry. Maimonides was a famous physician, rising to the position of court doctor to the sultan Saladin and the royal family. In his medical writings, he described conditions such as asthma, diabetes, hepatitis, and pneumonia, and he emphasized moderation and a healthy lifestyle. His greatest rabbinic work, the 14-volume *Mishneh Torah* (1180), was a systematic statement of Jewish law and belief and is still used as a standard compilation of halakha (the collective body of Jewish law observed by orthodox Jews). His greatest philosophical work, *Guide for the Perplexed* (1190), was written in Arabic and attempted to rationalize Jewish theology by using Aristotle's principles tinged with Neoplatonist ideas. The book also formulated a proof of the existence of God and tried to clarify baffling religious and philosophical (especially metaphysical) problems.

303. (B) Sunni Muslims ruled al-Andalus, the Arabic name given to the territory in Spain (and Portugal) governed by Muslims between 711 and 1492. Al-Andalus generally consisted of the central and southern part of Spain, but the boundaries underwent constant change because of attacks from Christian kingdoms to the north. The Spanish emirate at Cordoba was created at the beginning of the Abbasid Caliphate in 756 by Abd al-Rahman (731–788), a member of the Umayyad family who fled to Spain. The Muslim rulers in al-Andalus governed a wide range of peoples, including Jews and Christians. Many Christians adopted so much of the new language and culture that they were called Mozarabs ("like the Arabs"). The official Cordoba Caliphate began when Abd al-Rahman III (c. 889–961) took the title of caliph in 929. The caliphate declared that all religious groups in al-Andalus possessed religious freedom of worship and an equal opportunity to rise in the civil service. This openness helped make Cordoba the cultural center of al-Andalus. It was noted for its mosques and as a center of the translation of ancient Greek texts to Arabic, Latin, and Hebrew. Important advances in science, history, geography, and philosophy also occurred during the Cordoba Caliphate. In 1031, the caliphate broke up, as rulers of small, independent regions called *taifa* took power.

304. (B) The Toledo School of Translators was a group of scholars that worked together in Toledo (in present-day Spain) in the 12th and 13th centuries. These scholars translated many important philosophical and scientific works from Arabic, Greek, and Hebrew into Latin, a language available to every educated person in Europe. Traditionally, Toledo was a center of multilingual culture and important as a hub of learning and translation. The most famous translator was probably Gerard of Cremona (c. 1114–1187), who translated Arabic scientific works found in the abandoned Arab libraries of Toledo. His translated books include Ptolemy's *Almagest*; many of the works of Aristotle; and books by Archimedes, Euclid, al-Kindi, al-Farabi, and Rhazes. Other important translators were John of Seville, Michael Scot, Yehuda ben Moshe Cohen, and Dominicus Gundissalinus. The work attracted scholars from all over Europe, who came to Toledo to study books of astronomy, astrology, algebra, medicine, optics, and philosophy that had not been available to Europeans for centuries.

305. (E) The principal medieval Islamic architectural types are the mosque, the tomb, the palace, and the fort. All four types are represented in the answer choices, and all are UNESCO World Heritage sites. The Taj Mahal is a mausoleum located in Agra, India. It was built by the Mughal emperor Shah Jahan from 1632 to 1653 in memory of his wife. It is the finest example of Mughal architecture, a style that combines elements from Persian, Turkish, and Indian architectural styles. The Alhambra is a palace and fort in Granada, Spain. It was constructed in the mid-14th century by the Muslim rulers of the emirate of Granada. The Selimiye Mosque is an Ottoman mosque in Edirne in European Turkey. The mosque was commissioned by Sultan Selim II and built according to plans by the famous architectural genius Mimar Sinan between 1568 and 1574; Sinan considered it his masterpiece. He was the chief Ottoman architect for the sultans Suleiman I, Selim II, and Murad III, and he built more than 300 major structures. Sankore Madrasa is one of three ancient centers of learning located in Timbuktu. Along with three ancient mosques, it makes up the famous medieval University of Timbuktu. (The Cairo Geniza is a collection of more than 250,000 Jewish documents and manuscript fragments found in the *geniza* (storeroom) of the Ben Ezra Synagogue in Cairo, Egypt.

306. (E) Mecca, in present-day Saudi Arabia, is the holiest city of Islam and the birthplace of Muhammad. It is located in a narrow valley about 45 miles from the Red Sea port of

Jidda. Even before Islam, the city was a center of commerce and a place of great sanctity for polytheistic Arab sects. Meccan caravans sold Bedouin products to more urbanized areas in the north. The Kaaba, a religious shrine surrounded by 360 idols, served as a sacred place where violence was prohibited. The Quraysh tribe controlled the shrine and benefited by taxing pilgrims as well as selling them food and drink. Muhammad's flight (*Hijra*) from Mecca in 622 began the rise of Islam. In 624, he led an outnumbered force to ambush a huge Meccan caravan. The small battle of Badr had large consequences; Muhammad's followers killed 49 Meccans, took numerous prisoners, and confiscated rich booty. The battle of Badr was a great triumph for Muhammad, and he consolidated his position in Medina. In 630, he captured Mecca with 10,000 men, assuring the Quraysh of leniency and offering alliances to its leaders. He destroyed the idols and declared Mecca the holiest site in Islam and the center of Muslim pilgrimage. He also declared that no non-Muslim would be allowed inside the city so as to protect it from the influence of polytheism. Although Mecca never lost its sanctity, it declined in commercial importance after its capture by the Umayyads in 692.

307. (D) Henri Pirenne (1862–1935) was a Belgian historian concerned with the socio-economic history of medieval Europe. The Pirenne thesis tried to date the point of transition from the Roman Empire to the Middle Ages and was spelled out in his posthumous essay titled *Mohammed and Charlemagne* (1937). Pirenne argued that real change in Europe came with the rise of Islam and not the German invasions. He believed the Roman Empire was mainly a maritime domain oriented around the Mediterranean; the sea provided trade routes, political administration, and military supervision. He hypothesized that the Muslim conquest of northern Africa split the Mediterranean world in two and cut western Europe off from markets in the east. As a result, individual regions in Europe could no longer produce some goods for market and use the proceeds from their sale to buy other needed goods. Instead, each region had to be self-sufficient, and a subsistence economy developed in Europe in the eighth century. Trade and urban life declined, and the Carolingians created a local land-for-service, self-sufficient economy that became the basis for medieval society. Pirenne's thesis has been widely attacked and partially discredited over 75 years, but it remains an important conceptual tool to envision the impact of the rise of Islam on western Europe.

308. (A) When Muhammad unexpectedly died of an illness in 632, a succession crisis followed. The first caliphs did not come from the traditional elite but from the new circle of men close to Muhammad who had been participants in the *Hijra*. The first two caliphs ruled peacefully, but the third was not so lucky. Uthman (reigned 644–656) was a member of the Umayyad family and a son-in-law of Muhammad. His reign aroused discontent, and he was accused of favoritism in distributing offices and revenues. His opponents supported Ali, also a son-in-law of Muhammad, a member of the Hashim clan (to which Muhammad had belonged), and the husband of Muhammad's only surviving child (Fatimah). After a group of soldiers murdered Uthman, a civil war broke out between the two factions. Ali was killed by one of his own followers, and the Umayyad caliphs remained in power until 750. However, the faction supporting Ali (the Shiites) refused to accept the caliphs who were supported by mainstream Muslims (the Sunni). Shiites saw Ali as a symbol of justice and righteousness, and they awaited the arrival of the true leader, the imam, who would only come from the house of Ali. (Eschatology is a part of theology that deals with death, judgment, and the final destiny of the soul and humankind.)

309. (D) A hadith (also plural) is a saying or an act that is ascribed to Muhammad or that had his tacit approval when it was said or done in his presence. Hadith are regarded by traditional Islamic legal schools of thought as important tools for understanding the Koran, and for a thousand years, they have been viewed as second only to the Koran as a source of authority. Modern scholars continue to refer to hadith in matters of Islamic law and history. Hundreds of hadith—too many to be taken seriously—appeared after Muhammad's death. Abbasid scholars determined which hadith were authentic and should be followed and which hadith were simply composed for political or theological purposes. In the eighth and ninth centuries, Islamic scholars evaluated hadith and gathered them into large collections. They carefully judged the chain of transmission of the hadith, as well as considering the content as a source of religious authority. Hadith exist in two main collections corresponding to the Sunni and Shiite divisions within Islam.

310. (B) The Arab (Oriental) slave trade originated before Islam and lasted more than a thousand years. There were several main sources of slaves. Native Africans might be sent across the Sahara, Red Sea, or Indian Ocean, and non-Muslim prisoners might be captured in jihad. The first Muslims took a practical view of slavery. The Koran did not abolish it; in fact, Muhammad bought, sold, and owned slaves. However, the Koran did preach that slaves must be treated kindly, and later caliphs discouraged the enslavement of free Muslims. However, as Muslim armies swept across India, North Africa, and Spain, rebellious people in the lands they conquered were often enslaved. Arab rulers in Africa sometimes conducted raids to the south and captured slaves by claiming that their raids were jihads. They sold some of these African slaves to Islamic areas such as Persia or Arabia; others were purchased by Christians in present-day Spain, Portugal, and Italy. The Arab slave trade was never as large as the European transatlantic slave trade. However, an average of about 10,000 slaves left Africa across the Sahara, Red Sea, and Indian Ocean every year for centuries. It is impossible to be precise, but most estimates claim that between 8 and 20 million Africans were enslaved by Arab slave traders between 650 and 1800. Arabs also enslaved substantial numbers of Europeans; perhaps as many as a million were captured by North African raiders between 1500 and 1800.

311. (C) Ibn Sina (980–1037), known in Europe as Avicenna, wrote books on logic, the natural sciences, and physics. He wrote more than 400 treatises, of which about 240 have survived. Of his surviving works, approximately 150 are philosophical in nature and 40 concentrate on medicine. His *Canon of Medicine* organized earlier Greek and Arab treatises and reconciled them with his own experiences as a doctor. Avicenna noted the contagious nature of some infectious diseases and discussed how to test new medicines effectively. *The Canon of Medicine* was translated into Latin and then spread in manuscript and printed form throughout Europe. It remained a standard medical textbook in Europe until the 17th century. Avicenna also wrote *The Book of Healing*, an encyclopedia of science and philosophy that became another popular textbook in Europe. (Rhazes [865–925] wrote *The Comprehensive Book of Medicine*, which distinguished between measles and smallpox and was also popular in Europe. Albucasis [936–1013] wrote an encyclopedia of medicine that included descriptions and diagrams of more than 200 surgical instruments, many of which he developed. The surgery section was translated into Latin by Gerard of Cremona in the 1100s and was still being reprinted in the 1770s.)

312. (C) The Macedonian renaissance was a Byzantine intellectual movement that lasted from about 870 to 1025; it takes its name from the imperial dynasty from Macedonia that began with Basil I. The Carolingian renaissance describes the cultural explosion in the empire of Charlemagne and the kingdoms of the Carolingian Dynasty (northern and western Europe) in the ninth century. Political unification during the eighth century preceded the Macedonian, Islamic, and Carolingian renaissances that began in the ninth century. The consolidation of political power and the wealth of rulers in these three regions allowed for the sponsorship of art and scholarship. This trend also created centralized communities of scholars, such as the Great House of Study in Baghdad. The Islamic renaissance was particularly dazzling in urban centers such as Cordoba and Cairo. Compared to the ninth-century Byzantine and European movements, the scholars of the Islamic renaissance were more interested in mathematics. Most of the mathematical knowledge of medieval Europe came from the writings of Al-Khwarizmi and Ibn al-Haytham (Alhazen), who wrote studies on cubic and quadratic equations. So great was Muslim mathematical prestige that the numbers one, two, and three—although they were invented in India—were known as Arabic numbers when they were introduced to western Europe in the 12th century.

313. (E) Rodrigo Diaz (c. 1043–1099), also known as El Cid, was born into the lowest rank of Castilian nobility. In 1081, he was exiled from the court of Alfonso VI of Leon and Castile and signed up with with the Islamic emir of Saragossa. He commanded this Moorish army for several years with great success; there was nothing unusual in such cross-religious alliances until the invasion of the Almoravids. While working for the emir, he received the Arabic title of sayyid (lord), which was Hispanicized as Cid. After the Christian defeat at the battle of Sagrajas (1086), Alfonso VI talked El Cid into commanding a combined Christian and Moorish army against the Almoravids. El Cid used his military and political skills as well as his knowledge of Spanish Muslim politics to create his own fiefdom in the coastal city of Valencia. He managed to fight off the Almoravids and held the city until his death in battle in 1099. El Cid's military exploits made him a mythic folk hero who has been immortalized in plays, movies, folktales, and songs.

314. (A) At Manzikert (1071), Seljuk Turks under Alp Arslan annihilated Byzantine forces, and Muslims took control of almost all of Anatolia. After Manzikert, the Byzantines were never again a major military force. At Hattin (1187), Saladin crushed King Guy of Jerusalem and ended any European control of the Holy Land. As a direct result of the battle, Islamic forces reconquered Jerusalem; Europeans would not regain it until World War I. At the second battle of Taraori (1192), Muslim Afghans defeated the Rajputs and took control of northern India. The area would be ruled by Muslims until the fall of the Mughal Dynasty in 1857. At Constantinople in 1453, the Ottoman Turks finally destroyed the Byzantine Empire and opened Europe to the spread of Islam. The Ottomans would be the dominant Muslim group until the 20th century. The exception to these victories was Tours (Poitiers) in 732. At this battle, Charles Martel defeated Abd ar-Rahman and ended the Muslim threat to western Europe.

315. (C) Islamic thinkers had a tremendous influence on medieval Europe. Most mathematical knowledge of medieval Europe came from the writings of Al-Khwarizmi. His book on equation theory (written c. 825) became so well known in Europe that the word *al-jabr* in the title became the English word *algebra*. Ibn al-Haytham (965–c. 1040), known in Europe as Alhazen, contributed to the principles of optics. His *Book of Optics* (1021) was famous for his early use of an experiment based on the scientific method. Alhazen rejected Ptolemy's theory that light was emitted by the eye, insisting instead that light rays entered the eye. The Latin translation of his *Book of Optics* influenced many later European scientists, including Roger Bacon and Johannes Kepler. Ibn Sina's (Avicenna's) *Canon of Medicine* was the most advanced medical knowledge in Europe until 1500, and Ibn Rushd (Averroes) wrote important commentaries on Aristotle that greatly influenced European philosophy.

316. (D) *Jihad* is an Arabic word for "striving" or "struggle," although it is typically translated into English as "holy war." A person engaged in jihad is called a mujahid (plural, mujahideen). The word *jihad* appears 41 times in the Koran, usually in an expression meaning "striving in the way of God." Jihad is a principal religious duty of Muslims, but it is not one of the Five Pillars of Islam. Muslims use the word to refer to three different types of struggles: an internal struggle to maintain faith, the struggle to improve Muslim society, or the struggle to defend Islam. In the last sense, jihad grew out of the traditional Bedouin tribal practice of seizing booty from other peoples. In medieval Islam, Muslims were allowed to enslave non-Muslim prisoners taken in jihad. In 1302, the famed Muslim jurist Ibn Taymiyyah issued the Mardin fatwas in which he declared that jihad against the Mongols was not only permissible but obligatory, even though the Mongols had converted to Sunni Islam. He based this ruling on the grounds that the Mongols were not true Muslims, because they used the Yassa code rather than sharia, so they were living in a state of pre-Islamic pagan ignorance. Historically, Sunni and Shiite Muslims have forbidden acts of suicide, kidnapping, and war against civilians.

317. (A) Ibn Battuta (1304–c. 1369) was a Moroccan Islamic scholar and traveler known for his vast travels, which he wrote about in *Rihla* (The Journey). His journeys spanned more than 20 years and covered almost the entire known Islamic world. Nearly everything that is known about Ibn Battuta's life comes from his own writings; he set out from his native Tangier on the hajj to Mecca in 1325 and did not return to Mecca until 1349. According to one estimate, he traveled more than 75,000 miles, a record that may not have been surpassed until the 1800s. His travels reveal the webs of interconnection that stretched across the Muslim world from Spain to China and from Kazakhstan to Tanzania. (Nur ad-Din [1118–1174] was a Muslim leader in Syria who fought against the Crusader kingdoms. Tariq ibn Ziyad was a Berber commander from northern Africa who began the Muslim conquest of Spain in 711. Hasan ibn Sabah [d. 1124] was a leader of the Nizaris, a heterodox Islamic sect. He is credited with organizing and training the Assassins. Hakim [985–1021] was a possibly insane Fatimid caliph famous for his persecution of Christians and Jews.)

318. (D) The Outremer (from the French word for "overseas") was the name for the Crusader states established after the First Crusade. The last major city of the Outremer was Acre, which had been captured by Christians in 1104 in the First Crusade. The Crusaders turned Acre into their chief port in Palestine, and it became the main port of the eastern Mediterranean. After the battle of Hattin, Saladin conquered Jerusalem and Acre; the Christians did not regain Jerusalem until the 1900s, but they reconquered Acre in the Third Crusade (1191). For the next hundred years, Acre was the Crusader base of operations and the capital of the kingdom of Jerusalem. In 1229, Acre was placed under the control of the Knights Hospitaller. It was the final stronghold of the Crusader states and fell to the Mamluks in 1291 after a bloody, 43-day siege. Although the crusading ideal continued for several more centuries in Europe, the capture of Acre marked the end of further crusades to the Holy Land. The Outremer continued to exist on the island of Cyprus, where the Latin kings schemed to recapture Jerusalem. However, they lacked the necessary money, men, and willpower and never succeeded. One last effort was made by King Peter I in 1365, when he successfully landed in Egypt and sacked Alexandria. Once the city was pillaged, however, the Crusaders speedily returned to Cyprus to divide up their booty.

319. (B) In 622, Muhammad made the *Hijra* to Medina, an oasis about 200 miles north of Mecca. This journey was crucial to his fledgling movement. At Medina, Muhammad found followers ready to listen to his religious message and to regard him as the leader of their community. (After Muhammad's death, the year of the *Hijra* (622) became the first year of the Islamic calendar.) However, if the Muslims wanted to expand, it was essential to take control of Mecca, a revered holy place. The Meccan merchants made considerable money from the pilgrims who came to honor the numerous Arab gods. The fierce rivalry between Mecca's clans and Medina's Muslims began to spill over into the rest of the Arabian peninsula as both sides competed to win converts. At the battle of Badr in 624, Muhammad and his outnumbered forces ambushed a Meccan caravan. The success gave him the prestige to convince other clans to convert. In 630, two years before his death, Muhammad and his followers conquered Mecca and created a government dedicated to the worship of the one God, Allah.

320. (B) Ibn Rushd (1121–1189), known in Europe as Averroes, was a Muslim philosopher, physician, and astronomer. He lived in Cordoba (present-day Spain) and Morocco when he was in favor with the caliphs. However, he was banished, probably for heresy. Averroes is most famous for his commentaries on Aristotle; his interpretations remained influential well into the European renaissance. He attempted to separate the domains of faith and reason in Islam, insisting that the two did not conflict. He declared that philosophy was the highest form of inquiry and tried to demonstrate the importance of engaging religion critically to achieve deeper insights and correct understandings of God. Averroes vociferously defended Aristotelian philosophy against claims from Islamic theologians such as al-Ghazili (1058–1111) that philosophy would contradict the teachings of Islam. Ironically, Ibn Rushd was far more influential in European Christian and Jewish circles, where he was known simply as the Commentator. In the University of Paris in the late 1200s, a group of philosophers who identified with the Aristotelian philosophy presented by Ibn Rushd were known as Averroists. These Christian philosophers sparked a controversy in the Christian church about the relationship between philosophy and theology and between reason and faith.

Chapter 10: Sub-Saharan Africa

321. (B) The Ghana Empire existed from about 800 to 1200 CE. It was located in present-day southeastern Mauritania and western Mali. The introduction of the camel, which preceded Islam by several centuries, brought about a gradual change in trade routes and permitted the resources of western Africa to be sent north for manufacturing. As these routes flourished under Arab and Berber traders, western African states grew around depots for the desert crossings. The Ghana Empire grew rich from the trans-Saharan trade in gold and salt. Jade was associated with distant locations such as China. Trade in ivory and animal skins was more important in the central and eastern regions of sub-Saharan Africa and the

Indian Ocean. Huge quantities of cowries from the Maldives were introduced to Africa during the period of slave trade after 1500 CE.

322. **(D)** Africa is extremely rich in natural resources, including minerals, wood, and rubber. However, many rivers are unfavorable to transportation and communication because of falls and rapids. Mountains, deserts, and rainforests also impede economic development. The pervasiveness of insects like mosquitoes (which carry malaria) and the tsetse fly (which carries "sleeping sickness") have helped destroy the effectiveness of manpower and animals in sub-Saharan Africa.

323. **(D)** The Kush lived in northeastern Africa in present-day southern Egypt and the Sudan. As early as 2000 to 1500 BCE, the kingdom of Kush may have controlled a 750-mile stretch (from the first to the fourth cataract) of the Nile Valley. After the collapse of the New Kingdom of Egypt, the Kushites invaded Egypt in the eighth century BCE, and Kushite kings ruled as pharaohs of the 25th Dynasty of Egypt for about a century. These pharaohs have been called the "black pharaohs" or the "Ethiopian pharaohs." The 25th Dynasty was based at Napata (in present-day Sudan) until the Kush were expelled in 656 BCE. The Kush then retreated to their own capital at Meroë (farther south than Napata), which became a center for ironwork and trade. Women apparently played a key role in the government of the Kushite kingdom, a situation almost unique in the ancient world. One of the largest of the Kushite pyramids was built for a woman, Queen Shanakdakheto (170–150 BCE). The kingdom of Kush began to fade as a power in the first and second century CE, sapped by the war with the Roman province of Egypt.

324. **(A)** Axum (also spelled Aksum) was a powerful, urban, Iron Age kingdom in Ethiopia that flourished from about 400 BCE to about 500 CE. The city of Axum was situated on a plateau about 7,200 feet above sea level. In its prime, Axum's commercial influence extended to both sides of the Red Sea. The kingdom of Axum had its own written language called Ge'ez and also developed a distinctive architectural style characterized by giant obelisks.

325. **(C)** Archaeological, linguistic, genetic, and environmental evidence all support the idea of a significant Bantu migration out of western Africa. However, many aspects of this migration, such as attempts to trace the exact route or to correlate it with genetic or archaeological evidence, are disputed. One possible interpretation suggests that about 2000 to 1500 BCE, farmers in the Niger and Benue River valleys in western Africa (the proto-Bantu) began migrating south and east. The earliest speakers settled along rivers and cultivated yams and oil palms. As they migrated, they took along their languages and their knowledge of agriculture and iron metallurgy. These Bantu migrations continued for at least 2,000 years. The evidence for this expansion is mainly linguistic; the languages of southern Africa are similar to each other, and scholars think it unlikely that they began diverging more than 3,000 years ago. The Bantu migration was a slow process, although major movement may have occurred between about 700 and 500 BCE. When a farming settlement could no longer support its population, part of the group left to form a new settlement. Bantu speakers gradually moved into areas occupied by nomads or hunter-gatherers such as the Khoisan (Bushmen) and the Mbuti (Pygmies). Some nomads simply moved on, and some adopted the more sedentary culture of the Bantu.

326. **(D)** Mansa Musa (fl. 1312–1337 CE) was a famous king (or emperor) of the Malian Empire. He was a devout Muslim, and his famous and extravagant pilgrimage to Mecca made him well known across northern Africa and the Middle East. According to Arab historians, Mansa Musa spent so much gold in Cairo that he inflated the currency for years. His reign probably brought the Malian Empire to its greatest wealth and power. He embarked on a grand building program, raising numerous mosques and madrasas in Timbuktu and Gao. Mansa Musa is especially known for his patronage of the Sankore Madrasa.

327. **(B)** The Kanem Empire (c. 1000–1380 CE) was located to the northeast of Lake Chad in present-day Chad, Nigeria, and Libya. A later incarnation, known as Kanem-Bornu, lasted as an independent kingdom until about 1900. Kanem's origins are the subject of dispute. However, in the early 11th century, Kanuri-speaking tribes moved into the area. Some of them may have converted to Islam, but the faith was not popular until the 13th century. Kanem's wealth came from its ability to control trade in the area from Libya to Lake Chad to Hausaland. Almost all commercial traffic in northern Africa passed through these strategic areas. Kanem's main exports were ostrich feathers, slaves, and ivory. The people rode horses imported from the north and had a powerful cavalry. Kanem reached the height of its power under the long rule of Mai Dunama Dibbalemi (1210–1248). Dibbalemi declared jihad against surrounding chiefs and began to conquer neighboring areas. However, over the next 100 years, a combination of overgrazing, civil strife, and attacks from neighbors led the rulers of Kanem to move to Borno, a Kanuri kingdom south and west of Lake Chad. This kingdom endured various ups and downs until it collapsed around 1900.

328. **(B)** Timbuktu is in present-day Mali about 10 miles north of the Niger River (not the Congo). The historic town is located where the Niger flows northward into the southern edge of the Sahara Desert. Timbuktu became a permanent settlement early in the 12th century. After a shift in trading routes, the city flourished from the trade in salt, gold, ivory, and slaves, and it became part of the Malian Empire early in the 13th century. At its peak, Timbuktu's many Islamic scholars established an important book trade that turned the city into a scholarly center in Africa. Books became more valuable than almost any other commodity, and private libraries grew in the homes of local scholars. Timbuktu soon had three universities and 180 Koranic schools. By the end of Mansa Musa's reign (c. 1340 CE), the Sankore Madrasa probably had the largest collection of books in Africa (possibly 400,000 manuscripts) since the library at Alexandria. Ibn Battuta, the famous Muslim traveler, visited Timbuktu in 1352 and admired its splendor and lack of crime. In the first half of the 15th century, the Tuareg tribes took control of the city for a short period until the expanding Songhai Empire absorbed it in 1468. It began a long decline after 1600, and today, Timbuktu is an impoverished town of about 60,000.

329. **(B)** The kingdom of Zimbabwe (c. 1100–1500 CE) dominated a major portion of southeastern Africa to the coast of the Indian Ocean. The archaeological discoveries of glass beads and porcelain from Asia demonstrate trade connections between Asia and Zimbabwe through the Arab port of Sofala. The capital city of Great Zimbabwe was near a trade route that connected the gold mines of central Africa with Sofala. Zimbabwe gained control of this route in the 1200s and prospered by collecting commercial taxes. The most impressive feature of Great Zimbabwe was its massive stone walls, built without mortar; the word

Zimbabwe means "stone dwelling" in the Shona language. The ruins at Great Zimbabwe are the largest ancient stone construction south of the Sahara. For 400 years, many scholars believed Indians, Egyptians, or Phoenicians built these impressive structures. They insisted that native dark-skinned people could not have been skillful enough to construct the buildings, carve the sculptures, and mold the pottery. The former white-controlled government of the country (when it was named Rhodesia) supported this view. However, excavations and carbon dating show that the structures were built by the Shona, a native Bantu-speaking group. The dating is unclear, with estimates ranging between the 9th and 15th centuries. Reasons for the decline of Great Zimbabwe in the 16th century are also unclear; internal strife, soil exhaustion, overgrazing, movement of trade routes, famine, and water shortages have all been suggested.

330. (A) The origins and early history of coffee are shrouded in mist. However, botanical researchers speculate that the history of the coffee bean began on the plateaus of central Ethiopia. The Ethiopian ancestors of today's Oromo people seem to have been the first to recognize the energizing effect of the coffee bean plant. However, the story of the ninth-century Ethiopian goatherd who supposedly discovered coffee did not appear in writing until 1671 and is not considered historical. From Ethiopia, coffee supposedly spread to Yemen, where it has been cultivated since the sixth century CE. The earliest evidence of coffee drinking appears in the mid-1400s in the Sufi monasteries of Yemen. By the 16th century, coffee drinking had spread to Cairo and Mecca and then to Persia, Turkey, and North Africa. As of 2008, Brazil was by far the largest coffee producer in the world (36 percent of total production), but Ethiopia was 4th (5 percent of total production); Uganda was 10th, and the Ivory Coast was 12th.

331. (B) The kingdom (or empire) of Ghana was located in southeastern Mauritania and western Mali, but the modern country of Ghana is named after the ancient kingdom even though there is no shared territory. The kingdom of Ghana (fl. c. 800–1200 CE) grew rich from the lucrative trans-Sahara trade in gold and salt. The ambiguity of the written Arabic sources and the archaeological record have led to several different theories regarding when and how Ghana declined and fell. One possibility is that long-term drought affected the ability of the land to sustain cattle and cultivation. Some historians suggest that Almoravid Muslims invaded Ghana from the north, although others suggest that the Almoravid influence was gradual. In the 11th and 12th centuries, new gold fields were mined at Bure (in modern Guinea) out of the commercial reach of Ghana. At the same time, new trade routes opened up farther east, and Ghana became the target of attacks by the Sosso and the Malinke. By about 1200 CE, Ghana was totally eclipsed by the Malian Empire.

332. (C) The cause of the Bantu migrations is disputed. Some possible causes include population increase or the introduction of new crops (such as the banana), which allowed more efficient food production. It is possible that the expansion was caused by the increasing sophistication of proto-Bantu culture, such as developments in agriculture, the making of ceramics, and the use of iron, which allowed new ecological zones to be exploited. Another theory is that climate changes made the present-day Sahara Desert too dry to live in. People moved south out of the Sahara and into the proto-Bantu's homeland, which in turn pressured the proto-Bantu to move to the forests of central Africa. However, scholars believe that the Bantu did not know livestock husbandry until after their migrations began;

they apparently learned it from other people they met in eastern and southern Africa, and they in turn passed the knowledge on to hunter-gatherers. Herding practices reached the far south of Africa several centuries before any Bantu-speaking migrants.

333. **(E)** Sonni Ali (born Ali Kolon) reigned from about 1464 to 1492 CE as the first great king of the Songhai Empire. He was the 15th consecutive ruler of the Sonni Dynasty (begun in 1335) to rule Songhai, which was centered around its capital city of Gao on the Niger River. Under Sonni Ali's rule, Songhai expanded to cover a great portion of the Niger River area and gained control of crucial trading cities such as Timbuktu (captured in 1469) and Djenne (captured in 1475). Sonni was noted for his repressive policy against the scholars of Timbuktu, as well as a fleet he built to patrol the Niger River. He mixed an unorthodox observance of Islam with traditional African animism. His historical legacy is disputed; Muslim historians called Sonni Ali "the Celebrated Infidel" or "the Great Oppressor," while Songhai oral tradition painted him as the righteous ruler of a mighty empire.

334. **(E)** The kingdom of Kongo (c. 1400–1914 CE) was located in western central Africa in parts of present-day Angola, the Republic of the Congo, and the Democratic Republic of the Congo. Sometime after 1000, the settled Bantu people began to create centralized states. The kingdom of Kongo was already a highly developed state at the center of a vast trading network when the first Portuguese explorers reached it in 1483. The kingdom was rich in natural resources, such as ivory, and manufactured and traded copperware, iron goods, cloth, and pottery. Early Portuguese travelers described the capital, Mbanza-Kongo, as perhaps the largest city in sub-Equatorial Africa. By 1600, the city had a population of about 100,000, almost 20 percent of the kingdom. This concentration permitted resources, soldiers, and surplus food to be available easily at the request of the king. At its greatest extent, the kingdom reached from the Atlantic Ocean in the west to the Kwango River in the east and from the Congo River in the north to the Kwanza River in the south.

335. **(B)** The Swahili coast is a stretch of east African coastline in present-day Kenya and Tanzania. It has been the site of cultural and commercial exchanges between eastern Africa and the outside world since at least the second century CE. Early coastal communities were formed by Bantu-speaking people who farmed and fished in the rivers. Between 500 and 800, they shifted to a sea-based trading economy and began to migrate south by ship. The incredible wealth generated by the trade in goods from the African interior—gold, ivory, and slaves—led to the development of powerful kingdoms and market towns such as Mogadishu, Sofala, Shanga, Kilwa, and Mombasa. By about 900, Africans, Arabs, and Persians who traded on the coast had developed Swahili, a language based on the Bantu language Sabaki that uses Arab and Persian loanwords. By the 1400s, many of the old mud-and-wood outposts had become fortified cities with stone and coral mosques, public buildings, and international residents. These cities had different fates. Mombasa, now the second-largest city in Kenya, has almost a million people. Shanga (Kenya), Kilwa (Tanzania), and Sofala (Mozambique) are little more than historic sites or archaeological ruins. (Abidjan is the largest city in the Ivory Coast [in West Africa] and, with 5 million people, the fourth-largest French-speaking city in the world.)

336. **(D)** The Songhai Empire ruled much of western Africa from the early 15th to the late 16th century CE. It was one of the largest Islamic empires in history, replacing the Malian

Empire that had ruled the same general area from about 1200 to 1400. The Songhai Empire included three of the greatest trading cities on the Niger: Gao (the capital), Timbuktu, and Jenne (present-day Djenne). All three had once been part of the Malian Empire. This gave the Songhai Empire effective control over the lucrative Niger River trade of gold, kola, grain, and slaves. The cities also belonged to the important trans-Saharan trade route system, which brought caravans of salt and copper, as well as goods from the Mediterranean coast. However, when the Portuguese established trading posts on the African coast, the importance of the trans-Saharan trade declined. The Songhai eventually fell in 1591 to a Moroccan force that used gunpowder and cannons.

337. (E) All four answer choices are African rivers with lengths of more than a thousand miles that are in the top 100 longest rivers in the world. The Zambezi (mostly in Zambia) and the Limpopo (mostly in South Africa) are the two longest African rivers that drain into the Indian Ocean. The Zambezi's most spectacular feature is Victoria Falls. The Orange River is the longest river in South Africa and, like the Limpopo, forms part of South Africa's international boundary. The Kasai River is a lengthy tributary of the Congo River, located in central Africa around Angola and the Democratic Republic of the Congo. Most of the Kasai River's watershed consists of equatorial rainforest.

338. (A) Originally, the Bantu were organized into agricultural communities based on family and kinship groups. These stateless societies of several hundred individuals were led by a family member who served as leader of the clan. Eventually, many of these villages came to be ruled by chiefs with varying degrees of power and authority. Within Bantu society, there were also age sets (or age grades), a type of cohort group that could sometimes have a great deal of political or military power. In general, rulers and religious leaders were the elite of Bantu society. Private property was an unknown concept to the Bantu; all property was held in common. Most Bantu were animistic and believed that spirits inhabited the features of the natural world; they especially revered the spirits of their ancestors. Tribal traditions were passed on orally through storytellers (sometimes called griots). Because much of the African topsoil layer was extremely thin and easily eroded, the land wore out frequently, necessitating frequent migration. Among the Bantu, both men and women might share the duties of planting and harvesting, but there were gender distinctions between various tasks. Traditionally, despite their important economic and social responsibilities, women's roles were subordinate to those of men.

339. (E) African converts to Islam did not totally give up their tribal beliefs. For example, Sonni Ali, the ruler of the Songhai Empire, mixed an unorthodox observance of Islam with traditional African animism. In general, the sub-Saharan elite were more interested in converting to Islam than the common people. Rulers were aware that acceptance of Islam was a commercial advantage; the Mali and Songhai were both Islamic empires. Contacts with Islam were generated by Indian Ocean and Mediterranean (not transatlantic) trade. Many African women had more privileges than Islamic women; this probably slowed sub-Saharan conversions to Islam.

340. (B) The Akan people are an ethnic group of more than 20 million in western Africa. Most Akan peoples live in Ghana, where they settled in migratory waves beginning in the 11th century CE; others live in the eastern part of the Ivory Coast and parts of Togo. From the 15th to the 19th century, the Akan people dominated gold mining and trade in the region. They were especially noted for the crafting of bronze or brass gold weights, which were created using the lost-wax technique. Akan gold weights were used as a system for weighing gold dust; the weights were made of brass, not gold. Each weight had a known measurement that ensured merchants traded fairly with each other. The status of a man increased if he owned a complete set of weights. Geometric weights are the oldest forms, dating from about 1400, while those made in the images of people, animals, and buildings first appeared around 1600.

341. (B) Axum was a powerful, urban kingdom in Ethiopia that flourished from about 400 BCE to about 500 CE. During the first century CE, it rose to prominence by trading through the port of Adulis to the Red Sea trade network and then to the Roman Empire. Trade through Adulis also connected Axum to India, Ceylon, Persia, and Arabia, making the kingdom an intermediary between Rome and Asia. The Axumites exported gold, ivory, rhinoceros horn, hippopotamus hide, and slaves. In exchange, they imported cottons; silks; knives; swords; drinking cups; metal for local manufacture; and luxury goods such as gold and silver plate, military cloaks, olive oil, and lacquerware. Axum reached its apogee under King Ezana in the fourth century CE. Around that time, the king and most of the population converted to Christianity. Ezana apparently expanded Axum to the north and east, conquering Kush and burning the Nile Valley city of Meroë. He constructed much of the monumental architecture of Axum, including a reported 100 stone obelisks (or steles), the tallest of which was 98 feet and weighed 517 tons. Axum flourished until about the sixth century; it declined in importance when the rise of the Persian Empire and then Islam redrew the trade routes.

342. (C) A fetish is an object of magic or a man-made object that has power over others. The concept is very important in African culture and art, although the term is considered outdated. The word *fetishism* was first used by the Portuguese sailors who landed in western Africa in the 16th century CE; it described the so-called primitive African culture's religion as the worship of inanimate things and animals. The word *fetish* derives from the French, via the Portuguese, and Latin; it has no root in any African language. For the next few centuries, Europeans often discussed African art and artifacts as the creations of "uncivilized" people. The term *fetish* is often used condescendingly in reference to a belief in superstitions and the sense that Europeans are above Africans in the scale of human progress. Some people would now consider the term derogatory. Instead, they suggest using descriptive terms such as "dance staff" and "fertility figure" to better address the functions of objects formerly known as fetishes. Nonetheless, even if the term is discarded, the concept is important. African art objects were rarely constructed solely as decoration or for display; their context and function is crucial to understanding them. Ironically, the term *fetish* has shifted from a derogatory description of African art to a term with extremely complex Freudian and Marxist applications.

343. (B) The banana originated in southeastern Asia; some scholars believe it was probably first domesticated in Papua New Guinea before 5000 BCE. Bananas were transported by Malayan sailors across the Indian Ocean to the island of Madagascar off the southeastern coast of Africa. This has been established by the similarities in the languages of Malaysia and Madagascar, although the date of the movement is disputed. From Madagascar, the banana spread north and west across Africa, probably following in reverse the path of the migratory Bantu. The arrival of the banana provided the additional calories and nutrients that caused an increase in the population of the Bantu. In modern times, bananas are among the most widely consumed foods in the world.

344. (D) Nok is a small village in present-day central Nigeria. The discovery of ancient terra-cotta figures there gave the name to Nok culture, which flourished from about 500 BCE to 200 CE. Nok terra-cottas are the oldest-known figurative sculpture south of the Sahara. Most Nok sculpture is hollow and coil-built like pottery, and it appears to be portrait heads and bodies. Nok head fragments are so unique that they were probably sculpted individually rather than cast from molds. However, there are certain common styles such as triangular eyes; bold, abstracted features; and elaborately detailed hairstyles and jewelry. The sophistication of Nok terra-cottas has led some scholars to believe that an older, as yet undiscovered tradition must have preceded Nok terra-cotta arts. Some pottery figures appear to depict subjects suffering from sicknesses such as elephantiasis and facial paralysis. These "diseased" faces may have been intended to protect against illness, but like the rest of Nok sculpture, their actual meaning is unknown. Nok culture was also one of the earliest African centers of ironworking. Yet it seems to have mysteriously vanished around 500 CE. Some scholars have speculated that the society eventually evolved into the later Yoruba kingdom of Ife.

345. (D) There are two species of camels: the dromedary, or Arabian camel, has a single hump, and the Bactrian camel has two humps. Camels were probably domesticated in the third millennium BCE. They appeared in the Sahara region in the second millennium BCE but seem to have disappeared around 900 BCE. The Persian invasion of Egypt under Cambyses (c. 525 BCE) reintroduced domesticated camels to the area. These Persian camels were not well suited to travel over the desert; rare trans-Sahara journeys were made in horse-drawn chariots. The stronger and more durable dromedaries first began to arrive in northern Africa in about the third century CE. However, it was not until the Islamic conquest of North Africa that these camels became common. Dromedaries were well suited to long desert journeys and could carry a great deal of cargo. This allowed substantial trade across the Sahara for the first time. By the late 700s, Islamic traders used camels to transport goods across the Sahara. Soon, some oases in the desert along the trans-Sahara trade routes began to turn into cities and towns. New occupations, including camel dealers and caravan traders, appeared.

Chapter 11: European Middle Ages

346. (C) Feudalism is a political and economic system based on the holding of all land in fief, or fee. In this type of system, vassals and tenants owe their lords homage as well as legal and military service. If they fail to provide these things, they risk forfeiting their land. Spain was part of the Islamic Empire and did not experience the extreme governmental disintegration that caused the rise of feudalism in other parts of medieval Europe. Japan developed a feudal political system from about 1100 to 1600. Japanese feudalism, with its code of Bushido (chivalry) and its daimyo (lords) and samurai (knights), was similar in many ways to feudalism in medieval western Europe.

347. (A) From 1378 to 1417, the Roman Catholic Church had two different popes at the same time. The popes disagreed over whether the papacy should be located in Avignon or Rome and how independent it should be of the rising French state. The Great Schism seemed impossible to solve until several scholars at the University of Paris came up with a new idea. They claimed that popes were not supreme in the Roman Catholic religion but had to obey the wishes of general councils. This was called the conciliar theory or conciliarism. The Council of Pisa (1409) deposed both popes—Gregory XII in Rome and Benedict XIII in Avignon—and chose a third pope, Alexander V, who died 10 months after his election. John XXIII (reigned 1410–1415) followed him. Now there were three popes, each with his own supporters and Sacred College of Cardinals. In 1414, after difficult negotiations, the Council of Constance forced Gregory XII to resign, deposed John XXIII and Benedict XIII, and elected yet another new pope, Martin V (reigned 1418–1431). When Martin V moved the papacy back to Rome in 1420, the Great Schism finally ended. This schism weakened the power of the pope and the prestige of the papacy, and it delayed reforms in the Catholic Church. This would play a part in the Protestant Reformation in the 1500s. (The term *Great Schism* is also sometimes used to describe the split between eastern and western Christianity in 1054.)

348. (C) The word *monasticism* comes from the Greek word *monos*, meaning "single" or "solitary." Christian monasticism began in Egypt during the fourth century when communities of men and women withdrew from everyday society to lead lives of self-denial. Monks initially lived alone but then began to form communities to provide mutual support in their quest for holiness. The first community of monks, or coenobitic monastery, was organized by Pachomius in Egypt in about 323 CE. The concept spread to western Europe, where it became popular after the creation of the moderate Rule of Saint Benedict in the sixth century. Christian monks and nuns often worked among the poor and needy of their communities, and they were famous for copying books by hand during the Middle Ages. Both monks and nuns are found in Buddhist monasteries.

349. (C) The Black Death probably originated in central Asia and entered Europe via Constantinople in 1348. The plague was recorded in China in 1331, and from Asia, it was carried west along trade routes by merchants and Mongol soldiers during the era of Pax Mongolica. Plague-infected fleas probably hitched rides in the manes of horses, on the hair of camels, or on black rats that snuck into cargoes or saddlebags. The Black Death is estimated to have killed about one-third of China's population and 25 to 50 percent of Europe's population. The effect in Europe varied widely by area, and population decline probably preceded the arrival of the plague. However, successive waves of plague spread across Europe in 1362, 1374, 1383, 1389, and 1400. Scholars estimate that the population of England in 1400 was only about half of what it was in 1300. Between 1340 and 1450, the population of Germany and Scandinavia is estimated to have declined from 11.5 million to 7.5 million and the population of France, Belgium, and Holland from 19 million to 12 million. These population declines led to labor shortages, social unrest, and a resulting rise in wages. Because of the social turmoil, the strict hierarchy of feudal society became somewhat more flexible.

350. (A) The concept of chivalry flourished in western Europe between about 1150 and 1500. The word is derived from the French *cheval*, meaning "horse," and it was applied primarily to aristocratic fighting men. Chivalry developed its basic institutions and conventions in the 12th and 13th centuries. The code was influenced by the church and popularized by artwork, music, poetry, and epics such as the *Song of Roland* and Thomas Mallory's *Le Morte d'Arthur*. Above all, the code of chivalry was about loyalty; a knight swore on his honor to serve his lord on earth and his lord in heaven. Initially, Christianity had a tremendous impact on chivalry, softening the virtues of ferocity, bravery, and courage in battle by preaching a degree of respect for human life and dignity. However, chivalry soon emphasized the secular attributes of the ruling military aristocracy in ceremonies such as the dubbing of the knight and the adoption of distinguishing emblems. The tournament became the iconic institution of the chivalric world, and it flourished despite the disapproval of the church. Because women attended tournaments, the ideas of courtly love and service to women also became entangled with the notion of the ideal warrior. Ultimately, chivalry slowly (and incompletely) softened the rude and violent European military society of the early Middle Ages.

351. (A) Ibn Rushd (1121–1189), known in Europe as Averroes, was a Muslim philosopher, physician, and astronomer. Averroes is most famous for his commentaries on Aristotle and his attempt to separate the domains of faith and reason in Islam. Ironically, he was more influential in European Christian and Jewish circles, where he was known simply as the Commentator. At the University of Paris in the 1260s and 1270s, Siger de Brabant, Boethius of Dacia, and some other scholars identified themselves with the Aristotelian philosophy presented by Ibn Rushd. Later known as Averroists, these Christian philosophers sparked a controversy in the Roman Catholic Church about the relationship between philosophy and theology, and reason and faith. The quotation is an attack on Siger de Brabant by Thomas Aquinas in about 1270. Averroist doctrines on personal immortality and the eternity of the world were eventually condemned by Christian authorities.

352. (B) The Saxons lived in ancient times in present-day northern Germany. From there, they expanded to the south and the west as far as present-day France and England. The Saxons were first mentioned in Roman writings in the second century CE. They were excellent farmers and warriors, and they built tentlike huts in forest clearings or near rivers. Saxon society was divided into nobles, free people, and serfs, and they held a regular meeting of all freemen who were able to carry arms. The Saxons followed the nature religion of the Germanic tribes of western Europe and Scandinavia; they believed in many gods, demons, and giants. Charlemagne, the famous king of the Franks, fought a bloody war with the Saxons from 772 to 804. In the end, Charlemagne defeated them, forced the people to convert to Christianity, and incorporated them into the Christian Frankish kingdom.

353. (C) The Rule of Saint Benedict is a book of guidelines written by Saint Benedict of Nursia (c. 480–553) for monks living together under the authority of an abbot. From about the seventh century, it was adopted by communities of women. For the last 1,500 years, it has been the leading guide in European Christianity for monastic living. Benedict's rule was heavily influenced by the writings of John Cassian in the east (c. 360–435) and is similar to the so-called Rule of the Master from the sixth century. However, Benedict tried to find a middle ground between individual zeal and strict regulation. The spirit of Saint Benedict's rule is summed up by *pax, ora, et labora* (meaning "peace, pray, and work"). His monastic code prescribed the monks' daily routine of prayer, scriptural readings, and manual labor. The rule divided the day into seven parts, each with a compulsory service for prayer and lessons. The required worship for each part of the day was called the office. Benedict's code did not isolate the monks from the outside world or deprive them of sleep, adequate food, or warm clothing. Instead, it established order, helped people live together in a community, and provided a system to support and strengthen a person's spiritual growth. Saint Benedict is sometimes regarded as the founder of European monasticism.

354. (A) The *Carmina Burana* is a collection of Latin songs attributed to students and wandering scholars of the 12th and 13th centuries. The collection was compiled by an anonymous editor in the mid-1200s, possibly at the abbey of Benediktbeueren in Bavaria. The songs poke fun at the existing order; rejoice in the poetry of love; and express delight in nature, youth, and student life. The work of the Archpoet (c. 1135–1165), one of the finest poets of the Middle Ages, is known through this collection. The poems are a famous product of the 12th century, revealing the vigor of urban communities and the enthusiasm of groups of students gathered around the schools and new universities of western Europe.

355. (E) Craftspeople and others involved in commerce formed guilds to protect their products and trades. Guilds were local collective organizations of artisans who usually worked in the same trade. These organizations served the economic, religious, and even social needs of their members. Guilds might maintain chaplains, pay for prayers for the dead, or serve as welfare institutions for sick and poor brethren and their families. Some began as prayer associations, but they evolved into organizations that guaranteed each member a place in the market by controlling production. Guilds did not eliminate competition between artisans, but they did regulate a member's work hours, materials, prices, and quality standards to prevent one artisan from gaining an unfair advantage over another. By the 13th century, guilds had become complex corporations defined by statutes and rules. Women did not ordinarily join them, even though mothers, wives, daughters, and female apprentices often knew how to make shoes, weave cloth, or sell goods.

356. (D) Henry II (1133–1189) attempted to assert royal authority by destroying the castles of English barons and confiscating their lands. He also extended monarchal power by expanding the royal system of courts. He enlarged the role of the crown in both criminal and civil cases through a system of judicial visitations called eyres. Under this system, royal justices made regular trips to every locality in England. Henry declared that some crimes, such as rape, murder, and arson, were so heinous that they came under the king's jurisdiction no matter where they were committed. The strongest opposition to Henry's system of royal courts came from the church, which had had a separate system of trial and punishment available to the clergy for centuries. The punishments for crimes given by these clerical courts were usually quite mild, so churchmen naturally refused to submit to Henry's courts. The ensuing contest between Henry II and his appointed archbishop, Thomas Becket (1117–1170), became the greatest battle between church and state of the 12th century. Eventually, Henry's nobles murdered Becket in Canterbury Cathedral in 1170, accidentally turning him into a martyr. Although Henry's role in the murder is unclear, he did public penance for the deed, and Becket's tomb at Canterbury became a national shrine. Ultimately, however, the royal courts continued to expand.

357. (A) The Fourth Lateran Council was an important ecumenical council held in 1215 and called by Pope Innocent III to reform clerical and lay discipline. One canon required Christians to attend Mass and to confess their sins to a priest at least once a year; another proclaimed marriage a sacrament. The Eucharist was declared to truly contain Christ's body and blood, even though it looked like bread and wine on the altar. The final canons stated that Jews and Muslims should wear special clothing so they could be distinguished from Christians. The longest canons dealt with heresy; the council laid down the mechanism of persecution and created a range of sanctions against those convicted. The sanctions originally designed for heretics were now adapted for use against Jews, lepers, homosexuals, prostitutes, and other minority groups that did not fit with the orthodox view of society. (Gutenberg's printing press dates from the 1440s. The Hundred Years' War began in 1337. The First Crusade occurred from 1096 to 1099. Thomas Becket was murdered in 1170.)

358. (C) Clovis (c. 466–511) was king of the Franks from 480 to 511 and is recognized as the founder of the French monarchy. During his rule, he won crucial victories over the Alemanni and the Visigoths and controlled most of Gaul, except for the Mediterranean coast. His power was enhanced by his conversion to Catholic Christianity at a time when most of the Germanic tribes were Arian Christians. Clovis combined elements of both the Germanic and Roman traditions. His law code, reflecting many traditional practices, was published in Latin and is known as the Salic law. Clovis's code promoted social order through clear penalties for specific crimes. He created a system of fines to defuse vendettas between individuals and clans. The most famous part of this system was the *wergild*, the payment a murderer had to make as compensation for his crime. Most of the money was paid to the victim's kin, but the king received about a third of the amount. The fine depended on the status of the person murdered: murdering a woman of childbearing age cost 600 gold coins, while a freeborn male was valued at 200, and ordinary slaves at 35. No distinction was made between murder and manslaughter until the Holy Roman imperial law in the 12th century. Payment of the wergild was gradually replaced with capital punishment around the 9th century; by the 12th century, the wergild had disappeared.

359. (C) In the Carolingian period, landlords began reorganizing their estates to run more efficiently. Heavy plows that could turn the thick northern soils came into wider use. Horses, which were more effective than oxen, often were harnessed to pull the plows. Most important was the transition from a two-field system to a three-field system. In the three-field system, farmers planted one third of the arable land with a winter crop, one third with a summer crop, and left the final third fallow to restore its fertility. The fields were rotated, so that land use was repeated only every three years. At any given time, two-thirds of the arable land was producing crops, as opposed to the two-field system, in which only half the land was used. The result was higher yields, surplus food, and a better standard of living for nearly everyone. From the end of the Middle Ages to the 20th century, European farmers practiced a three-year rotation of rye or winter wheat, followed by spring oats or barley, and then let the soil lie fallow.

360. (A) Musicians developed new musical forms in the 13th and 14th centuries that bridged the sacred and the secular. These innovations are most obvious in the spread of the motet, an example of polyphony (music that consists of the simultaneous performance of two or more melodies). By about 1000, vocal polyphony was used in church to add ceremonial importance to specific moments of the liturgy. Before 1215, most polyphony was sacred, and secular polyphony was not common before 1300. The motet originated in Paris and typically has three melody lines (or voices). The lowest, usually from a liturgical chant melody, has no words and may be played on an instrument rather than sung. The remaining melodies have different texts, whether Latin or French (or one of each), which are sung simultaneously. The Latin texts are usually sacred, whereas the French ones are secular, dealing with themes such as love and the seasons. The motets used the music of ordinary people, such as the calls of street vendors and the songs of students. In turn, polyphony influenced every form of music from the Mass to popular songs. Yet the church was not pleased to have secular music merging with the sacred. Certain instruments and types of music were actually forbidden in the church because they were related to secular music. Pope John XXII banished polyphony from the liturgy in 1322 and warned in his 1324 bull, *Docta sanctorum patrum*, against the unbecoming elements of this musical innovation.

361. (B) The absurdly named "Gothic" style of architecture began around 1135 with the project of Abbot Suger to remodel the Church of Saint Denis in Paris. By the mid-1200s, this style was adopted across Europe (with regional variations), and it lasted until the 16th century. Gothic was an urban architecture centered on the big cathedrals and did not rely on monastic patronage. The large, jewel-like, stained-glass windows and the soaring spires reflected the pride and confidence of wealthy urban merchants, artisans, and bishops. Gothic techniques included ribbed vaulting, which gave a sense of precision and order; the pointed arch, which produced a feeling of soaring height; and flying buttresses, which took the weight off the walls. The buttresses permitted much of the wall to be cut away and the open spaces filled with glass. Gothic sculpture, which decorated the cathedral, evolved from the stiff and elongated style of Romanesque into a spatial and naturalistic feel in the late 12th and early 13th centuries. Romanesque sculptures were carved on flat surfaces, whereas Gothic figures were sculpted in the round, turning, moving, and interacting with one another. Gothic sculpture often depicted complex stories or scenes. Nicola Pisano (c. 1220–c. 1284) was an Italian sculptor who is considered the pivotal figure between Gothic and Italian Renaissance sculpture. His most famous work was the pulpit of the Pisa baptistery. Gian Lorenzo Bernini (1598–1680) was the greatest naturalist sculptor of the Italian baroque style.

362. (D) The most profound challenge to papal authority in the late Middle Ages came from Bohemia. John Huss (c. 1369–1415) was a Czech religious reformer who preached in Czech at the University of Prague. Huss was concerned with the moral reform of the church, but he did not support a break with Rome. He attacked the sale of papal indulgences and challenged papal claims to head the church. The reform movement attracted support from most Czech-speaking social groups but opposition from the German minority. Huss was given safe conduct to attend the Council of Constance; there, he was arrested, condemned for heresy, and burned in 1415. The resulting scandal led to a revolt of his followers on both religious and nationalist grounds. The Hussites gathered at Mount Tabor in southern Bohemia and began to restructure their community according to the Bible, practicing communal ownership and collecting tithes from peasants. Taborite leaders were radical priests who ministered to the community in the Czech language, exercised moral and judicial leadership, and even led people into battle. The Taborite army, led by military genius Jan Zizka (c. 1360–1424), repelled five attacks by "crusader" armies from neighboring Germany. Zizka pioneered the use of new military technology and strategy, and the Hussite infantry defeated larger armies and helped change medieval warfare. The Czechs eventually gained some autonomy until they were defeated at the battle of White Mountain in 1620.

363. (B) Pope Gregory I (540–604), also known as Gregory the Great, was pope from 590 until his death. He was the first pope to come from a monastic background and is known for his merging of spiritual and temporal power. During his reign, the pope became the greatest landowner in Italy. Gregory organized the defenses of Rome and paid for its army. He heard court cases, made treaties, and provided welfare services. He sent a missionary expedition to England and worked to convert the Visigoths from Arianism. He also simplified the ideas of church fathers like Saint Augustine and made them accessible to a wider audience. *Pastoral Rule*, his practical handbook for the clergy, was matched by practical reforms within the church. He tried to impose regular elections of bishops and clerical celibacy in Italy. Gregory the Great is often depicted as a transitional figure between the Roman and Germanic worlds and between the ancient and medieval eras.

364. (A) L'Anse aux Meadows on the northernmost tip of Newfoundland is the only known site of a Norse village in Canada. The site is notable for possible connections with the attempted colony of Vinland, established by Leif Ericsson around 1003. The Vikings made their first historical appearance in about 790; they did not take part in the invasions of Rome. They first settled Iceland in 874, and Iceland has been occupied ever since. The Vikings also traded with Kievian Rus around 900. Apart from two or three representations of ritual helmets, no depiction of Viking Age warriors' helmets, and no preserved helmet, has horns.

365. (E) The climate of Europe in the Middle Ages was generally warmer than the so-called Little Ice Age that followed (c. 1590–1850). However, there was a major weather change between 1310 and 1330. During this time, northern Europe saw some of the worst periods of bad weather in the entire Middle Ages, characterized by severe winters and cold, rainy summers. Usually, medieval food production and distribution could sustain the population in peacetime. It was not until after 1300 that protracted famine occurred in western Europe. Two general causes have been suggested: climate change and overpopulation beyond what the economy could support. From 1000 to 1300, the population of Europe had exploded, reaching levels not matched again in some places until the 1800s. During the Great Famine (1315–1317), the price of bread tripled in a month in many northwestern European cities, and thousands starved to death. Estimates place the death toll at 10 to 25 percent of the population of many cities and towns. The Black Death (1349) and subsequent outbreaks of plague exacerbated the problems. The Great Famine marks a clear end to the early medieval period of growth and prosperity.

366. (C) The church condemned some groups, not on doctrinal grounds, but because they allowed their lay members to preach. This challenged the authority of the church hierarchy. The Waldensians, or Vaudois, were followers of a Christian movement of the later Middle Ages that preached the benefits of poverty. According to the most widely accepted story, the sect received its name in Lyon in the 1170s when a rich merchant named Peter Waldo decided to take Matthew 19:21 seriously: "If you wish to be perfect, then go and sell everything you have and give to the poor." The same message had inspired countless monks and would later be the basis for Saint Francis's preaching. Waldo's followers lived in poverty but refused to retire to monasteries. They also preached the Gospel in the vernacular so everyone would understand it. Pope Alexander III examined Waldo and his followers at the Third Lateran Council, and although their way of life found approval, they were forbidden to preach without permission from the local bishop. The members of the group were declared schismatics in 1184 in France and then heretics by the Fourth Lateran Council in 1215. This radicalized the Waldensians, and they began rejecting the authority of the clergy. They wandered to Languedoc, Italy, northern Spain, and the Moselle Valley (Germany), where they were almost wiped out in the 1600s. However, active congregations still exist in Europe, South America, and North America.

367. (D) The great English peasant revolt of 1381 is one of the best-documented peasant revolts. The Black Death (1349) and subsequent epidemics caused a population decline that affected peasant-landowner relations. Peasants resented the Ordinance of Laborers (1349), a reactionary labor law that attempted to freeze wages and tie workers to lords. Religious dissent based on the preaching of John Wycliffe (c. 1328–1384) also stirred unrest; the radical priest John Ball was an example of the many common priests who supported the revolt. Peasants also complained about the English government, especially unpopular advisers; the costly war with France; taxes such as the poll tax passed by Parliament in 1377; and the administration of justice. Government action against tax evasion sparked the uprisings, with Wat Tyler, a soldier who had served in France, emerging as the leader. The rebels entered London unopposed and met with Richard II, who agreed to their demands, including the abolition of serfdom. Tyler was then killed by the mayor of London, the rebels dispersed, and Richard revoked his concessions. The uprising of 1381 began a century of regional unrest, including Jack Cade's revolt in 1450 and the Cornish revolt of 1497. Although these peasant revolts failed, they did help to limit taxation, reduce military expenditures, and trigger resistance to serfdom in England.

368. (B) At a great ceremony in Rome on Christmas Day in 800, Pope Leo III crowned Charlemagne emperor of the Romans. This signified an important link between Charlemagne's Frankish kingdom and the old Roman Empire. Leo III's action exalted a European king and downgraded the authority of the Byzantine emperor. The pope was effectively reviving the western Roman Empire and nullifying the legitimacy of Empress Irene of Constantinople, whom Leo did not consider a legitimate claimant to the Byzantine throne because she was a woman. The Byzantines thought this was outrageous, especially since they viewed Charlemagne as an upstart barbarian. The coronation also implied a privileged position of power for the pope as an "emperor maker." Charlemagne may have been displeased because he feared offending the Byzantines or perhaps because he did not like the idea that the pope held a position of authority higher than his own.

369. (C) In Spain, the Visigoth king Leovigild (reigned 569–586) established his rule through military might. However, he still could not attain the support of the powerful landowners and bishops. His son, Reccared, converted to Catholic Christianity, and at the Third Council of Toledo (589), most of the bishops also converted from Arianism. Afterward, Visigoth kings gave bishops and churchmen the freedom to establish their own hierarchy. In return, the bishops supported the Visigoth king. They anointed the king in a ritual that paralleled the ordination of priests, and rebellion against the king became synonymous with rebellion against Christ. The great landowners also supported the king by supplying him with troops. Ironically, this centralization of power helped bring down the Visigoths. When the Arabs invaded in 711, they only had to defeat a single army and kill the king to achieve victory. The situation in Spain differed from the situation in northern Italy, where the Lombards had to deal with a hostile papacy and fiercely independent dukes.

370. (E) Pope Boniface VIII (c. 1235–1303), was pope from 1294 until his death. He put forth some of the strongest claims to temporal and spiritual power of any pope. Yet at the same time, both France and England began to tax the clergy to finance their ongoing wars against each other. Boniface viewed this taxation as an assault on traditional church rights and issued the bull *Clericis laicos* (1296), forbidding secular taxation of the clergy without the pope's approval. Philip IV retaliated by denying the exportation of money from France to Rome, funds that the church needed to operate. The feud between the two peaked in 1302, when Boniface issued *Unam sanctam*, one of the most important papal bulls in Catholic history. It declared officially that both spiritual and temporal powers were under the pope's jurisdiction and that kings were subordinate to the power of the church. Boniface declared that it was "absolutely necessary for salvation that every human creature be subject to the Roman pontiff." It is ironic that this extreme statement of papal supremacy should be issued at a time when the monarchies of France and England were beginning to build strong state systems with close control over their respective churches. Boniface had overreached, and French reaction to *Unam sanctum* was quick and brutal: the pope was captured, roughly handled at Anagni, and died from the harsh treatment he received in 1303.

371. (E) Joan of Arc (1412–1431), sometimes called La Pucelle ("the maid" or "the virgin") d'Orléans, is the national heroine of France and a Catholic saint. She was a peasant girl from eastern France who claimed to have received mystical instructions from heaven that ordered her to rally the French armies and recover her homeland from English domination in the Hundred Years' War. The uncrowned king Charles VII sent her to the siege of Orléans as part of a relief mission, and her presence and leadership helped lift the siege in nine days. Several swift victories followed, and she stood next to Charles VII at his coronation in Rheims in 1429. This strengthened Charles's legitimacy and settled the disputed succession to the throne. The following year, she was captured by the Burgundians, sold to the English, tried by an ecclesiastical court for heresy and witchcraft, and burned at the stake (1431). She was 19 years old. To the lasting shame of Charles VII, he did nothing to help her. Twenty-five years later, Pope Callixtus III pronounced her innocent and declared her a martyr. After Joan's death, the English position slowly crumbled. The duke of Burgundy recognized Charles VII as king of France, and Charles entered Paris in 1437. The English were eventually driven from France, retaining only the port of Calais when hostilities ceased in 1453.

372. (B) Gregory of Tours (c. 540–594) wrote the *Historia Francorum*, a chronicle that covered the history of the world from creation to 591 CE but contained many details about sixth-century affairs. Bede (632–735) wrote *The Ecclesiastical History of the English People*, which relates the story of the conversion of England to Christianity and the history of the English church until the time of his writing in 731. Bede popularized the dating of events from the birth of Christ. Einhard (c. 770–840) was a Frankish scholar and court official during the Carolingian renaissance who is best known for his biography of his friend Charlemagne. Geoffrey of Monmouth (c. 1100–1154) was famous for his *Historia Regum Britanniae* (1136–1138), which freely mixed material from Welsh legend and early British sources. Despite its lack of historical accuracy, the book was popular in the Middle Ages and provided the basis for the later tradition surrounding characters such as King Arthur and Merlin the wizard.

373. (D) Frederick II (1194–1250) was Holy Roman Emperor from 1220 to 1250, German king from 1212, and king of Sicily (1198–1250) and Jerusalem (1225–1228). He was the son of Emperor Henry VI and Constance of Sicily and the grandson of Frederick Barbarossa. Frederick II inherited Sicily and Germany and tried to control both places. In 1215 and 1220, he promised to go on crusade but delayed until Pope Gregory IX excommunicated him. He finally went on the Sixth Crusade (1227–1229), secured Jerusalem and other important places through negotiations instead of warfare, and returned triumphantly to Italy. In 1231, he promulgated the Constitutions of Melfi for Sicily, a group of laws that established a system of salaried governors who worked according to uniform procedures. The constitutions called for most law cases to be heard by royal courts, standardized commercial privileges, and established a system of taxation. At the same time, Frederick's involvement in the affairs of northern Italy in the 1230s brought him into conflict with Gregory IX (who called him the Antichrist) and then Innocent IV, who excommunicated and deposed him at the Council of Lyons (1245). Frederick was one of the most controversial men of the Middle Ages; Matthew Paris called him *stupor mundi* ("the amazement of the world"). He spoke six languages, was an enthusiastic patron of science and poetry, and wrote a book on falconry.

374. (A) Innocent III (c. 1160–1216) was a zealous church reformer and one of the strongest medieval popes. During his reign (1198–1216), he consistently claimed that the pope had the right to intervene in any issue where sin might be involved. He presided over the Fourth Lateran Council, which tried to regulate all aspects of Christian life for both the laity and the clergy. One canon required Christians to attend Mass and to confess their sins to a priest at least once a year; another proclaimed marriage a sacrament. The Eucharist was declared to truly contain Christ's body and blood, even though it looked like bread and wine on the altar. The Fourth Lateran Council also blasted heretics and ordered Jews to wear badges to indicate their religion. Innocent III's Lateran Council marked a high point of papal prestige in the Middle Ages. He supported the Franciscans and Dominicans despite noting the similarities between their teachings and some heresies. He worked to separate Germany from Italy, keep northern and southern Italy apart, and protect the power of the Papal States. He preached the crusade against the Albigensians in Languedoc; this was the first time a pope offered warriors fighting an enemy in Christian Europe the same spiritual and temporal benefits as Crusaders to the Holy Land. Innocent also preached the Fourth Crusade that sacked Constantinople in 1204.

375. (E) The Magna Carta was a royal charter, sealed and issued by the English king John at Runnymede on the Thames near Windsor in 1215. It was the result of more than two years of negotiations between the king and his barons. Initially, it consisted of 63 relatively brief and often unrelated clauses, but several reissues omitted certain clauses. The barons intended the Magna Carta to be a conservative document defining the "customary" obligations and rights of the nobility and forbidding the king from breaking these customs without consulting his barons. It also maintained that all freemen in England had certain rights in common and that the king must uphold those customs and rights. The most important rights were the vaguely worded statements against oppression of all subjects that later generations interpreted as guarantees of trial by jury and of habeas corpus (but are not explicit in the Magna Carta itself). In the Middle Ages, the barons invoked the Magna Carta whenever they felt the need to oppose royal tyranny. Eventually, as the definition of *freemen* expanded to include all the king's subjects, the Magna Carta became a milestone in the movement toward government by law.

376. (E) Renewed religious fervor in Europe in the 1100s led to new movements that stimulated individual piety for both laywomen and laymen. Some women joined convents, a few became recluses, and others joined new lay sisterhoods. The Beguines formed in northern Europe at the end of the 1100s. They were laywomen who lived in religious community houses (*béguinages*) but without permanent vows or an established rule. In this way, they imitated the convent lives of nuns but did not submit to male clerical control. They chose to remain celibate and devoted their lives to philanthropy, such as the care of lepers, the sick, and the poor. They later became influential in the weaving of cloth. Although their daily occupations were prosaic, the Beguines' internal lives were often emotional and ecstatic. For example, the renowned Mary of Oignies (1177–1213) envisioned herself as a pious mother entrusted with the Christ child. The Beguine movement spread along the trade routes of northwestern Europe, and in the 1300s, *béguinages* sprang up throughout the urban areas of Belgium, Holland, and the Rhineland. The movement represented the desire of many urban women to achieve salvation through piety and good works. They became closely connected with the Franciscans, but their relations with the institutional church were uneasy throughout the Middle Ages. The Beguines were often suspected of heresy but never officially declared heretical. Their male equivalents were known as Beghards.

377. (A) Lollardy was a name given to opponents of the established order within the English church at the end of the 1300s. They professed to be followers of John Wycliffe (c. 1330–1384), who rejected the ecclesiastical hierarchy in *On the Church* (1378) and denied the doctrine of transubstantiation in *On the Eucharist* (1379). Lollardy combined intellectual dissent, social unrest, and nationalist sentiment into a powerful anticlerical movement. Wycliffe and his disciples actively promoted the use of English in religious writings and attempted to translate the Bible into English and popularize it by reading it to all ranks of society. In the opening years of Henry IV's reign, the government took savage action against the Lollards under the terms of the statute *De Heretico Comburendo* (1400). A rebellion led by Sir John Oldcastle after Henry V's accession in 1413 was cruelly suppressed. However, Lollardy seems to have survived to provide some independent religious experience in which the emphasis was on studying the scripture in the vernacular and the rejection of priestly authority. Lollard beliefs resurfaced in the convulsive religious conflicts of the 16th century known as the Reformation.

378. (D) The Hanseatic League was a federation of north German towns formed to protect their mutual trading interests. German expansion along the coast in the 12th and 13th centuries enabled German merchants to establish a monopoly over the Baltic Sea trade. This trade, centered on the island of Gotland, dealt in fur, wax, and luxury goods from the east and helped to stimulate older trading links with England and Flanders. At first, Baltic towns negotiated small-scale agreements; then they formed a more powerful union in 1356 when some German towns met to try to resolve common trading problems in Flanders. The Hanseatic League reached its peak in the late 14th century, with more than 70 members and a network of rich trading routes hinging on the *Kontors* (foreign trading centers) in London, Novgorod, Bergen, and Bruges. The league was created to protect commercial interests and privileges granted by foreign rulers in cities and countries visited by the merchants. The

Hanseatic cities had their own legal system and furnished their own protection and mutual aid. The town of Lübeck usually took the lead in Hanseatic affairs, generally summoning the council (*Hansetag*) and using its seal on behalf of the league. The Hanseatic League began to decline during the 15th century because of challenges in the Baltic by non-Hanseatic merchants and the growing threat of territorial rulers.

379. (E) The Magyars (Hungarians), nomadic latecomers to Europe, arrived about 899 in the Danube basin. Until then, the region had been primarily Slavic, but the Magyars came from the east and spoke a language unrelated to any other in Europe except Finnish. From their bases in present-day Hungary, the Magyars raided far to the west, attacking Germany, Italy, and even southern Gaul. The battle of Lechfeld (955) is often viewed as the crucial event for stopping Magyar raids into western Europe. Fought south of Augsburg on a flood-plain that lies along the Lech River, the German king Otto I (reigned 936–973) decimated a Magyar raiding party in the battle. This increased Otto's prestige (he would eventually become Otto the Great) and made him a hero to his contemporaries. The victory also contributed to the establishment of a settled Hungarian kingdom. However, some historians believe the containment of the Magyars had more to do with their internal transformation from nomads to farmers than with their military defeat.

380. (C) The troubadours were poet-musicians of the courts of southern France. William IX of Aquitaine (1071–1127), widely considered the first troubadour, wrote songs that ranged from bawdy to sensual and refined. There are different ideas regarding the beginning of the troubadour tradition; the most commonly held theory is that it had Arabic origins. The notions of love for love's sake and exaltation of the beloved lady have been traced back to Arabic literature of the 9th and 10th centuries. Famous European troubadours included Jaufre Rudel (who developed the theme of love from afar); Bernart de Ventadorn (who established the classical form of courtly love poetry); the Comtessa de Dia (a noted female troubadour); Bertran de Born (who reveled in bloody warfare); Peire Cardenal (of whose works, almost 100 survive); and Guiraut Riquier (who wrote songs in praise of the Virgin Mary). Troubadours varied their rhymes and meters to dazzle their audiences with brilliant originality. They celebrated the doctrine of *fin'amors* (courtly love), the glorification of women, and the cult of true love. Eleanor of Aquitaine and other aristocratic women patronized the troubadours, but both men and women appreciated troubadour poetry, which recognized and praised women's power even as it eroticized it. Troubadour music was always sung, typically by a jongleur (musician). No troubadour music existed before 1200, but by the 13th century, music was written on four- and five-line staves. Troubadours exerted a profound influence on the lyric poetry and literature of Europe and even on its social attitudes.

381. (C) Charlemagne's son and successor, Louis I the Pious (reigned 814–840) was also crowned emperor by the pope. After his death, a period of family alliances and tragedies led to the Treaty of Verdun (843), which partitioned Charlemagne's empire among Louis's three sons. Louis the German received the eastern portion (later Germany); Charles II (Charles the Bald) became king of the western portion (later France); and Lothair I received the central portion (Belgium, Holland, Lorraine, Alsace, Burgundy, Provence, and most of Italy) and also kept the imperial title. The Treaty of Verdun represented the breakup of Charlemagne's empire into political units that foreshadowed the nations of western Europe.

382. (A) Saint Francis (c. 1182–1226) founded the famous orthodox religious movement named after him. He was a spellbinding preacher who advocated the benefits of poverty, simplicity, and helping others. Franciscan friars often sought town life, sleeping in dormitories on the outskirts of cities. They became part of urban community life, preaching to crowds and begging for their daily bread. Saint Francis converted both men and women; in 1212, his teaching particularly inspired an 18-year-old noblewoman named Clare (1194–1253). As a result, she assembled a community of pious women that eventually became the Orders of the Sisters of Saint Francis (Poor Clares). At first, the women worked alongside the friars, but Francis and the church disapproved of their activities in the world. Soon, Franciscan women were confined to cloisters under the Rule of Saint Benedict. Although they were an enclosed order, the Poor Clares lived a life of great poverty and austerity and became extremely popular in the 1200s and early 1300s. Franciscan nuns, unlike their male counterparts, lived in strict seclusion. Yet they ministered to the world by taking in the sick. Francis died in 1226 and was canonized by 1228. The rapid growth (and wealth) of the medieval Franciscans has been viewed as both the fulfillment and the abandonment of his ideals.

383. (E) In the early Middle Ages, slavery was widespread throughout Europe. It was inherited as an institution from both Roman and German sources and common in the neighboring Byzantine and Islamic states. The attitude of the Christian church was ambivalent. Jesus once said, "Whatever you wish that men would do to you, do so to them, for this is the law." But Jesus never actually spoke out against slavery. A famous passage from the Bible told slaves to "be obedient to those who are your earthly masters, with fear and trembling." The early Christian church did not oppose Roman slavery. Instead, it preached that slaves could look forward to freedom in heaven. Until then, they should follow the example of Jesus, who suffered in silence rather than using force to fight back. Paul's letter to Philemon, the shortest book of the New Testament, exemplified Christianity's ambivalence toward slavery. The medieval church opposed the sale of Christian slaves to non-Christians but accepted slavery as a result of humanity's sinful nature. Eventually, the rise of a manorial economy favored the use of serfs over slaves. The Vikings sold Slavs at slave markets and helped give the term *slave* to Europe. By 1100, however, most of the Scandinavian and Slavic people had been Christianized. Although chattel slavery persisted in some areas in the 1100s, the enslavement of Christians by other Christians became increasingly regarded as unethical and unprofitable.

384. (D) In the Old Testament, Deuteronomy 23:20 stated, "You shall not deduct interest from loans to your countryman, whether in money or food or anything else that can be deducted as interest." Jews interpreted this to mean that interest could be charged to strangers but not to other Jews. The early church opposed any payment of interest (which it called usury) in principle. However, the commercial revolution of the 11th and 12th centuries spread the use of contracts for sales, exchanges, and loans and increased the need for flexible capital. Because Christians forced Jews out of most professions, Jews were pushed into marginal occupations such as moneylending. Thomas Aquinas believed that usury was a violation of natural moral law, because all things are created for their natural end, but money is not an end but a means of buying goods and services. Lending money to generate more money was therefore unnatural and evil; it made something that should be sterile into something productive. Canon 29 of the Catholic Council of Vienne (1311) stated, "If indeed someone has fallen into the error of presuming to stubbornly insist that the practice of interest is not sinful, we decree that he is to be punished as a heretic." As a result, interest in western Europe was often disguised as a penalty for late payment under the rules of a contract. Interest of any kind is forbidden in Islam, forcing the creation of specialized banking rules for investors wishing to literally obey the Koran.

385. (D) *The Mabinogion* is a collection of 11 prose stories from medieval Welsh manuscripts of the 1300s. The tales draw on pre-Christian Celtic mythology, international folktales, and early medieval historical traditions. The first four tales, which are collectively called "The Four Branches of the Mabinogi," are roughly based on the story of Prince Gwri (Pryderi). In the first tale, he is born and raised, inherits the kingdom, and marries; in the second, he is barely mentioned; in the third, he is imprisoned by enchantment and released; and in the fourth, he falls in battle. Five of the subsequent stories are early examples of legends involving King Arthur.

386. (D) The papal reform movement is most closely associated with the controversial Gregory VII (c. 1020–1085). He began as a lowly cleric and rose slowly through the hierarchy. His anxiety over the moral state of the church was the motivating force for most of his actions. He was always a passionate advocate of papal primacy and unafraid to clash with the German emperor Henry IV (1050–1106) in the Investiture Controversy. However, this was only part of larger reforms Gregory promulgated, including the celibacy of the clergy (which would distance European clerics even further from their Byzantine counterparts), the end of simony, and the autonomy of the church from secular leaders. In 1074, Gregory published an encyclical absolving people from obedience to bishops who allowed married priests. The next year he enjoined them to take action against married priests and deprived these clerics of their revenues. Both the campaign against priestly marriage and that against simony provoked widespread resistance. Gregory also emphasized the importance of the sacraments and the special nature of the priest, whose chief role was to administer them. Not until the 1100s did people regularly come to be married by a priest in church, and churchmen began to stress the sanctity of marriage. The reform movement also proclaimed the special importance of the Mass.

387. (B) The Inquisition was a Catholic court that tried to eliminate heresy (beliefs that contradicted Catholic teachings). The foundation of the papal Inquisition can be attributed directly to Pope Gregory IX's bull *Excommunicamus* (1231), which established inquisitorial courts answerable directly to the pope and laid down procedures by which professional inquisitors were to be sent out to trace heretics. Inquisitors, aided by secular authorities, rounded up virtually entire villages and interrogated everyone. The judges assigned relatively lenient sentences to those who were unaware that they held heretical beliefs or those who quickly recanted. However, unrepentant heretics were given to secular powers to be burned at the stake. In the 13th century, long-term imprisonment also became a tool to repress heresy, even if the heretic confessed. Inquisitors used imprisonment to force people to recant, to give the names of other heretics, or to admit to a conspiracy against the church. In 1252, Innocent IV permitted the use of torture to obtain a confession. The Inquisition's reputation suffered from the squalid actions taken against the Knights Templars in France in the early 1300s and against the Spiritual Franciscans. One of the most famous inquisitors was Bernard Gui (1261–1331), who worked to eradicate heresy in southern France from

1308 to 1323. The Inquisition was not effective against later reforming movements, but it was reactivated in Spain under Isabella and Ferdinand, who used it as a tool of the national government.

388. (A) Hildegard of Bingen (1098–1179) was a multitalented writer, music composer, philosopher, and mystic. She was elected a *magistra* (abbess) by her fellow nuns in 1136, and she founded the monasteries of Rupertsberg (1150) and Eibingen (1165). At a time when few women wrote, Hildegard produced major works of theology and visionary writings. Her *Scivias* (1140s) denounces vice in almost apocalyptical terms. She wrote treatises about natural history and the medicinal uses of plants, animals, trees, and stones. She is perhaps the first composer of music with a known biography. One of her works, the *Ordo Virtutum*, is an early example of liturgical drama. Hildegard was consulted by and advised famous men such as Saint Bernard of Clairvaux and Frederick Barbarossa. In her old age, she wrote *Liber de Operatione Dea*, which attempted to explain the inner motivations of humans and reconcile the physical and the spiritual.

389. (D) The Seljuk Turks were a Turco-Persian dynasty that ruled parts of central Asia and the Middle East from the 11th to the 14th centuries. The Seljuks entered Baghdad in 1055 and, under Alp Arslan, crushed the Byzantine army at Manzikert (1071) and occupied Anatolia. They also captured Jerusalem in 1071 and Antioch in 1085; the Seljuk expansion was the direct cause of the First Crusade (1096–1099). In 1095, the Byzantine emperor Alexius I appealed for help to Pope Urban II, hoping to get new mercenary troops for a fresh offensive. The pope chose to interpret this request differently. At the Council of Clermont (in France) in 1095, he moved outside and addressed the crowd, saying, "Oh, race of Franks . . . race beloved and chosen by God . . . Enter upon the road to the Holy Sepulcher; wrest that land from the wicked race, and subject it to yourself." The crowd reportedly responded with one voice, "God wills it." Although historians disagree on Urban II's motives, the goal was to reclaim the Holy Land from the Muslims. In 1099, the Crusaders conquered Jerusalem, massacred many Christian and Jewish inhabitants, and established the Crusader states (Outremer) of the kingdom of Jerusalem, the county of Tripoli, the principality of Antioch, and the county of Edessa.

390. (C) At Christmas 1085, 20 years after his conquest of England, William I ordered a massive survey and census of England, popularly known as the Domesday Book. It received its name (from *doomsday*, meaning "day of judgment") in the 12th century because there was supposed to be no appeal against its judgment. One of the main purposes was to determine what taxes had been paid under Edward the Confessor. The Domesday Book was the most extensive inventory of land, livestock, taxes, and population that had ever been completed in Europe. The king's men conducted local surveys by consulting Anglo-Saxon tax lists and taking testimony from local jurors. From these inquests, scribes wrote voluminous reports filled with statements from villagers, sheriffs, priests, and barons. The reports were then summarized in the two-volume Domesday Book. The survey provided the king and his officials with information about land and revenue, especially regarding the Danegeld. One of the interesting findings of the Domesday Book is that chattel slavery was an important institution in England; it is estimated that slaves formed between 2 and 10 percent of the country's population.

391. (D) Geoffrey Chaucer (c. 1340–1400) was one of the greatest English writers and poets. This excerpt is from the Prologue to *The Canterbury Tales* (written after 1386). Chaucer was also a businessman and active in the court under the patronage of John of Gaunt. He traveled widely, especially to Italy in the 1370s. He chose to write in Middle English at a time when the triumph of English over French was uncertain. Using a blend of realism and imaginative insight, Chaucer painted an ironic and critical portrait of English society at the end of the 14th century. *The Canterbury Tales* is told by a party of pilgrims, a cross-section of contemporary society, on the journey from Southwark to the shrine of Thomas Becket at Canterbury. Chaucer's work borrowed from Boccaccio's *Decameron*, but Chaucer populated his tales with "sondry folk" rather than Boccaccio's fleeing nobles. In the Prologue, Chaucer describes not the tales to be told but the people who will tell them. In this way, he hints to the reader that the book's structure will depend on the characters rather than a general theme or moral.

392. (D) The Cistercians (known as the "white monks") were one of the new orders (such as the Carthusians) that appeared in the early 1100s in response to calls for greater asceticism. They were founded in 1098 by Robert, the abbot of Molesme, and the movement took its name from the location of its first house in Citeaux, France. The Cistercians aimed to live exactly according to the Rule of Saint Benedict. Their greatest expansion took place under Saint Bernard (c. 1090–1153), the abbot of Clairvaux. By 1200, there were more than 500 Cistercian houses throughout Europe, including Norway, Sicily, and Romania. The Cistercians accepted two separate classes of monks: choir monks, many of whom were well-educated priests, and lay brothers who tilled the fields. In this way, they provided an opportunity for ordinary men from nonaristocratic backgrounds to lead monastic lives. The Cistercians developed a spirituality of intense personal devotion and emphasized Christ's and Mary's humanity. The Cistercian God was approachable, protective, and even nurturing. The order's monastic buildings had little or no decorative details and were often similar to each other in construction; they lacked wall painting and sculpture and were much plainer than those of the contemporary Benedictines. To resist worldly temptations, the Cistercians chose secluded spots for their abbeys. Thus, they played a crucial economic role in settling marginal European lands and turning them into productive agricultural tracts.

393. (A) By 1000, most Jews lived in cities, many in the flourishing commercial region of the Rhineland. Under Henry IV, the Jews in Speyer and elsewhere in the empire received protection from the local bishop in exchange for paying a tax. Within these cities, Jews lived in their own tightly knit communities. Although officials occasionally spoke out against them, they were not persecuted systematically until the First Crusade. In his chronicle of that crusade, Solomon bar Simson wrote, "At this time . . . Frenchmen and Germans, set out for the Holy City [Jerusalem] . . . as they passed through the towns where Jews dwelled, they said to one another, . . . Here, in our midst, are the Jews—they whose forefathers murdered and crucified [Christ] for no reason. Let us first avenge ourselves on them and exterminate them. . . . On the eighth day of Iyar, on the Sabbath, the foe attacked the community of Speyer and murdered 11 holy souls who . . . refused to defile themselves by adopting the faith of their foe." Jews were killed in many Rhineland cities such as Metz, Speyer, Worms, Mainz, and Cologne. The First Crusade marked a milestone in the late medieval hostility against the "other"—Jews, witches, heretics, lepers, and homosexuals. After the Fourth Lateran Council (1215) and the establishment of the Inquisition, all these groups suffered much greater hostility and legal persecution.

394. (A) Investiture is the ceremony in which a churchman is given his office. Before the Investiture Controversy, the ruler gave a church appointee his office by symbolically investing the priest or bishop with the church and lands that accompanied that office. The Concordat of Worms was an agreement reached between Pope Callixtus II and Holy Roman Emperor Henry V in 1122 near the city of Worms. This agreement ended the first phase of the power struggle between the papacy and the Holy Roman Empire. It was a compromise that relied on a conceptual distinction between the spiritual and the secular parts of investiture. The ceremony would be divided between clerical and secular authorities. A member of the clergy would give the church appointee the spiritual signs of his office (a ring and a staff), while the emperor or his representative would give him the symbols of material goods. Elections of bishops in Germany would take place "in the presence" of the emperor. In Italy, they would take place before the pope. In the end, secular rulers continued to have a part in choosing and investing churchmen, but few people claimed the king was the head of the church. The Investiture Controversy was an early milestone on the way to the separation of church and state.

395. (B) The Investiture Controversy and the subsequent civil war (1075–1122) strengthened the German princes and weakened the kings. This situation changed under Frederick Barbarossa (1122–1190), the king of Germany from 1152 until his death. Frederick affirmed royal rights, even when he handed out duchies and allowed others to name bishops. He expanded his theoretical power by requiring princes to concede formally and publicly that they held their rights and territories from him as their lord. By making them vassals, Frederick defined them as powerful yet personally subordinate to him. Historians often date the origin of the so-called Holy Roman Empire to his reign, even though the term was first used in 1254. Frederick dreamed of restoring the empire to its former glory, and this required constant conflict with Italy. He invaded Italy six separate times, alternately fighting and negotiating with the cities in the north, especially Milan. On his fifth try, he met disaster at the battle of Legnano (1176), where he was defeated by the forces of the Lombard League. The battle marked the triumph of the city over the crown in Italy, which would not have a centralized government until the 1800s. Frederick finally won a foothold in Italy by marrying his son Henry to Constance, heiress to the kingdom of Sicily. Frederick supported the Third Crusade and drowned in the Saleph (now Goksu) River in Turkey on his way to fight against Saladin.

Chapter 12: The Mongols

396. (E) Hakata Bay is famous for its role in the Mongol invasions of Japan in 1274 and 1281. Both invasions were undertaken by Kublai Khan to conquer Japan after he had already reduced Korea (Goryeo) to the status of a puppet state. The failure of these invasions limited Mongol expansion, and the memory of them remains a major part of Japanese self-definition. One of the reasons for the Japanese success were the huge damages the Mongol invasion fleet suffered both times as a result of major storms. The invasions are therefore the earliest events for which the word *kamikaze* ("divine wind") is widely used. The Mongols' failed invasions were the closest that Japan had come to being conquered by a foreign power until its occupation in 1945 at the end of World War II. The destruction of the Mongol fleets guaranteed Japan's independence but also created a power struggle in the Japanese government that eventually led to the military's control of the emperor.

397. (A) The Yuan Dynasty developed from the Mongol invasion of China in the 1200s. During this period, the territory, economy, and trade routes of China expanded greatly. Although China generally flourished under Yuan rule, the Mongols essentially established a caste system that left the native Chinese (especially the southern Chinese) with little opportunity for advancement. In 1368, Yuan rule ended after a successful Chinese uprising.

398. (D) Karakorum was the capital of the Mongol Empire in the early 13th century. Its ruins lie on the Orhon River in present-day north-central Mongolia. In 1220, Genghis Khan established his headquarters at Karakorum and used it as a base from which to invade China. However, until 1235, Karakorum was little more than a yurt town. In that year, Ogodei, Genghis Khan's son and successor, surrounded Karakorum with walls and built a huge palace. At its height, the city included many brick buildings, 12 shamanistic shrines, and 2 mosques. Karakorum was also noted for its sculpture, especially its great stone tortoises. Under Ogodei and his successors, the city became a major site for world politics. Mongke Khan had the palace enlarged and a great stupa temple completed. William of Rubruck, a papal envoy to the Mongols, visited Karakorum in 1254 and described the town as cosmopolitan and religiously tolerant. The silver tree he described as part of the palace has become the symbol of Karakorum. In 1272, Kublai Khan moved the capital to Khanbaliq (present-day Beijing), and Karakorum became a provincial backwater of the Yuan Dynasty. The city briefly revived as capital of the Northern Yuan in the 14th and 15th centuries but then declined until it became nothing more than ruins.

399. (A) The battle of Ayn Jalut in 1260, although a relatively small battle, had extremely large consequences. In 1258, Genghis Khan's grandson, Hulagu, sacked Baghdad and then conquered Aleppo and Damascus in 1260. He was aiming for Jerusalem and Egypt when he received the news that Mongke the Great Khan had died. Although advised by his generals not to return to Mongolia, Hulagu departed, leaving a greatly reduced army behind. This Mongol force was confronted by the Mamluks (Egyptian soldiers of slave origin) under the command of the wily Baibars. The two forces met at Ayn Jalut (Goliath's Well), about halfway between Jerusalem and Acre (present-day Israel) in 1260; the number of soldiers on both sides is disputed. The Mamluks defeated the Mongols and checked their advance, essentially the first Mongol defeat in history. The establishment of the Mamluk Dynasty following the battle revitalized Islam after the disaster at Baghdad. Complicated political maneuverings followed Ayn Jalut, but a united Mongol force never again threatened Egypt.

400. (A) The precise causes of the Mongol expansion in the early 1200s are not clear. In the late 12th century, various nomadic tribes of mixed ethnic origins lived in the north Mongolian plateau; these tribes never seemed to stop fighting each other. Genghis Khan (c. 1162–1217), the brilliant Mongol leader, united the varied ethnic tribes and established the Mongol khanate in 1206. He fused the nomadic tribes into an aggressive army, creating a cavalry so powerful it seemed invincible. Recently, some scholars have speculated that climate changes had reduced the grasslands that sustained the Mongols' animals and their nomadic way of life. In the 13th century, they began to migrate from the steppes of central Asia to better grazing lands in the south and southwest. If that were the case, economic necessity impelled the Mongols to expand. However, their advance out of Mongolia also represented the definite political strategy of Genghis Khan, who believed that military offensives would keep the tribes united under him.

401. (A) The Mongol invasions in eastern Europe brought the cultures of Asia into contact with the European world. At its largest extent, the Mongol Empire touched Europe and very nearly reached Japan; it also stretched southward to Persia and India. The unification of Eurasia under the Mongols greatly diminished competing tribute gatherers throughout the trade network and ensured greater safety in travel. Thus, the Mongols were among the first people to tie the so-called Eastern world to the West and open up trade relations across regions formerly separated by language, religion, and political regimes. This allowed the spread of Christianity to Asia and stimulated the European search for exotic goods. Under Mongol rule, trade flourished, ideas circulated, and diverse cultures existed side by side. This is sometimes called Pax Mongolica.

402. (F) Despite the military power of the Yuan Dynasty, its rulers never subjugated Vietnam or Laos. The other answer choices were all ruled by the dynasty. Xinjiang is in northwest China in Silk Road country. Tibet is a plateau region in Asia, north of the Himalayas. Yunnan is a mountainous area located in the far southwest of China. The capital of the area is Kunming, and the area borders present-day Burma, Laos, and Vietnam. Taiwan, previously known as Formosa, is an island in the western Pacific Ocean off the southeast coast of China.

403. (C) The Mongols dominated Russia for about 200 years. Their most important victory was the capture of Kiev in 1240. They made the mouth of the Volga River their power center in Russia. During their rule, they standardized tax collection and based the recruitment of troops on a population census. However, they also used much of the local government machinery, allowing Russian princes to continue to rule as long as they paid homage and tribute to the khan. (The Mongol overlords exempted the Russian church from taxes.)

404. (E) In 1256, Hulagu Khan (Genghis Khan's grandson) led a Mongol force into Iran, defeated the Assassins at Alamut, and turned toward Baghdad. In 1258, after a relatively short siege, the Mongols breached the walls of Baghdad and spent eight days sacking the city. They massacred most of the inhabitants, including the Abbasid caliph Al-Musta'sim; estimates of fatalities range from 100,000 to a million. The Mongols also destroyed large sections of the city, including its libraries, universities, mosques, artistic treasures, and the canals and dikes that formed the city's irrigation system. The sack of Baghdad ended the Abbasid Caliphate, a blow from which Islamic culture arguably never fully recovered. Baghdad remained depopulated and in ruins for several centuries; its destruction is usually regarded as the end of the so-called Islamic golden age.

405. (B) Mongol khans and generals developed sophisticated military tactics, strategies, and organization that helped them conquer large parts of Asia, the Middle East, and eastern Europe. The Mongols organized their campaigns far in advance of the planned attack. Their armies traveled light and lived mostly off the land. While an army of the Roman Empire might cover 25 miles a day, Mongol horsemen could traverse 90 miles. Although the Mongols were ruthless in battle, they displayed extraordinary military discipline. Their primary weapon, the Mongol bow, had a range of more than 200 yards and was the best of its time. The Mongols also used sophisticated tactics such as two- and three-flank operations. For example, the Mongol invasion of Hungary was two-pronged: one division arrived from Russia, while the other moved through Poland and Germany. At the battle of Mohi in 1241, Mongol forces crushed the Hungarian army. After the invasion, about a quarter of the

Hungarian population died by slaughter or epidemic. Yet although the Mongols claimed control of Hungary, they could not occupy the fortified cities. The Mongols excelled where cavalry operated best. While they could use siege warfare successfully (for example, at Baghdad), it was not their strong point. They realized this deficiency and tried to surmount it by using foreign technical experts (such as at Xianyang) and adapting new technologies when faced with strong defensive fortifications.

406. (A) Ivan III (1440–1505) is also known as Ivan the Great or the Gatherer of the Russian Lands. He was a grand prince of Moscow who tripled the territory of his state, ended the dominance of the Mongols over Russia, and renovated the Kremlin. He reigned for 43 years (1462–1505). The Mongol invasion, reinforced by the breakup of Kievan Rus in the 12th century, led to the rise of the grand duchy of Moscow. In 1476, Ivan refused to pay the customary tribute to the grand khan. He then expanded his territory to the south and east by pushing the Mongols to the Volga River. Ivan III was the first Muscovite prince to claim an imperial title, referring to himself as tsar (or czar, from the name Caesar). In 1471, Ivan defeated the city-state of Novgorod, Moscow's possible competitor for control of Russia. In following years, he abolished Novgorod's local government and forcibly relocated leading families to lands around Moscow. By the time of his death, he had laid the foundations of the Russian state. (Ivan the Terrible was Ivan IV (1530–1584), grand prince of Moscow and the first ruler to be crowned tsar of all Russia.)

407. (B) A rich cultural diversity developed in China during the rule of the Yuan Dynasty. Some of the major cultural achievements were the development of drama, especially the music drama. The Yuan suppressed Confucianism, with its emphasis on conservative conformity, and this meant the arts received new freedom. The Yuan rulers abolished the imperial examination system, lowering the status of intellectuals to a position only slightly higher than beggars. Scholars found an outlet for their talents as professional playwrights. The result was a wealth of plays to be sung, spoken, acted, or mimed. The Chinese playwrights gleefully mocked and satirized their Mongol oppressors to the delight of their audiences. They wrote stories of injustice and vengeance, love and death, gods, ghosts, and dragons. They set up the Scholars Association, which encouraged playwriting; the Yuan era was one of the golden ages of Chinese theater.

408. (E) After Kublai Khan's successful conquest of China, the Mongols again looked to expand. However, the costly invasions of Burma, Champa, Annam, and Sakhalin only turned them into client-states. At the same time, Mongol invasions of Japan and Java failed completely. The Yuan Dynasty invaded present-day Vietnam three times: from 1257 to 1258, from 1284 to 1285, and from 1287 to 1288. In the end, the Mongols withdrew their troops, although Dai Viet and Champa became tributary states of the Yuan. The Mongols invaded the kingdom of Burma in 1277 and 1283; in 1287, they sacked Pagan, ending the kingdom's 250-year rule of the Irrawaddy River valley. Burma would not be unified again for another 250 years. The Mongols launched six major campaigns against Korea (Gorveo) between 1231 and 1270; ultimately, Korea was forced into an alliance with the Yuan for almost 80 years. Of all the Mongol campaigns in southeastern Asia, Java was the most remote. The invasion began in 1292, but the heat, tropical environment, and diseases led to the invaders' withdrawal from Java within a year.

409. (A) The Mongol conquest of southern China's Song Dynasty was the final step for the Mongols to rule all of China. It was also the Mongol Empire's last great military achievement. The decisive moment was the siege of Xianyang between 1268 and 1273, which led to the establishment of the Yuan Dynasty. Between the 1220s and the 1260s, the Song managed to turn back several major Mongol offensives. The key fortress was Xianyang on the Han River, with the almost equally strong city of Fancheng directly across from it. The walls of Xianyang were supposedly about 20 feet thick, and the main entrances to the city led through a waterway that was impossible to ford in the summer and an impassable swamp and series of mudflats in winter. Xianyang and Fancheng controlled the main route to the Yangtze River valley, which the Mongols needed to capture to reach the Song capital of Hangzhou. After a five-year siege, the Mongols finally took the two cities in 1273. Once the Mongols occupied Xianyang, they could easily travel by ship down the Han River into the Yangtze. Hangzhou surrendered in 1276, although Song loyalists continued fighting until the battle of Yamen in 1279. That battle marked the official end of the Song Dynasty and the beginning of the Yuan Dynasty.

410. (A) Marco Polo (c. 1254–1324) was a member of a Venetian merchant family who traveled to China as a young man (c. 1271). He supposedly served Kublai Khan as an envoy for 24 years before returning to Venice. He was captured by Genoans in a battle with Venetians and, while a prisoner, dictated his adventures in Asia. The book, known as *The Travels of Marco Polo*, astounded Europeans when it appeared around 1299, and it became an international best seller. There is no definitive version of Marco Polo's book; about 150 manuscript versions exist in a variety of languages. Marco Polo was released from captivity in 1299; he eventually became a wealthy merchant, but he never left Venice again. His book gave Europeans their first in-depth look at China; there is not much analysis but a good deal of description. Polo emerges from the book as curious, relatively tolerant, and devoted to Kublai Khan. The extent of his accuracy has been questioned for centuries, and a few historians have hypothesized that he never went to China at all but just repeated stories he had heard from other travelers. However, most modern scholars believe that Polo did actually go to China. If nothing else, he stirred the interest in exploration that led to the age of European ocean voyages.

411. (D) The Mongols were initially pastoral nomads organized into families, clans, and tribes. The leaders of the Mongols were always men, but women were allowed to speak in the tribal councils. In an unusual case, Toregene Khatun was the great khatun (female version of the khan) and regent of the Mongol Empire from the death of her husband, Ogodei, in 1241 until the election of her eldest son in 1246. In this role, she exercised enormous power in a society traditionally led only by men. Marriages in the Mongol Empire were usually arranged, but men were permitted to practice polygamy. Each wife had her own yurt; women worked by loading the yurts, herding and milking all the livestock, and making felt. In addition to these jobs, they cooked and sewed for their husbands, children, and elders. If a man died, his wife rarely remarried; instead, a woman's youngest son or youngest brother took care of her. In general, Mongol women enjoyed more freedom than those in the countries they conquered. They refused to adopt the Chinese practice of foot binding and did not wear chadors or burkas. Mongol women were also allowed to move more freely in public than their non-Mongol counterparts. At the end of the Mongol Empire, however, the increasing influence of other cultures caused greater limits to be placed on Mongol women.

412. (E) In some ways, the Mongol conquest damaged China. The Yuan Dynasty forbade marriage between the Mongols and the Chinese and prevented the Chinese from learning the Mongol language. Yet these restrictions also had some benefits. Because the Chinese were not allowed to Mongolize, they preserved their own ethnic identity. When the Mongols were evicted from China in 1368, the Chinese established the Ming Dynasty under traditional Chinese practices they had never lost. The Mongols classified the population of China into a hierarchy of four groups: Mongols; non-Han (mostly Islamic); northern Chinese; and at the very bottom, the southern Chinese. The Mongol rulers distrusted the Confucian scholar-officials of China and dismissed many of them. These scholars and other native Chinese were not eligible for some of the top positions in the ruling government. The Mongols eliminated civil service examinations, which remained banned until 1315. Even after the ban was lifted, they were no longer the only means to an official position in the Yuan Dynasty.

413. (B) The impact of Mongol invasions on European and Asian countries was uneven. While the Mongols generally brought peace and prosperity to China (under Yuan rule), their conquest of Russia resulted in the destruction and emigration of many native Russians. While ruling China, the Mongols adopted some elements of Chinese culture and society, especially the use of a strong central bureaucracy to run the government. This idea diffused to other lands through the Pax Mongolica. The Mongols did not spread Islam to China and Russia. They did occupy Korea during Kublai Khan's reign but never successfully occupied Japan or Egypt.

414. (C) Technically, the Mongol invasion of Europe began at the battle of the Kalka River in 1223 between a small Mongol force and several Russian princes. However, 15 years of peace followed. Most historians date the Mongol invasions of Europe to the full-scale attack on Russia, Poland, and Hungary from 1237 to 1242. These invasions, under the leadership of the great Mongol general Subotai, effectively destroyed east Slavic principalities such as Kiev and Vladimir. The Mongols then attacked the kingdom of Hungary (in the battle of Mohi in 1241) and Poland (in the battle of Legnica). By late 1241, Subotai was discussing plans to invade the Holy Roman Empire. Only the death of Ogodei (the great khan) and subsequent disputes over succession prevented an assault on Germany. Over the objections of Subotai, the Mongol princes withdrew the army to Mongolia for the election of a new great khan. The timing of Ogodei's death thus ended the Mongol invasion of Europe. The Mongols would later raid Poland in 1259 and from 1286 to 1287, but these raids were not aimed at conquest. A recent view is that the Mongol invasion of Europe was simply a diversion meant to frighten the Europeans and keep them out of Mongol affairs in the Middle East. For the Mongols, the European invasions were only a third (and least important and lucrative) theater of operations, after the Islamic Middle East and Song China.

415. (A) The Mongol Empire became too large to be governed by one ruler, so it was subdivided into five khanates. These were independent kingdoms, each supposedly subject to the great khan. The Golden Horde conquered Russia; the word *golden* probably refers to the color of their leader's tent, and *horde* comes from a Turkish word meaning "camp." Il-Khanate comprised Persia and most of the Middle East. The Yuan Dynasty was the Mongol Empire in China that replaced the Song Dynasty, and the Changhadai khanate consisted of western China and parts of southern Asia. After Kublai Khan's death, the office of the great khan was abolished and the empire fragmented. At its peak (c. 1340), the territory of the Golden Horde included most of eastern Europe from the Urals to the Danube, extending east to Siberia and south to the Black Sea and the Caucasus Mountains.

416. (E) Genghis Khan (c. 1155–1227) was the founder and khan (ruler) of the Mongol Empire. He came to power by uniting many of the nomadic tribes of northeast Asia. As ruler, he abolished aristocratic privilege and instituted a quasi-meritocracy in Mongol society. He downplayed family ties and tribal identities, especially in the army. After his early conquests, Genghis Khan instituted the great law (Yassa), which was designed to keep peace on the steppes. Militarily, he put absolute trust in his generals such as Muqali and Subotai, allowing them to make their own decisions when they fought far from Mongolia. One of his strengths was that he was curious and tolerant of different religions. Genghis Khan had five sons who were eligible to succeed him, and they constantly jockeyed for position. However, he clearly picked Ogodei (1189–1241), his third son, to be his successor.

417. (B) The secular code of Mongol law was written by Genghis Khan and is known as the Yassa (Great Law). It was the principal law under the Mongol Empire, even though no copies were publicly available. It decreed strict rules and punishments and helped to suppress many of the traditional causes of tribal feuding such as wife stealing and livestock rustling. In this way, the Yassa helped to create a peaceful trading and traveling environment throughout the Mongol Empire. Harsh penalties (such as restitution of nine times the value of stolen goods) helped deter theft on Mongol roads. The Yassa also proclaimed complete religious freedom, ensuring that Buddhists, Muslims, and Christians could all travel freely throughout the empire. Religious leaders, doctors, lawyers, teachers, and scholars were all exempt from taxation. One of the Yassa's strengths was its flexibility; it was often modified in remote parts of the empire.

418. (C) Some historians have suggested that the Mongol system of service to rulers deeply affected the way Russian rulers conceived of the national state. Ivan III and his descendants considered themselves, at least to some degree, heirs to the empire of the Mongols. They thought of Russia as a private dominion, emphasized autocratic power, and divided the population into a landholding elite that served the tsar and a vast majority of taxpayers. These historians have argued that the Muscovite princes created a national state that was more similar to the autocratic political tradition of the central Asian steppes and the Ottoman and Byzantine Empires than to that of western Europe.

419. (A) Tamerlane (1336–1405), also known as Timur, conquered vast portions of Asia. Though not related to Genghis Khan, he came from similar central Asian roots and imagined himself the successor to the great conqueror. Tamerlane roamed across an area from present-day Turkey to India and from Russia to Syria. By 1396, he had conquered Iraq, Azerbaijan, Armenia, Mesopotamia, and Georgia. Along the way, he left a trail of death and destruction, although he was also known as a great patron of the arts. Much of the architecture he commissioned still stands in his capital at Samarkand (in present-day Uzbekistan). While central Asia thrived under his reign, places such as Baghdad, Damascus, Delhi, and other Arab, Persian, and Indian cities were sacked and destroyed and their populations massacred. He also weakened the Christian church in much of Asia; in 1400, he invaded Christian Armenia and Georgia and captured more than 60,000 people as slaves. While Tamerlane claimed to be a good Muslim, some of his most vicious attacks were against Mongols and fellow Muslims, destroying the jewel cities of Islam and slaughtering their inhabitants. His legacy remains controversial.

420. (D) Under Mongol rule, trade flourished, ideas circulated, and diverse cultures existed side by side. The development of the Silk Road trade across Eurasia under the Mongols resulted from their promotion of commerce and creation of an infrastructure that ensured safe conditions for travel. The Pax Mongolica ended with the political breakup of the Mongol Empire and the outbreak of the Black Death in Asia in the 1330s. Ironically, the Pax Mongolica allowed the plague to spread along trade routes to much of the world. In 1331, the plague was noted in China. From eastern Asia, merchants and soldiers carried it on the protected trade routes, where it killed an estimated one-third of China's population and a quarter of Europe's.

Chapter 13: Tang/Song China and Southeastern Asia

421. (A) Li Po (c. 701–762 CE) and Tu Fu (712–770 CE) are considered two of the greatest poets in Chinese history. They lived during the Tang Dynasty (618–906), when poetry was extremely important and no occasion or event was considered complete without a poem. Poems were written for birthdays and weddings, to honor emperors and friends, to celebrate the change of seasons, and to mourn the passage of time. The Chinese call this period their golden age of poetry, and Li Po and Tu Fu were the greatest masters of the time. Tu Fu was very involved in politics, although he failed to pass the civil service examination on two different occasions. Some of his poems reflect his disappointments. He also wrote about his feelings on being separated from his family and his sympathy over the destruction caused by the An Lushan Rebellion. Li Po's work often uses Taoist imagery. He portrays himself as a neglected genius and a lover of wine, the moon, nature, friends, and women. His colloquial speech and confessional celebration of sensuality and his own failings made him the most popular Chinese poet in English. Li Po is influential in Europe and the United States partly due to Ezra Pound's (1885–1972) versions of some of his poems that helped establish a conversational and intimate tone in modern American poetry.

422. (B) The order is Shang (c. 1800–1100 BCE); Han (c. 200 BCE–220 CE); Tang (618–907 CE); Song (960–1279 CE); and Ming (1368–1644 CE).

423. (D) Papermaking was invented in the Han Dynasty. The oldest known Chinese piece of hard, hempen wrapping paper dates to the second century BCE. The standard papermaking process was supposedly invented by Cai Lun (c. 50–121 CE) in 105. The oldest extant piece of paper with writing on it was found in the ruins of a Han watchtower that had been abandoned in 110 CE in Inner Mongolia. The other answer choices were all accomplishments of the Song Dynasty.

424. (B) Wu Zetian (624–705 CE) was the first and only empress of China. The Tang Dynasty (618–906) was a time of relative freedom for women when they did not bind their feet or lead totally submissive lives. Wu was born into a rich and noble family and was taught to play music, write, and read the Chinese classics. At a young age, she was known for her wit, intelligence, and beauty, and she was recruited to the court of Emperor Taizong

(599–649), one of the greatest emperors in Chinese history. She soon became his favorite concubine and then married his son who came to power as Emperor Gaozong (628–683). She ruled as empress dowager and regent following her husband's death. In 690, she announced the founding of the new Zhou Dynasty (interrupting the Tang). Three years later, she took the title Divine Empress Who Rules the Universe, in effect creating a Buddhist state. These moves caused a brief rebellion, which she suppressed before she died of natural causes in 705. Wu Zetian has been described as malicious, cunning, devious, power hungry, and ruthless, especially to her adversaries. However, she also demonstrated great compassion for the peasants, reducing their taxes and boosting agricultural production. Her rise to power and reign were harshly criticized by Confucian historians who considered her a woman who had inappropriately overstepped her bounds. However, her reputation has been positively revised since the 1960s.

425. (C) In Korea, the Silla Dynasty was overthrown in 935 CE and replaced by the Goryeo Dynasty (from which the name Korea derives). The Goryeo Dynasty (918–1392) had a strong Buddhist influence that shaped many of its cultural achievements. Buddhist temples flourished, producing a need for fine vessels to be used during the many ritual ceremonies. In the mid-10th century, Korean artists, some of whom had been schooled in China, began creating celadon by using inlay and copper glazing techniques. These methods were first developed in China but perfected by Korean artisans. The term *celadon* (for the pottery's pale, jade green glaze) was coined at a later date by European buyers. Actually, celadon glazes can be produced in a variety of colors, including white, gray, blue, and yellow. Korean celadon was noted for its pale green glazes with beautiful inlay work. The level of quality surpassed that of other areas and came to be revered by even the Chinese for its elegant yet simple beauty. The Goryeo royal court also used some of the best examples of celadon pottery in their palaces as vessels for daily use and as art objects. The finest examples of Korean celadon were produced during the late 11th century by anonymous artisans. The Mongol invasions, beginning in 1231, caused a decline in Goryeo culture and the quality of the pottery. By the beginning of the Chosun Dynasty (1392–1910), most of the Korean manufacturing techniques for celadon had been lost.

426. (E) The heaviest commercial traffic on the Silk Road took place during the first half of the Tang Dynasty (618–907 CE). This world-famous network experienced its golden age before the An Lushan Rebellion (755–762). The Chinese imported gold, gems, ivory, glass, perfumes, dyes, and textiles, and they exported furs, ceramics, spices, jade, silk, bronze, iron, and lacquer. Chang'an (present-day Xian), the eastern terminus of the Silk Road, became an international metropolis during the Tang Dynasty and possibly the largest city in the world. Tang trade also benefited because competing empires to the west, such as the Byzantines and the Arabs, were relatively stable during this period and willing to build commercial relations with China. Tang China, like Rome, also boasted roads that linked all parts of the empire. The Tang emperors paid special attention to the vast so-called western regions of eastern central Asia. Important garrison posts (such as at Kucha and Tokmak) guarded the Silk Road, and the Tang court sent military governors as far west as Teheran. All these factors led to commercial prosperity along the Silk Road and frequent cultural exchanges between the West and the East. Despite minor setbacks, the Tang dominated central Asia until the battle of Talas in 751, when the Islamic Arabs decisively defeated the Chinese. Tang trade along the Silk Road began to decline after the An Lushan Rebellion and never recovered its former glory, although it did undergo a revival until the Pax Mongolica of the late 13th century.

427. **(C)** China's rulers used the so-called mandate of heaven to explain the decline of one dynasty and the takeover by another until the end of the empire in 1912 CE. The concept of the mandate of heaven originated with the Zhou Dynasty to justify its overthrow of the Shang. The notion was supported by Mencius, an influential Confucian philosopher. The mandate of heaven supposedly granted a dynasty the authority to rule. Whenever a dynasty fell, Chinese sages declared that it had lost the moral right to rule, which was given by heaven alone. In this sense, *heaven* did not mean a personal god but a universal all-encompassing power. However, unlike the European concept of the divine right of kings, the mandate of heaven depended on the conduct of the ruler in question. The idea was adopted by the rulers of the Tang and Song Dynasties to rationalize their assumption of power.

428. **(A)** Zhu Xi (1130–1200 CE) was a Song Dynasty scholar and the most influential neo-Confucian in China. His main contribution to Chinese philosophy was assigning special significance to *The Analects of Confucius*, *The Book of Mencius*, *Great Learning*, and *Doctrine of the Mean* (the so-called Four Books). Zhu Xi not only selected these classical Confucian texts, but he also edited and compiled them with commentary. By doing so, he redefined the Confucian tradition, restoring its original focus on moral cultivation. The Four Books became required reading for the imperial civil service examination system from the Yuan Dynasty until the civil service system was abolished near the end of the Qing Dynasty in 1908. Zhu Xi's teachings dominated the Chinese movement known as neo-Confucianism. While older Confucianism had focused on practical politics and morality, the neo-Confucianists borrowed Buddhist ideas about the soul and the individual. The influence of neo-Confucianism eventually spread to Korea and Japan, both of which partially adopted the imperial examination system and admired Zhu's intellectual achievements. (The White Cloud Sect was a type of Buddhism that became popular during the Song Dynasty and still survives today. Adherents believe that reciting the name of the Buddha, renouncing meat, and studying are three factors that can help bring salvation.)

429. **(A)** Tibet emerged in the seventh century CE as a unified state but quickly divided into a variety of territories. Some of these retained their independence; others fell under the control of the Mongols or the Chinese. Tibetan cuisine differs from that of its neighbors because only a few crops (not including rice) will grow at the country's high altitudes. Barley is the most plentiful crop; wheat, rye, buckwheat, and potatoes are also cultivated, but the main occupation is raising livestock. Bon is the ancient religion of Tibet, but it has almost been replaced by Tibetan Buddhism, which merges Mahayana and Vajrayana (Tantric) ideas. A common motif in Tibetan Buddhism and art is the representation of wrathful deities, who are often depicted with angry faces, circles of flame, or the skulls of the dead as necklaces. Their wrath represents their dedication to the protection of the dharma (divine law). The Potala Palace is a UNESCO World Heritage site and the best example of Tibetan architecture. Construction began in 1645; it has 13 stories with more than 1,000 rooms, 10,000 shrines, and about 200,000 statues. *The Epic of King Gesar* dates from the 12th century. It tells the story (in poetry and prose) of the heroic deeds of Gesar, the fearless lord of the legendary kingdom of Ling. It is still sung throughout central Asia and is well known as one of the only oral epic traditions in the world to still survive as a performing art.

430. (D) The Vietnamese people adopted many Chinese ideas, such as the civil service and bureaucracy, Confucian writings, Buddhism, and Chinese agricultural techniques. However, differences between Chinese and Vietnamese cultures sparked animosity to Chinese rule. Women in Vietnamese society were used to wider privileges, especially in local business and commerce, than their Chinese counterparts. The Vietnamese won their independence after a thousand years of Chinese control in 939 CE, shortly after the fall of the Tang Dynasty, when Ngo Quyen (897–944) defeated Chinese forces at the Bach Dang River. Vietnamese rulers of the Li Dynasty (1009–1225) established a capital at Hanoi and conquered peoples to the south. The subsequent Tran Dynasty (1225–1400) was considered the golden age of music and culture. During this dynasty, the Vietnamese people repelled three Mongol invasions, Buddhism flourished as the state religion, and the Vietnamese language was used for the first time as the second language at court.

431. (B) After the fall of the Han Dynasty, China broke into numerous regional governments. The Sui Dynasty (589–618 CE), powerful but short-lived, restored the central government and united the Chinese people by constructing public works. They built granaries and palaces and also repaired many of China's defensive walls. The Sui Dynasty is probably best known for the construction of the Grand Canal, which linked northern and southern China. The Grand Canal is more than 1,100 miles long from Beijing to Hangzhou, with roads on either side of it. It is the longest canal in the world. The oldest parts date back to the fifth century BCE; the Sui Dynasty built the connecting links between the various sections. The Grand Canal provided an effective and economical way to transport rice and other crops from the Yangtze River valley to the northern portions of China. Until the invention of railroads in the 1800s, the Grand Canal was China's main economic link. The Sui launched a series of costly and unsuccessful campaigns against Korea between 598 and 614. The dynasty's tyrannical demands on the people, who bore the burden of taxes and compulsory labor, caused its rapid fall after the assassination of Emperor Sui Yangdi (569–618). This dynasty is often compared to the earlier Qin Dynasty because of its ruthless accomplishments.

432. (C) The Song Chinese were world leaders in shipbuilding. Watertight bulkheads improved buoyancy and protected cargo. Stern-mounted (sternpost) rudders improved steering. Sounding lines were used to determine depth. Some ships were powered by both oars and sails and held several hundred men. The Song also perfected the compass. The fact that a magnetic needle would point north-south was already known, but in Song times, the needle became smaller and was attached to a fixed stem instead of floating in water. In some cases, it was put in a small protective case with a glass top, making it suitable for sea travel. The first reports of a compass used this way date to 1119 CE. These improvements led the Song to create China's first permanent navy. The dynasty also relied on new naval weapons such as gunpowder, catapults, and incendiary devices. Between 1132 and 1189, the Song navy introduced paddle-wheel warships, some so large that they had 12 wheels on each side of the vessel. The Song also used ships for trade; for the first time in Chinese history, maritime trade exceeded overland foreign trade. In 1973, a Song-era vessel that had been shipwrecked in 1277 was excavated off the south China coast; it was vastly superior to European ships of the same period. (Astrolabes date back to the Hellenistic world.)

433. (E) The position of Chang'an (present-day Xian), the capital of Tang China, played a crucial role in the dynasty's outward-looking worldview. The city was first constructed about 200 BCE and also served as capital to the Han and Sui Dynasties. It grew because of its location as the eastern terminus of the Silk Road, which connected it to the vast caravan trails that extended through central Asia to the Middle East, India, and the Mediterranean. All trade goods from northern Africa, the Byzantine Empire, and the Islamic world had to pass through Chang'an. From the city, one of the best transportation networks in the world distributed these goods by canal, river, and coastal shipping throughout China and south-eastern Asia. At its height, Chang'an—along with its competitors, Baghdad and Constantinople—was one of the world's largest cities and may have had a population of as many as one million. It was also a tolerant city; its rulers created special quarters for merchants and religious practitioners of Nestorian Christianity, Judaism, Islam, and Zoroastrianism, and there were many Buddhists and Taoists. Much of ancient Chang'an was destroyed during the fall of the Tang Empire.

434. (B) Sejong the Great (1397–1450 CE) reigned from 1418 to 1450 as king of the Yi Dynasty of Korea. During his reign, he created a phonetic writing system called Hangul that is essentially the same system used in Korea today. Before the creation of Hangul, only members of the highest Korean classes were literate. A person would have to learn complex Chinese characters in order to read and write Korean. In 1446, Sejong introduced a 28-letter Korean alphabet. In the preface to *Hunmin Chongum* (The Proper Sounds for Instructing the People), he wrote, "The spoken language of our country is different from that of China and does not suit the Chinese characters. Therefore among uneducated people there have been many who, having something that they wish to put into words, have been unable to express their feelings in writing. I am greatly distressed because of this, and so I have made 28 new letters. Let everyone practice them at their ease and adapt them to their daily use." Hangul is the only alphabet made by a specific individual for which the theory and motives behind its creation have been fully explained.

435. (D) The Han brought Chinese culture to Vietnam when they occupied the country in 111 BCE. However, Han attempts at imposing Chinese values and institutions brought conflicts between the Chinese-influenced elite in larger towns and valleys and those living in more remote areas. When Chinese authorities executed a popular local leader in 39 BCE, his widow (Trung Trac) and her sister (Trung Nhi) organized a revolt, and their militia drove the Han garrison out of the region. The Chinese returned two years later and over-whelmed the Trung sisters' forces; the sisters drowned themselves rather than be taken alive. It was more than a thousand years before Vietnam was independent again. The Trung sisters are revered in Vietnam; many temples are dedicated to them, and many Vietnamese observe a yearly holiday to commemorate their deaths.

436. (A) The art of metallurgy during the Song Dynasty built on the achievements of earlier Chinese dynasties. Steelmaking was known in the Han Dynasty as early as the first century BCE. However, Song Dynasty inventors discovered new ways to make steel. Between 806 and 1078 CE, the per capita output of iron in China rose 600 percent. According to one estimate based on government tax receipts, by 1078, Song China was producing 125,000 tons of iron per year. This massive increase in output resulted in manufactured products such as weapons, cooking utensils, farm implements, coins, musical bells, artistic statues, and components for machinery. (The greatest volume of goods was traded along the Silk Road during the first half of the Tang Dynasty.)

437. (A) At some time in the first millennium BCE, the people of the Malay peninsula became daring sailors and began to travel long distances to ports as far away as Africa and Madagascar. These so-called Malay sailors carried plants such as bananas and coconuts as well as cinnamon, which originally came from southern China. The sailors discovered how to ride the predictable monsoon; they sailed for thousands of miles with the wind at their backs, waited until it changed direction, and then sailed home. By the first century CE, regular maritime traffic connected India to the Malay peninsula and southeastern Asia. In the fifth century, a well-defined maritime route between India and Asia regularly used the Strait of Malacca and the South China Sea. This paved the way for the rule of the far-flung Hindu/Buddhist Srivijaya Empire between the 7th and 13th centuries. For six centuries, the rulers of Srivijaya controlled the areas around the Malay peninsula by controlling the two passages between India and China: the Sunda Strait and the Strait of Malacca. The empire reached its peak in the 10th century between the fall of the Tang and the rise of the Song.

438. (E) The unified Silla Dynasty (668–935 CE), with its capital at Gyeongju, marked a turning point in Korea's cultural development. The country had previously been conquered by the Han Dynasty, which had introduced a Chinese centralized government. In the mid-600s, the Silla Dynasty drove out the Chinese, and for the first time, the Korean peninsula was unified and controlled by native peoples. Under the Silla, the Koreans continued to construct Buddhist monasteries and create Buddhist art objects. They also modified the writing system based on Chinese characters. However, despite Chinese influences, Korean society under the Silla was divided into distinct classes, with a large semislave population supporting an aristocratic minority. The last century of the Silla Dynasty was filled with almost constant civil war. Warlords in the north eventually overthrew the Silla Dynasty in 935, and it was followed by the Goryeo Dynasty (918–1392).

439. (D) As commerce brought Buddhism to China, the nature of the religion changed. The Chinese, influenced by the Confucian emphasis on the family and the distrust of celibacy, were never totally at ease with Theravada Buddhism. As the religion advanced via the Silk Road, the Chinese preferred Mahayana Buddhism, which emphasized the divinity of the Buddha and surrounded itself with rituals that were unknown to Indian Buddhism. In some cases, Chinese Buddhism blended with Taoist beliefs to form a faith that depended on meditation and enlightenment called Chan Buddhism (Zen Buddhism in Japan). The Buddhist speculation on the nature of the soul also influenced neo-Confucianism, and the new interest in metaphysics made it more attractive to the scholar-officials of the Song period than the pure Buddhist religion. Buddhism also affected land distribution in Tang China, because large tracts of land were taken up by Buddhist monasteries.

440. (A) In the 10th century, the Song Dynasty (960–1279 CE) again restored centralized rule to China. This dynasty was characterized not by military rule but rather by an emphasis on education and the arts. However, the Song Dynasty maintained a strong, centralized state and the most urbanized society of its time. Under the Song, the Confucian civil service was expanded to include opportunities for more men to study Confucian philosophy and to take the exam. Song China faced some threat from nomadic invasion, but there were no Islamic incursions during this period.

441. (C) Wood-block printing is a technique for printing text or images that is used throughout eastern Asia. The technique originated in China before 220 CE; the earliest existing fragments of wood-block printing are Chinese silk printed with flowers in three colors from the Han Dynasty. (The earliest Egyptian printed cloth dates from the fourth century; it is unclear if Egyptian printing was learned from China or developed separately.) The oldest existing wood-block book is the Diamond Sutra, dating from 868. This book is so technically advanced that historians presume wood-block printing must have begun much earlier. Because Chinese writing has at least 40,000 characters, wood-block printing suited it better than movable type. In the former, only the characters used in the text needed to be created. In addition, the Chinese focused on printing and reprinting Buddhist texts. Even if these required 130,000 woodblocks, the blocks could be maintained for centuries. If a text needed to be reproduced, the original woodblocks could be reused, while the same book produced with movable type would need new, possibly error-prone editions. Ironically, although the Chinese invented movable type with baked clay in the 11th century (and metal movable type was invented in Korea in the 13th century), they continued to prefer woodblocks because of the difficulties inherent in typesetting Chinese text. The difference between Asian wood-block printing and the European printing press affected the comparative development of book culture and book markets in Asia and Europe.

442. (A) In the sixth century CE, the Khmers (Cambodians) created an empire in present-day Cambodia and Laos. The capital was established in Angkor (not Phnom Penh) by King Yasovarman I (reigned 889–900). The Angkor period (889–1434) was the golden age of Khmer culture, when the empire reached its greatest extent into parts of present-day Thailand and Vietnam. At this time, Angkor was one of the largest urban centers in the world. The Khmer Empire was influenced by Indian culture, especially Buddhism and Hinduism; many Indian scholars, artists, and religious teachers were attracted to the Khmer court, and Sanskrit literature flourished under royal patronage. The greatest achievements of the Khmers were in architecture and sculpture, especially evidenced by the construction of Angkor Wat by Suryavarman II (reigned 1113–1150). Angkor Wat is a temple complex dedicated to the Hindu god Vishnu and a magnificent blend of Indian and southeast Asian cultures. Another noted temple complex is Angkor Thom, constructed by Jayavarman VII (reigned 1181–c. 1218). Khmer temples were filled with bas-relief sculptures that depicted Khmer life in great detail. The Khmer Empire declined in the late 1300s and early 1400s for reasons that are still disputed.

443. (E) Foot binding probably originated among court dancers in the early Song Dynasty, but it spread to upper-class families and even to lower socioeconomic groups. According to one estimate, about 40 percent of Chinese women had bound feet in the 1800s, with the number rising to almost 100 percent for the upper classes. Foot binding was the practice of tightly wrapping the feet of young girls (usually between two and five years of age) with strips of cloth. This would break some bones in the foot, preventing the girl from walking easily. It was generally painful for life. The belief was that men found the tiny, narrow feet extremely erotic and that such feet made a woman's movements more feminine. The procedure also was a display of high social standing and a way to control a girl's behavior. Since foot binding made it impossible for a woman to do most agricultural work or even walk without pain, it demonstrated that a family was so wealthy that it did not need to send its women into the fields to work. Their disability also made Chinese women with bound feet completely dependent on their husbands or other male family members. The practice did not die out until the early 20th century.

444. (C) The An Lushan Rebellion (755–763 CE), sometimes known as the An Shi Rebellion, was the turning point in the history of the Tang Dynasty. For the next 144 years, the Tang were greatly weakened, and their rule was a far cry from the dynasty's glorious days under the emperors Taizong (599–649) and Xuanzong (712–756). The troubles began in 755 when An Lushan, a disaffected general, began a revolt against the dynasty. The subsequent civil war devastated a large portion of the Tang Empire until, after many ups and downs, the rebels were finally defeated at unbelievable cost. The 754 census recorded a population of about 53 million, while the 764 census listed only about 17 million. It is unlikely that the population really declined to this extent, but it does indicate the severity of the rebellion's impact. After the An Lushan Rebellion, distant provinces broke away, reducing the influence of the central government in Chang'an. The need for soldiers from neighboring tribes reduced the prestige of the Tang Dynasty among "barbarians," who began raiding Tang settlements again. The Tang also lost control over the western regions in eastern central Asia along the Silk Road when the troops there returned to central China to crush the rebellion. The An Lushan Rebellion also caused a crisis of conscience among many Tang intellectuals; it had a major impact on poets like Tu Fu and Li Po.

445. (D) The decline and fall of the Southern Song Dynasty had multiple causes. However, the main reason for the collapse was outside invasion. In the early 1100s CE, nomadic northern peoples such as the Khitan and the Jurchen began demanding tribute and overrunning the northern part of China. The Northern Song could not repel the Jurchen invasions; in 1127, the Jurchen captured the Northern Song capital of Kaifeng and created their own Jin Dynasty (1115–1234). This limited the Song Dynasty to the south; the border between the two parts comprised the Yellow (Huang He) and Yangtze Rivers. Between the 1220s and the 1260s, the Song did turn back several offensives by the Mongol Empire. However, the Mongols were victorious at the siege of Xianyang (on the Han River) between 1268 and 1273. Once the Mongols occupied Xianyang, they easily traveled by ship down the Han River into the Yangtze. Hangzhou surrendered in 1276, although Song loyalists continued fighting until the battle of Yamen in 1279. That battle marked the official end of the Southern Song Dynasty and the beginning of the Yuan Dynasty (1280–1368).

Chapter 14: The Americas

446. (A) Cahokia is located near present-day Collinsville, Illinois, about 15 miles east of St. Louis, Missouri. It was one of the world's greatest cities and larger than London, England, in 1250 CE. The Mississippians who lived here were master builders and erected a wide variety of structures, from practical homes to monumental public works. Cahokia was abandoned by 1400. However, the agricultural practices of Mississippian culture—such as the use of flint hoes and the superior strains of corn, beans, and squash—spread across eastern North America.

447. (B) Until about 3000 BCE, Americans were nomadic hunter-gatherers. The first farmers probably lived in present-day Mexico, planting avocados, chili peppers, and cotton. However, agriculture as a way of life did not emerge in South America and Mesoamerica until about 2000 BCE. Inventive farmers of that time learned how to breed tomatoes, potatoes, and manioc (a fast-growing but not very nutritious root crop). In about 1500 BCE, native American societies in Mesoamerica discovered ways to domesticate maize (a variety of corn). Over the centuries, they bred maize into a much larger and extremely nutritious plant that was hardier and had a higher yield per acre than the staple cereals of Europe such as wheat, barley, and rye. In the first millennium CE, maize cultivation spread from Mexico into southwest America, and after 1000 CE, into the American northeast and present-day Canada. Native Americans also learned to cultivate beans and squash and to plant them in the same fields as corn, creating a mix of crops that provided a diet rich in calories and essential amino acids. This technique also preserved soil fertility and led to higher yields. The result was an agricultural surplus that led to the wealthy and populous societies of Mexico, Peru, and the Mississippi River valley. (Wheat was originally cultivated in the Fertile Crescent and contributed to the rise of city-states such as Assyria and Babylon.)

448. (C) Some pre-Columbian cultures, such as the Incas, did not have a system of writing. Instead, they used a method of record-keeping known as the *quipu*, a collection of cords of different colors on which were knots of different sizes and shapes. Each knot represented a different aspect of Incan life and government. The other answer choices are all Mesoamerican cultures with intricate and somewhat similar writing symbols. Those from Mesoamerican scripts are often called glyphs as a short form of *hieroglyph*. Many Mesoamerican glyphs are extremely ornate representations of real objects such as animals.

449. (B) The Ancestral Puebloans were an ancient American culture that thrived from about 100 BCE to 1350 CE in the present-day Four Corners area of the United States. They were sedentary agriculturists who excelled at irrigation and planted corn, beans, and squash in the river valleys. They also domesticated the turkey, gathered wild plants, and hunted game to supplement their diet. The Ancestral Puebloans organized their lives on a communal pattern, and their many kivas presumably show that their religious ceremonies were similar to those of the present-day Pueblo. They were remarkable builders and are best known for the stone and adobe dwellings built along cliff walls, particularly from about 900 to 1300 CE. They were also highly skilled potters, and shards of thousands of smashed pots litter their archaeological sites. The most common decorated pottery had black painted designs on white or light gray backgrounds. The Ancestral Puebloans built a complex system of ceremonial roads, many radiating out from the great house sites in Chaco canyon. Ironically, these people lived in the cliff dwellings for barely a century. By about 1300, many centers, such as Mesa Verde, were deserted. Several theories have been offered to explain the migration: climate change, drought and crop failure, overuse of land, deforestation, soil depletion, civil war, invasion, and/or social and political problems. Perhaps the people were simply looking for new opportunities elsewhere.

450. (E) The oldest of the highly developed Mesoamerican cultures was the Olmec, who flourished between about 1400 and 400 BCE. The Olmec were a somewhat mysterious people, often considered a parent culture for the Mesoamerican cultures that followed. They lived in the Gulf Coast regions of present-day Veracruz and Tabasco in Mexico, living off surpluses of corn, beans, and squash that they produced using irrigation techniques. They constructed large-scale buildings and developed noted ceremonial centers at San Lorenzo and La Venta. The Olmec developed markets, an administrative hierarchy, a standing army, a calendar, and a writing system. Olmec culture is most famous for its massive stone pieces such as stelae, altars, and especially colossal heads. Scholars believe these heads are the likenesses of certain rulers, perhaps dressed as players of the Mesoamerican ball game. Some of them are nine feet high and weigh more than 40 tons. The Olmec are somewhat unique as a culture because, although they had access to water from streams and small rivers, they did not develop in a major river valley. The reasons for the decline and dispersion of their culture are unknown. However, for some reason, between 400 and 350 BCE, the population in the eastern half of the Olmec heartland dropped sharply, and the area remained underpopulated until the 19th century CE.

451. (A) Among the many achievements of the Mayan culture was the development of both a lunar and a solar calendar that could record historical events. The solar calendar contained 18 months of 20 days each, with a final period of 5 days dedicated to religious observance. The Maya could perform complex mathematical and astronomical calculations because of their understanding of the concept of zero as a placeholder. Mayan scientists could predict solar and lunar eclipses with amazing accuracy. They also developed the most advanced writing system in the Americas, using glyphs to represent either symbols or words. With this system, they recorded the royal lineage of various city-states and noteworthy events such as wars and famines.

452. (E) Population estimates for the pre-Columbian Western Hemisphere are disputed. However, recent estimates place the population of the Americas in 1500 at about 70 million. Most of the people—probably about 45 million—lived in Mesoamerica. Another 15 million lived in lands to the north of the Rio Grande (the present-day United States and Canada), and about 10 million lived in South America. These so-called native Americans were divided into scores of language groups and hundreds of distinct cultural groups. American peoples lived in large empires, but many also lived in smaller agricultural communities in which kinship formed the primary bonds of society.

453. (A) The Incan Empire began as a small city-state. Under militaristic native rulers, the Inca eventually conquered much of western South America. The Incan Empire was known for its extensive system of roads, sophisticated farming techniques, lack of a writing system, and a strict class system established by the first Incan ruler. The empire remained strong until the mid-1500s when the Spanish invaded South America.

454. (C) In about 1325, the Aztecs claimed a small island area at the southwestern edge of Lake Texcoco; in 1376, Acamapichtli became their first ruler. In the early 1400s, a power struggle developed among the central valley communities. The Aztecs, with their capital at Tenochtitlan (present-day Mexico City), made an alliance with the cities of Texcoco and Tlacopan (the weakest of the three). These three city-states waged wars of conquest and expanded rapidly. They ruled the area in and around the Valley of Mexico from 1428 until they were defeated by the Spanish in 1521. The Aztecs, especially under Montezuma I (c. 1398–1469), eventually became the dominant partner in the alliance. (The Mixtec are a Mesoamerican people who live in the present-day Mexican states of Oaxaca, Guerrero, and Puebla. They were a major pre-Columbian culture after 1100 CE, producing fine stone- and metalwork. Their influence on other cultures was strong, but they were rarely friendly with the Aztecs.)

455. (E) The Hopewell culture (100 BCE–500 CE) is an ancient American culture that developed from the preceding Adena culture in Ohio. The Hopewell people lived in small villages scattered throughout the river valleys of southern Ohio. They increased their food supply by domesticating plants, which allowed clans to settle in cities. The people grew a variety of crops, including sunflower, squash, and other plants with oily or starchy seeds. They also gathered wild plants, hunted deer, and fished. The Hopewell culture is known for its gigantic burial mounds and earthen enclosures, as well as for handsome ornaments and pipes. People obtained exotic raw materials from great distances, such as shells from the Gulf of Mexico, copper from the Great Lakes region, mica from the Carolinas, and obsidian from the Rocky Mountains. Their cultural influence spread as far as present-day Wisconsin and Louisiana. However, the Hopewell cultural "explosion" was brief. By 400 CE, the culture's elaborate trading network had collapsed for reasons that are still disputed. Increasing conflict has been suggested for the abandonment of the earthworks and the far-flung trade routes.

456. (D) By 1500, the Incas ruled a large empire from present-day Ecuador to Chile and Argentina along the western coast of South America. With a population of possibly 10 million people of various ethnic and cultural backgrounds, the Inca Empire was one of the largest political units ever established in South America. The Incas were able administrators. They used quipus to record population counts, economic and financial matters, and religious concerns. They built an efficient system of roads that stretched the length of the empire. They did not collect tributes but instead required communities to participate in building projects, mining, or working the land. These shifts of labor were called *mita*. The vast majority of the Incan population consisted of peasant families living in towns and villages. Within Incan communities, small kin groups known as *ayllu* worked together to keep the community self-sufficient. Each *ayllu* owned a specific piece of land, and members of individual families within the group cultivated as much of this land as they needed to live. The members of the *ayllu* maintained a series of reciprocal obligations such as helping other members of the group build houses and cultivate land or providing communal support for the elderly, the infirm, widows, and orphans.

457. (B) The Aztecs, or Mexica, were nomads from northern Mexico who arrived in the Valley of Mexico around 1200 CE. For the next century, they migrated from one location to another, often forced to move because of their warlike disposition. In their wanderings, the Aztecs adopted many of the customs of other Mesoamericans, such as the cultivation of maize, ball games, the construction of truncated pyramids, picture writing, a solar calendar, and the legend of Quetzalcoatl. Because they borrowed so heavily from other cultures, they were not particularly noted for the development of more advanced traditions of their own.

458. (A) Most of the roles of women in ancient Mayan society can only be guessed from burial and ceremonial sites, as well as from glyphs, murals, steles, and vases. From this evidence, it appears that Mayan women typically cared for their household. They raised animals, helped with the harvest, prepared food, wove textiles, and made clothing. In many cases, men and women had complementary gender roles: men produced the raw materials (such as hunting deer), and women transformed them into objects of use (such as processing deer skins). Mayan families appear to have been patriarchal, although more prominent families traced their lineage through parallel descent (daughters inheriting from the mother and sons from the father). The Maya had several female divinities such as the moon goddess and Ixchel, the patron of midwifery and medicine. In the Mayan codices, a young female goddess of women, marriage, and sensual love appears frequently. The Maya preferred that rulership pass to sons, but there are examples of female rulers. The eighth ruler of Palenque was a woman named Yohl Ik'nal, who reigned for 20 years. At El Peru in northwestern Guatemala, archaeologists have discovered the burial tomb of an unknown Mayan queen from about 800 CE.

459. (D) The Chavin were a highly developed culture in the northern Andean highlands of present-day Peru from about 900 to 300 BCE who extended their influence along the Pacific coast. The Chavin appear to have lived mainly on potatoes and quinoa, crops that are somewhat resistant to the frost and irregular rain associated with high-altitude environments. However, some scholars have argued that Chavin culture depended on the cultivation of maize and the development of agricultural surpluses. The Chavin demonstrated advanced skills in metallurgy and used metal in their tools and weapons. They also used llamas as beasts of burden. The best-known archaeological site is Chavin de Huantar, north of present-day Lima. It was built around a large temple in about 900 BCE and was a religious and political center.

460. (E) The Mesoamerican ball game was played by the Olmecs, Mayas, and Aztecs from at least 1200 BCE until the Spanish conquest in the 1500s (and variants continue to be played today). More than 1,500 ball courts have been found in Mesoamerica. The game combined elements of present-day basketball, football, and soccer. Teams had to maneuver a heavy rubber ball around the courts, often using only their hips or arms, and the penalty for losing could be ritual sacrifice. The precise rules of the game varied from place to place and over time, but all versions shared two uniquely Mesoamerican innovations: team (as opposed to individual) participation and a ball made of rubber. While the rest of the world was emphasizing individual athletic skills such as jousting, footraces, and wrestling, Mesoamerican cultures were fielding teams of players who competed against each other on specially designed courts. The game was both a contest of athletic skill and a ritual spectacle in which the teams enacted the struggle between the opposing forces of day and night, good and evil, and life and death. The game appears to have been an attempt to impose order on a random universe, but it was also a lavish entertainment spectacle accompanied by music, dance, and drama. The ball game was an endless source of inspiration for Mesoamerican artists, who created ceramic figurines and vessels, stone sculptures, carved monuments, wall murals, and miniature ball courts packed with players and spectators.

461. (C) Beginning around 800 CE, Mayan culture declined for reasons that are unclear and disputed. This so-called Classic Maya collapse is one of the biggest mysteries in archaeology. It is particularly intriguing given the juxtaposition of the cultural sophistication of the Maya before 800 CE and the relative speed of abandonment of their cities and ceremonial centers. Numerous theories have been proposed to explain the Mayan decline. Scholars have proposed foreign invasion (by the Toltecs), civil war, epidemic diseases, deforestation, or perhaps soil depletion from overuse of the land. Revolutions, peasant revolts, and social turmoil have also been suggested. Some evidence implies that a two-century-long dry period may have caused a decline in population. According to this theory, the resulting economic crisis would have impelled overtaxed peasants to desert the temple cities and retreat to the countryside. Whatever the reason, by 900 CE, many Mayan religious centers had been abandoned. However, several cities did not collapse, and the Maya continued to influence the Gulf Coast and even the highlands of Mexico. After the so-called collapse, the Maya of the northern Yucatan prospered, and the rulers of Chichen Itza built an empire that briefly united much of the Mayan region. For these reasons, some scholars reject the term *collapse*. (Moral decay and the loss of civic virtue were reasons Edward Gibbon [1737–1794] famously proposed for the decline of the Roman Empire.)

462. (D) In Mesoamerica (and Mississippian culture), men as well as women worked in the fields. However, among Eastern Woodland peoples, men remained hunters and growing corn became women's work. Women prepared the ground with wooden hoes tipped with bone, flint, or clamshells. Then they planted the seeds and cultivated the plants. As women perfected their farming skills, they provided most of their society's food supply. By intensely cultivating two acres, an Indian woman could harvest 60 bushels of shelled corn—half the calories required by five people for a year. Among many tribes, women's role in food production enhanced their authority. For example, the Iroquois of New York had a matrilineal-based clan and inheritance system. In Iroquois tribes, use rights to land and other property passed from mother to daughter (rather than from father to son as in patrilineal European societies), and the senior women of each clan chose the male clan chief. The work of the two genders in Eastern Woodland culture often differed, but neither had priority. The common duties of native women included cleaning and maintaining the living quarters, nursing children, gathering plants for food, grinding corn, extracting oil from acorns and nuts, cooking, sewing, and packing and unpacking camps. They were also responsible for brewing dyes, making pottery, and weaving baskets and mats.

463. (A) The Ancestral Puebloans (Anasazi) lived in present-day northern Arizona and New Mexico. By 600 CE, they used irrigation to grow two crops a year. Although they grew squash, they depended on corn to survive, and they domesticated turkeys (not chickens). The Ancestral Puebloans developed large, multiroom stone structures and elaborate residential villages in steep cliffs. They built an elaborate ceremonial road system and several sophisticated astronomical devices. The culture fell into decline after about 1250, possibly because the fragile system of food production was disrupted by long periods of drought and invasions by nomadic Navajo and Apache. However, the descendents of the Ancestral Puebloans—including the Zuni and the Hopi—later built strong but smaller and more dispersed village societies. (Potatoes were South American plants.)

464. (B) Cahokia is the largest archaeological site related to the Mississippian culture. The Mississippians developed advanced societies in central and eastern North America more than five centuries before the arrival of Europeans. The city flourished from about 600 to 1300 CE. The 2,200-acre site includes 80 remaining human-built earthwork mounds over an area of six square miles. Cahokia was located at a strategic position near the confluence of the Mississippi, Missouri, and Illinois Rivers. It maintained trade links with communities as far away as the Great Lakes to the north and the Gulf Coast to the south, trading in exotic items such as copper and whelk shells. Cahokia began to decline after 1300, perhaps undermined by urban diseases such as tuberculosis and warfare among city-states over access to the fertile soils of the river valleys. It was abandoned a century before Europeans arrived in North America in the 1500s.

465. (B) The city of Teotihuacan was located about 40 miles northeast of what would become Tenochtitlan (the Aztec capital). Teotihuacan influenced most of Mesoamerica from about 100 to 500 CE before its mysterious decline and fall. Teotihuacan contains some of the largest pyramids in the Americas (the Pyramid of the Sun was as large at its base as the great pyramid of Cheops in Egypt) as well as huge, multi-floor apartments; the Avenue of the Dead; and many colorful, well-preserved murals. The residents of the city also produced a distinctive orange pottery style that spread through Mesoamerica. At its zenith in about 500, Teotihuacan was the largest city in the pre-Columbian Americas, with as many as 200,000 inhabitants. It contained more than 100 temples and about 4,000 apartment buildings. The archaeological site is about 25 miles northeast of present-day Mexico City and is among the most visited archaeological sites in Mexico.

466. (A) Mayan culture was located in the Yucatan Peninsula and in present-day Belize and Guatemala. It peaked (Classic Maya) from about 300 to 900 CE. Mayan cities, such as the capital at Tikal (with a population of about 20,000 in 300), and the ceremonial center at Palenque featured massive truncated pyramids and temples dedicated to Mayan gods. Agriculture formed the basis of Mayan life; maize, beans, and squash were the main crops. The various independent city-states were linked by trade, especially in jade, salt, flint, honey, feathers, and shells. Sometimes cacao beans were used as currency.

467. (B) The Aztecs filled the power vacuum created by the collapse of the Toltecs. From about 1000 to 1200 CE, the Toltecs had expanded southward and dominated the Maya of Yucatan. However, this larger Toltec Empire did not last long. Nomadic peoples (collectively termed the Chichimec) apparently brought about the fall of Tula (the capital) and the collapse of the Toltec in the 1200s. This opened the way for the rise of the Aztecs.

468. (C) The Moche culture flourished in northern Peru from about 100 to 800 CE. Moche was home to the Huaca del Sol, the greatest adobe pyramid ever built in the Americas, containing 143 million bricks. The Wari flourished in the south-central Andes and coastal area of present-day Peru, from about 500 to 1000. They established architecturally distinctive administrative centers in many places. They also created new fields with terraced field technology and invested in a major road network, both of which were later used by the Inca. The Chimu were the residents of Chimor, with its capital at Chan Chan, a large adobe city near present-day Trujillo, Peru. The culture developed about 900 and flourished until it was conquered by the Inca in about 1470. (The Adena lived in present-day Ohio around 500 and were noted for their large burial mounds.)

469. (E) There is archaeological evidence that the Toltecs traded obsidian (from northern Mexico) for the turquoise of the Ancestral Puebloans in the present-day southwestern United States. The Toltecs dominated southwestern Mexico around 900 CE after the fall of Teotihuacan. Their early history is obscure, but they were a warlike and formerly nomadic people who made their capital at Tula. They adopted many cultural beliefs and practices, such as temples and truncated pyramids, of sedentary Mesoamerican people. They began to expand to the south about 1000 and dominated the Maya of Yucatan from the 11th to the 13th centuries. The Toltecs were skilled artists and builders, and they knew how to smelt metals. Their polytheistic religion seems to have centered around Quetzalcoatl. Their ceremonies included human sacrifice, sun worship, and a sacred ball game. They are said to have discovered pulque (a fermented drink), and they developed considerable astronomical knowledge and a sophisticated calendar. The ambiguous information on the Toltec Empire has created extremely varied interpretations of its nature, geographical extent, and duration.

470. (A) All pre-Columbian people of South and Central America worshipped gods of nature. The Inca had no system of writing, although they were the only group noted for their administrative ability. The Toltecs carried on long-distance trade with the Ancestral Puebloans. The Aztecs did not integrate other groups into their society.

Chapter 15: Japan

471. (D) Feudalism is an economic system involving a grant of land in exchange for military and/or agricultural services. In the 13th century CE, both western Europe and Japan underwent a feudal period. In medieval Japan, landowners recruited warriors known as samurai to provide military protection for their lands. Each samurai swore an oath of loyalty to the emperor and to his *daimyo* (lord) and promised to follow a code of honor known as Bushido. In medieval Europe, the king gave land to his nobles, who promised to serve him and supply him with knights (warriors on horseback). Knights were expected to follow a code of chivalry. Historians disagree on how far the analogy can be extended. The countries in the other answer choices did not depend on feudal relationships.

472. (A) Between about 300 BCE and 300 CE, the Yayoi traveled to Japan from the Asian mainland. This marked a period of transition when influences from China and the Qin Dynasty began to be brought into the Japanese islands by way of the Korean peninsula. The Yayoi introduced wet rice cultivation, bronze, ironworking, and new pottery styles. They are named after the neighborhood of Tokyo where archeologists first uncovered artifacts and features from that era. (According to tradition, Buddhism was introduced to Japan in 552 CE by Korean missionaries.)

473. (C) The *kami* are the Shinto deities; the word *kami* is usually translated as "god" or "gods." However, the *kami* are not like the gods of monotheistic religions. In Shinto, there is no real notion of God's omnipotence, omnipresence, and omniscience. Shinto has numerous deities that are conceptualized in many forms. This belief system/religion looks to the physical world for meaning and stresses the individual's duty to live in harmony with his or her natural surroundings.

474. (B) The *Nihon Shoki* was written in classical Chinese and finished in 720 CE. According to this history, the emperor traced his ancestry to various *kami* who created the islands of Japan. With the acceptance of this myth, Japanese emperors were regarded as divine and the owners of all land on the islands. The *Nihon Shoki* begins with a creation story but continues to events of the eighth century. It has been an important tool for historians and archaeologists, because it includes the most complete surviving historical record of ancient Japan.

475. (D) The Heian period (c. 794–c. 1192 CE) is named after the capital city of Heian-kyo (present-day Kyoto). It was an unusual period in ancient Japan because of its general peace and prosperity. Japanese culture, especially poetry and literature, flourished during this period. Although Chinese influences were strong, the Japanese at the Heian court developed an independent culture that included their own system of writing. They also created a court culture with values and concepts that were uniquely Japanese—such as *miyabi* (courtliness), *makoto* (simplicity), and *aware* (sensitivity). This new culture was forged largely among the women's communities at court and is exemplified in the classic *Tale of Genji* by Murasaki Shikibu. Yet Chinese influences were also powerful in the Heian period. Buddhism and Taoism were at the height of their influence, and the capital was laid out as an exact replica of the Tang era's Chang'an. Although the imperial house of Japan officially ruled the country, the real power was in the hands of the Fujiwara clan, an aristocratic family that had intermarried with the emperor of Japan. (Japan was never occupied by the Mongols and never adopted Confucianism as a state religion. It did not really begin to explore and conquer until after the Meiji Restoration in 1868.)

476. (E) *The Tale of Genji* is a classic work of Japanese literature attributed to the Japanese noblewoman Murasaki Shikibu (or Lady Murasaki) in the early 11th century CE. It is sometimes called the world's first novel. *The Tale of Genji* relates the life and loves of Prince Genji and the affairs of his children and grandchildren. It is written in a prose style, with a vocabulary of more than 12,000 words and almost 800 embedded poems. The book was a product of the aristocratic court culture that flourished during the Heian period (794–1192 CE) in Japan. It is considered one of the great works of all Japanese literature and has been narrated and read in a variety of forms for more than a thousand years. The text is well known outside Japan. (*Kimigayo* is the national anthem of Japan; its lyrics are based on a *waka* poem written in the Heian period and sung to a melody written in the 19th century.)

477. (B) Zen is a subset of Mahayana Buddhism; the word *Zen* is derived from the Japanese pronunciation of the Chinese word *Chan*. Zen Buddhism emphasizes the wisdom of experience, rather than the study of theory, in order to attain enlightenment. In China, Zen emerged as a distinct school of Buddhism in the seventh century CE. From there, it spread south to Vietnam and east to Korea and Japan. A *koan* is a subject for meditation in Zen Buddhism, usually a saying of a great Zen master of the past. The paradoxical nature of the koan is meant to shock the student into spiritual intuition and the abandonment of reason that is necessary for enlightenment. The first collections of koans were compiled in the 11th century. The use of koans remains one of the main practices of some sects of Zen Buddhists today.

478. (C) Feudalism was the primary political and economic system in western Europe and Japan during the period known as the "Middle Ages." The main characteristics of feudalism are a decentralized power structure that stresses reciprocal alliances between nobles and monarchs. The main difference between Japanese and European feudalism was the size of the peasantry; the number of poor agricultural workers in Japan was much smaller than in western Europe.

479. (B) The rule of the Kamakura shogunate (1185–1333 CE) marked the beginning of Japan's medieval period. For about the next 700 years, the emperor, court, and traditional central government were left intact but relegated to ceremonial functions. De facto control of civil, military, and judicial matters was in the hands of the samurai class and the shogun. This period was filled with military violence. Increasing pessimism led to a search for salvation for many Japanese; this was the age of the great popularization of Buddhism, especially the new sects of Zen and Pure Land (Jodo Shu). It was also during the Kamakura period that the Mongols were defeated in 1274 and 1281. However, even though they were defeated, the invasion attempts caused problems for the Japanese. The war with the Mongols drained the treasury, and new taxes had to be levied to keep up defenses for the future. The invasions also caused disaffection among samurai who did not receive their expected rewards for their help in defeating the Mongols. Bands of roving *ronin* (masterless samurai) threatened the stability of the shogunate. The Kamakura period ended in 1333 with the destruction of the shogunate and the short reestablishment of imperial rule.

480. (C) Bushido was expected of both male and female members of the samurai class. Because of the value the Japanese placed on military ability, they only partially accepted the bureaucratic nature of Chinese government. During Japan's feudal period, the nation had a decentralized government of self-sufficient estates in which the samurai were expected to devote their attention to military service.

481. (B) A *ronin* was a samurai with no lord or master during the feudal period (1185–1868 CE) of Japan. A samurai became masterless after the death or exile of his master or after the loss of his master's favor or privilege. *Ronin* were in demand in times of war but a burden on society in times of peace. They sometimes became farmers, monks, soldiers of fortune, or even bandits, and their status varied over the centuries. Technically, according to Bushido, a samurai was supposed to commit *seppuku* (ritual suicide) on the loss of his master. A samurai who did not honor the code was on his own and sometimes suffered great shame. However, in some cases, such as in the work of the great Japanese dramatist Chikamatsu (d. 1724), the *ronin* were a model of loyalty and self-sacrifice that actually exemplified Bushido.

482. (A) The movement of Buddhism into Japan introduced a dramatic gender inequality in religious life. Women were deeply mistrusted in traditional Buddhism (as opposed to Shinto). Many Buddhists believed that salvation was impossible for women; Buddhist monastic communities were entirely male, and Buddhist monks only accepted men as students. Yet women found ways to make the religion work for them. As Buddhists, many women's religious lives centered on the Lotus Sutra, one of the only Buddhist sutras to specifically address the enlightenment of women. They also adopted Fugen as a personal bodhisattva because he was the protector of devotees of the Lotus Sutra. Women wrote the great poetry, tales, and diaries in the Heian period. Because they often focused on the inner lives of men and women, they provide a better understanding of the experience of gender in ancient Japan than in any other premodern culture. While the Buddhist religion did not always see women as equal to men, it did not have the Confucian restrictions against women as rulers. This horrified Confucianists, who believed that women should be subordinate to men and that a woman ruler would upset the natural order. Six of the rulers between 592 and 770 CE were women. However, after this period, only two women ruled as Japanese female emperors; both were children, and their reigns were brief.

483. **(C)** According to tradition, Korean missionaries brought Buddhism to Japan in 552 CE and began to convert the Yamoto and other clans to the new faith. Initially, there was conflict with the native Shinto priests, but the two faiths found common ground within a few decades. The first Buddhist temples appeared in the late sixth century, and a priesthood soon followed. The oldest surviving Buddhist temple is the Horyuji Temple near Nara, built in 607. By the seventh century, when the religion was firmly established, Japan had dozens of temple complexes, various orders of priests, and skilled artisans to craft the icons used in the faith. However, early Japanese Buddhism was not a mass religion but limited to members of the imperial court and educated priests whose official function was to pray for the prosperity of the state. This kind of Buddhism had little to offer the uneducated masses and led to the growth of "people's priests" with no formal Buddhist training. Buddhism did not really become popular with the Japanese masses until around the 13th century.

484. **(D)** Tennoism was the dominant political theory in Japan for more than a thousand years until the end of World War II (1945). The emperor of Japan was called the *tenno*, which literally means "heavenly sovereign." He was not only the head of the Japanese imperial family but also the highest authority of the Shinto religion. In the early seventh century CE, the emperor began to be called "son of heaven." The Taika Reforms of 645 declared that all land in Japan and all loyalty ultimately belonged to the emperor, who ruled by the decree of heaven and exercised absolute authority. For the Japanese, this theocracy distinguished them from other countries, because only the Japanese were ruled directly by a divine emperor. The Japanese retained their belief in the divinity of their emperor despite long declines in imperial power from 1185 to 1868, and the concept returned with a vengeance in the early 20th century. The idea still exists in some extreme conservative and marginal political movements in Japan.

485. **(E)** In the 12th century CE, the peace and security that was synonymous with the Heian period began to disintegrate. In the Japanese countryside, people tended to obey their clan elders rather than listen to the government bureaucrats sent from the capital. Tax revenue declined, especially because Buddhist monasteries and estates were tax exempt. Court disputes over regents for emperors and the increasing power of the outlying provinces forced the creation of the office of shogun—the emperor's chief military and political officer. From 1192 to 1867, the shogun would become the (usually) hereditary military dictators of Japan. The Genpei War (1180–1185) was a conflict between two powerful military clans—the Taira and the Minamoto—over dominance of the imperial court and control of Japan. The latter were ultimately successful, establishing Minamoto Yoritomo as the first shogun to rule all of Japan under the Kamakura shogunate (1192). This was a turning point in Japanese history; imperial rule ended in favor of direct military rule by the shogunate. (Edo was the seat of power for the Tokugawa shogunate that ruled Japan from 1603 to 1868.)

486. **(D)** *Kana* are the syllabic Japanese scripts, similar to letters, that are used in written Japanese. They were different from the logographic Chinese characters known in Japan as *kanji*. Kana is said to have been invented by a Buddhist priest in the ninth century CE. By the Heian period, Japanese writers had developed the syllable-based kana system, which used simple Chinese characters to represent the 50 sounds of the Japanese spoken language.

For centuries, classical Chinese would remain the language of men, but educated women wrote in kana. This was the style used by Murasaki Shikibu in the 11th-century masterpiece *The Tale of Genji*.

487. (B) There appears to have been very little that was taboo in the way of sexual activity in ancient Japan. Shinto had no special code of morals and did not teach sexual conduct in premodern Japan, so it was never a source of religious opposition to homosexuality. Early Japanese law codes penalized incest and bestiality but not homosexuality. Buddhist monasteries appear to have been early centers of homosexual activity in ancient Japan, even though all sexual activity was forbidden by the code of monastic discipline. From religious circles, same-sex love spread to the samurai class, where it was customary for a boy to undergo training in the martial arts by apprenticing to a more experienced adult man. The man was permitted, if the boy agreed, to take the boy as his lover until he came of age. This type of apprenticeship was called *wakashudo* (the way of the young). The older partner would teach martial skills, warrior etiquette, and the samurai code, while his desire to be a good role model for his *wakashu* would lead him to behave more honorably himself. *Shunga* is a Japanese term for erotic art, and large numbers of *shunga* scrolls appeared in the Heian period. They depicted every kind of sexual activity, including heterosexual and homosexual, old and young, and a wide range of fetishes. *Shunga* was widely enjoyed by men and women and carried almost no stigma.

488. (A) Hakata Bay faces the Tsushima Strait in the northwestern part of Fukuoka on the Japanese island of Kyushu. It is famous as the approximate site of the Mongol invasions that took place nearby; both invasions are sometimes referred to as the battle of Hakata Bay. In 1274 and 1281, Kublai Khan, the Mongol emperor of China (Yuan Dynasty), assembled enormous fleets to attack Japan. Both times, the fleets were almost completely destroyed by major storms. Samurai bands defeated the Mongols who survived these storms, and Kublai Khan made no further attempts to invade Japan. The invasions are the earliest events for which the word *kamikaze* ("divine wind") was widely used. The destruction of the Mongol fleets guaranteed Japan's independence but also created a power struggle in the Japanese government that led to the military's dominance over the emperor and the end of the Kamakura shogunate.

489. (E) By about 500 CE, aristocratic clans dominated Japan. In the following thousand years, they often reduced the emperor to a mere figurehead. The Japanese followed some aspects of the Chinese style of government. However, they emphasized noble birth as a key to power and ignored the Chinese concept of the civil service examination. The aristocratic clans accumulated increasing amounts of land while most of Japan was an uneducated, agricultural, village-based society. The common people were alienated from the Japanese aristocracy, who lived in a world of rich homes and palaces, silks, wealth, Chinese writing, and Buddhism. Although the Japanese did adopt Buddhism, Shinto retained much of its popularity.

490. (B) *Bushido* means "way of the warrior" and describes a Japanese code of conduct somewhat similar to the European concept of chivalry. Bushido developed from the samurai's moral code and stressed absolute loyalty, martial arts mastery, and the overwhelming importance of honor. It developed between the 9th and 12th centuries CE in Japan, combining the violent world of the samurai with philosophical trappings from Shinto and Buddhism. Bushido was followed by both men and women of the samurai class. Its code emphasized the preservation of family honor and willingness to face death rather than accept defeat or retreat. When faced with defeat, Bushido provided an honorable outcome through seppuku, or ritual disembowelment. Between the 12th and 16th centuries, Bushido had a wide influence across Japan, although the actual term rarely appears in the contemporary literature.

491. (E) Pure Land Buddhism (also known as Amidism), is a popular tradition of Mahayana Buddhism in eastern Asia. It is based on the Pure Land sutras that arrived in China around 150 CE. These sutras center on Amitabha (Amida in Japanese), a buddha of compassion and mercy, and his Pure Land paradise (Sukhavati). In Japan, Honen Shonin (1133–1212) established Pure Land Buddhism as an independent sect known as Jodo Shu; Shinran (1173–1263), a former Japanese monk, established Jodo Shinsu. Today, Pure Land is the main form of Buddhism in Japan. The central teaching is that nirvana can no longer be attained in the present degenerate age. Instead, a person must rely on the saving power of some benevolent entity—in this case, Amida. Focusing devotion on Amida will give a person enough karmic merit to go to the Pure Land. This is not an eternal destination but a pleasant place in which all karma disappears and nirvana is easier to attain. To its adherents, Pure Land Buddhism seemed more optimistic than traditional Buddhism. Its basic premise came from a Buddhist scripture in which Amida vowed to save anyone who would invoke his name with sincerity. Most Pure Land Buddhists focus on chanting a three-word mantra of devotion to Amida ("Namu Amida Butsu") as often as possible to create a proper and sincere state of mind and thus gain admission to the Pure Land. However, Pure Land's *sincerity* refers to an egoless psychological state that is actually quite difficult to attain.

492. (C) The Jomon period was Japan's Neolithic age and is usually dated from the end of the Ice Age (c. 14,000 BCE) to about 300 BCE. The first people to come to Japan probably originated on the Asian mainland; one estimate suggests that they came to Japan around 20,000 BCE when an ice bridge connected Siberia and northern Japan. They lived in matrilineal, clan-based societies and survived by fishing and domesticating a few local plants. Some of the world's earliest pottery (dated to the 14th millennium BCE) was produced in the Jomon period. The term *jomon* actually means "cord-patterned" in Japanese and refers to the pottery style of the culture, which has markings made from their construction using sticks with cords wrapped around them. All Jomon pots were made by hand without the aid of a potter's wheel; the potter built up the pot from the bottom with repeated coils of soft clay. Women almost certainly produced these early pots, as was the case in most Neolithic cultures. The manufacturing of pottery implies some form of sedentary life, because pottery is fragile and generally useless to nomadic hunter-gatherers.

493. (A) The Yamoto leaders of Japan adopted the Chinese concept of a centralized state and turned it to their own purposes. The Taika Reforms (645 CE), established by Emperor Kotuku, attempted to completely revamp the Japanese government along Tang Chinese lines and enhance the power of the imperial court. The independence of regional officials was severely restricted, and a centralized administration run by educated bureaucrats was organized. The reforms decreed the creation of a Confucian/Buddhist-type civil service, government ministries, conscription, a reformed tax system, and an official court protocol.

A permanent capital was erected at Nara (710–794) and then moved to a grander location called Heian-kyo (present-day Kyoto). Envoys and students were sent to China to study everything Chinese, including the writing system, literature, religion, and architecture. The Taika Reforms also abolished private ownership of land and established a semifeudal land tenure system. Lords could hold power and possess hereditary rights to land, but the reforms declared that all land ultimately belonged to the divine emperor. However, despite these decrees, the centralized government never really effectively gained control over the independent clans and aristocratic families of Japan.

494. (C) *The Pillow Book of Sei Shonagon* records the detailed observations of Sei Shonagon during her time as a court lady in Heian Japan from the 990s until about 1002 CE. In her book, Sei Shonagon included lists of all kinds, such as "annoying things" or "things which distract in moments of boredom." She also discussed poetry; court anecdotes; and personal thoughts on nature, religious ceremonies, and pilgrimage. The book is known for her wit, humorous observations, and caustic depictions of her contemporaries. Her style was unusual for the time in that she did not use many Chinese words. Sei Shonagon was a contemporary and sometime-rival of Lady Murasaki, whose novel, *The Tale of Genji*, fictionalized the same Heian court life. *The Pillow Book* is a great introduction to the daily concerns of the Heian upper class before the popularization of samurai values such as Bushido.

495. (C) *Waka* is a traditional form of poetry that has been composed in Japan for more than 1,300 years. The term *waka* ("Japanese poem") was coined during the Heian period, although the form may have existed as early as the seventh century CE. *Waka* originally distinguished Japanese-language poetry from *kanshi*, poetry written in Chinese by Japanese poets. The term eventually referred only to *tanka*, meaning a "short song." Traditionally, *waka* had no rhyme but was intended to be chanted aloud to music. The eighth-century *Manyoshu* (Collection of Ten Thousand Leaves) is the oldest existing collection of Japanese poetry. More than 4,000 of the anthology's 4,500 individual poems are written in *waka* form on subjects such as the beauty and evanescence of the natural world, human love, laments for the dead, and the affairs of ordinary people. It was customary in Japan for two writers, especially lovers, to exchange *waka* instead of prose letters. Making and reciting *waka* became a part of aristocratic culture in the Heian period; *The Pillow Book of Sei Shonagon* and *The Tale of Genji* both illustrate the use of *waka*.

496. (B) The Japanese tea ceremony (*sado*) is a way of preparing and drinking tea that was strongly influenced by Zen Buddhism. The ceremony consists of many rituals that have to be memorized; almost every hand movement is prescribed. The tea ceremony remains popular in modern-day Japan. Ikebana is the Japanese art of flower arrangement, emphasizing harmony, color, rhythm, and elegantly simple design. It is traced back to the sixth-century CE Buddhist ritual of offering flowers to the spirits of the dead, although the first classical styles of ikebana did not appear until about the 15th century. Noh is a form of classical Japanese musical drama that has been performed since the 1300s. Many characters are masked, with men playing male and female roles. Performances of Noh plays move slowly and combine singing, speech, instrumental music, dancing, and mime. Kabuki is a classical Japanese dance-drama known for the elaborate makeup worn by some of its performers. Kabuki uses more characters than Noh and features much more stage action. In both classical and modern forms, Kabuki continues to be popular in Japan, while Noh is restricted to a few theatrical groups. During the century of civil war (1467–1568), Noh, the tea ceremony, and Buddhism spread through all levels of society. (*Muqam* is the classical musical style used for more than 1,500 years by the Uyghurs in northwestern China and central Asia.)

497. (C) From about 800 to 1400 CE, a *shoen* described a private, tax-free, and often independent Japanese estate. The rise of the *shoen* undermined the political and economic power of the emperor and contributed to the growth of powerful local clans. *Shoen* became popular in Japan in the eighth and ninth centuries to counterbalance the system of state landownership established in the mid-600s by the Taika Reforms. The estates developed from land tracts assigned to officially sanctioned Shinto shrines or Buddhist temples or granted by the emperor as gifts to the imperial family, friends, or officials. As these estates grew, they became independent of the civil government and contributed to the rise of daimyos and powerful local clans. All people connected with the land—the patron, the owner, and the estate manager—benefited through rights to part of the income from the land. By the 11th century, *shoen* had completely replaced state possession as the typical form of land ownership in Japan. The Kamakura shogunate appointed stewards to weaken the power of these local landlords, but they did not disappear until the 1400s. At that time, villages became self-governing units, owing complete loyalty to a feudal lord (daimyo) who subdivided the area into fiefs and collected a fixed tax.

498. (B) In Japan, great tax-free estates were built up in the eighth century CE by giving land to members of the imperial family, friends, or officials who could not be supported at court. These estates were often managed by territorial barons, or daimyo. The daimyo established and administered their domains (*han*), built castles, established samurai armies, and created towns around their castles where their samurai retainers lived. The supreme military leader was called the shogun, and his government was called the *bakufu*, or "tent government." Daimyo were subordinate only to the shogun and the most powerful feudal rulers in Japan from the 900s to the middle of the 1800s. Warfare and destruction characterized much of this era in Japanese history, especially from 1185 to 1600. The rise of the samurai occurred as political power devolved from court nobles to warrior families. Military leaders ruled the land, while the emperor and his court remained in place but held no power. Samurai values of service to a daimyo and personal loyalty became central to Japanese cultural tradition over these centuries.

499. (E) The Ainu are an indigenous people of Japan. They may be descended from people who once lived in northern Asia and entered the Japanese islands before the Jomon period. According to one Ainu legend, "The Ainu lived in this place a hundred thousand years before the Children of the Sun came." At some (much disputed) point, more powerful invaders from the Asian mainland gradually forced the Ainu to retreat to the northern islands of Japan, Sakhalin, and the Kuril Islands in the east of present-day Russia. The Ainu religion was animistic; the people believed that everything in nature had a spirit inside and that there was a hierarchy of these spirits. One of their rituals centered on a bear cult. The Ainu are lighter skinned than their Japanese neighbors and have more body hair. In earlier times, when race was a more important concept, investigators proposed a Caucasian (European) ancestry for the Ainu. However, recent DNA tests have not shown any genetic similarity with modern Europeans. Most Ainu currently live on Hokkaido as fishers and small-scale farmers. In the early 2000s, official estimates placed the Ainu population at about 25,000, while the unofficial number was said to be more than 200,000. (*Burakumin* are a

Japanese social minority group. They are the descendants of outcast communities of feudal Japan, especially in occupations considered ritually impure such as executioners, undertakers, butchers, or tanners. The *burakumin* traditionally lived in their own secluded hamlets and faced [and continue to face] social discrimination.)

500. (C) *Kofun* are large tombs in Japan that were constructed between the third and seventh centuries CE; this was primarily the Yamoto period (c. 250–700). The tombs are so distinctive that the time period is sometimes called the Kofun period. Many of the *kofun* have an unusual keyhole-shaped mound unique to ancient Japan. They were constructed in the area around the Kanto plain on the central island of Honshu, where the Yamoto clan had created the beginnings of a state. *Kofun* range in size from several yards to more than 400 yards in length. The largest is in Sakai City and may be the tomb of the fourth-century emperor Nintoku. The large burial mounds indicated the new wealth and prestige of the Yamoto leaders.